Other books in The 'True Cases' Series

Tough Crimes: True Cases by Top Canadian Criminal Lawyers

Book One in the True Cases Series
Eds: C.D. Evans QC and Lorene Shyba

"Tough Crimes demonstrates that Crown prosecutors and criminal defence lawyers do not escape unscathed from serious trials. The disturbing memories remain."

— Hon. John C. Major, CC QC, Retired Justice of the Supreme Court of Canada

Tough Crimes is a collection of thoughtful and insightful essays from some of Canada's most prominent criminal lawyers. Stories include wrongful convictions, reasonable doubt, homicides, and community.

Price: $29.95 *Trade Paperback*
ISBN: 978-0-9689754-6-6

Shrunk: Crime and Disorders of the Mind

Book Two in the True Cases Series
Eds: Dr. Lorene Shyba and Dr. J. Thomas Dalby
Foreword: Dr. Lisa Ramshaw

"Shrunk's authentic portrayal of what mental illness is really like, and what it can do to people, sets it apart from other books of crime stories."

— Dr. Hy Bloom LLB, MD, FRCPC Consultant in Forensic Psychiatry

Shrunk is a collection of chapters by eminent Canadian and international forensic psychologists and psychiatrists who write about mental health issues they face and what they are doing about it.

Price: $29.95 *Trade Paperback*
ISBN: 978-0-9947352-0-1

Women in Silks: True Cases by Canadian Women in Criminal Justice

Upcoming: **Book Four in the True Cases Serie**
ISBN: 978-0-9947352-4-9

DURVILE PUBLICATIONS & UpRoute Books and Media Durvile.com

"More Tough Crimes is a fascinating collection of cases recounted by judges and lawyers who were actually involved. Their insights and observations are not those one would ever see in the reporting of those same cases by the press or through the other media. The authors contributing to *More Tough Crimes* are not just well known, preeminent judges and lawyers, they are very clearly articulate storytellers able to provide the reader with vivid pictures of the trials they describe. I would recommend this volume to anyone interested in hearing the inside story surrounding several of the more interesting and notorious criminal trials from Canada's recent past."

— *The Honourable Mr. Justice Richard D. Schneider*

"My Evidence students love the compelling case descriptions in *Tough Crimes*, all related in fascinating style by lawyers who have lived through the dramatic events. I look forward to introducing them to *More Tough Crimes*. Having had a sneak preview of Donald Bayne's account of the media circus that was the Mike Duffy trial, Mona Duckett's insightful commentary on the frightening impact of a Mr. Big sting, and Judge Raymond Wyant's heart-rending account of a grisly crime, the sequel is a must-read for anyone with an interest in Canada's criminal justice system."

— *Paul Atkinson, School of Law and Justice,*
Sir Sandford Fleming College

Praise for the True Cases Series

ABOUT *TOUGH CRIMES: TRUE CASES BY TOP CANADIAN CRIMINAL LAWYERS*
TRUE CASES SERIES BOOK ONE

"Incredible collection of memorable cases .... Readers go behind the scenes as lawyers prepare for difficult cases and see how they handle their clients, witnesses, and other evidence during and after trial."

— *Daryl Slade, The Calgary Herald*

"Well worth the read. There are lots of interesting stories and important lessons contained in them. I would certainly recommend every law student read this book.... *Tough Crimes* is a mentoring book. Reading stories from talented lawyers, seeing how they struggled with strategic and ethical concerns, is a great way for young and old lawyers to learn."

— *Steven Dykstra, Above the Law*

ABOUT *SHRUNK: CRIMES AND DISORDERS OF THE MIND*
TRUE CASES SERIES BOOK TWO

"[Shrunk] anthology takes a deep dive into the darkest, sometimes ugly, recesses of the minds of those whose deeds fill communities with shock, fear and revulsion."

— *Colin Perkel, Canadian Press*

MORE TOUGH CRIMES

True Cases by Canadian Judges & Criminal Lawyers

Books in Durvile Publications
'True Cases Series'

Book One in the True Cases Series
Tough Crimes
True Cases by Top Canadian Criminal Lawyers

Editors: C.D. Evans and Lorene Shyba

Authors: Edward L. Greenspan, Richard Wolson, Marilyn Sandford, Earl Levy, Peter Martin, John Rosen, Fred Ferguson, William Smart, Richard Peck, Noel O'Brien, Joel Pink, Patrick Fagan, Brian Beresh, Mark Brayford, Marie Henein, C.D. Evans, William Trudell, John Vertes, Thomas Dalby, Hersh Wolch

Paperback: ISBN 978-0-9947352-5-6,
E-book: 978-0-9952322-2-8 Audiobook: 978-0-9689754-8-0

Book Two in the True Cases Series
Shrunk: Crime and Disorders of the Mind
True Cases by Forensic Psychologists and Psychiatrists

Editors: Dr. Lorene Shyba and Dr. J. Thomas Dalby

Authors: J. Thomas Dalby, Sven A. Christianson, Patrick Baillie, Jack White, Joel Watts, Louise Olivier, Stephen Porter, Tianna Dilley, Donald Dutton, Barry Cooper, Jacqueline Kanipayur, Marc Nesca, Jeffrey Waldman, Lawrence Ellerby, Richard D. Schneider, David Dawson, William Trudell

Paperback: ISBN 978-0-9947352-0-1,
E-book: 978-0-9947352-3-2, Audiobook: 978-0-9952322-7-3

Upcoming, Book Four in the True Cases Series
Women in Silks
True Cases by Canadian Women in Criminal Justice

Editors: William Trudell and Lorene Shyba

Paperback: ISBN 978-0-9947352-4-9

MORE TOUGH CRIMES

True Cases by Canadian Judges & Criminal Lawyers

EDITED BY
William Trudell and Lorene Shyba
WITH A FOREWORD BY
Honourable Patrick LeSage

DURVILE PUBLICATIONS

Durvile Publications Ltd.

Calgary, Alberta, Canada
www.durvile.com

NATIONAL LIBRARY OF CANADA
CATALOGUING IN PUBLICATIONS DATA
Trudell, William and Shyba, Lorene

More Tough Crimes: True Cases by Canadian Judges and Criminal Lawyers
Issued in print and electronic formats
ISBN: 978-0-9947352-5-6 (print pbk) ISBN: 978-0-9952322-2-8 (epub)
ISBN: 978-0-9952322-9-7 (audiobook)

1. True Crime —collections
2. Canadian Law
3. Criminal Law
4. Canadian Essays—21st Century

II. Trudell, William, editor
II Shyba, Lorene Mary, editor

Book Three in the True Cases Series

We would like to acknowledge the support of the Alberta Government through the Alberta Book Fund. Printed by Houghton Boston Printers, Saskatoon, Saskatchewan. Durvile is a member of the Book Publishers Association of Alberta (BPAA) and Association of Canadian Publishers (ACP)

First edition, first printing. 2017

To all Canadians, in the 150th year of this great Nation,
who, through this True Cases Series might better
understand and value our system of criminal justice.

William Trudell and Lorene Shyba

FOREWORD

Photo: Ryerson University

Hon. Patrick LeSage

The Honourable Patrick LeSage spent twenty-nine years as a judge and until 2002 was the Chief Justice of the Ontario Superior Court of Justice. He received his legal education at Osgoode Hall Law School. In 2007, Justice LeSage was appointed a Member of the Order of Canada for his contributions to the Ontario judiciary, notably as Chief Justice of the Superior Court of Ontario, and for his ongoing dedication to public service.

THE CHAPTERS IN THIS BOOK reflect the personal experiences of the authors in particularly challenging cases. In every instance, these men and women have carried these memories for a long time. At some level, their life after the case/inquest/proceeding became different or they have an ongoing memory or concern for one or more of the participants in the case.

I understand this. Over my forty-one years in the criminal system, as a Crown attorney or a judge, I participated in cases that included incredible violence, cruelty, and inhumanity. While perhaps the best known of those cases for most people is *R. v. Bernardo*, there are others that come readily to my mind – not only cases I prosecuted or judged, but also ones conducted by other judges and lawyers who have opened up to me about their experiences.

More Tough Crimes, the third in this True Cases series, provides another opportunity for readers to take a glimpse into the sometimes very personal responses of highly regarded lawyers and judges in the course of and in the aftermath of a particular case. The cases they write about extend well beyond violent and vile crimes. They include the deaths of young Aboriginal students and the effect on their families and communities; the harms that can result from correctional failings; the calamity of wrongful convictions; the effects of faulty expert evidence; and the role of the media in reporting on and shaping public opinion. At the same time, you will read about good in people who have committed bad deeds. In the end, I suspect you will come to a better understanding of the challenges lawyers, jurors, judges, and other participants face, as well as challenges faced by victims, witnesses and, indeed, accused persons.

This book will highlight an important aspect of our criminal justice system, specifically the human element: the persons in the courtroom who work to ensure a fair trial, sometimes at great personal cost.

My experience in the criminal justice system began in 1963 when I was appointed an assistant Crown attorney in Toronto. It continued in the role of a judge from 1975 to 2004, including as Associate Chief and Chief Justice of the Ontario Superior Court. During that period, I was exposed to and involved with criminal cases of every nature from the minor 'cause a disturbance' to the most serious 'capital murder'. That experience provided me with the opportunity to intersect with a broad section of society. This included individuals whose very being had been violated physically, mentally, emotionally, as well as persons whose families and loved ones had been killed.

It is not just lawyers and judges who are affected by a particular case. I will always remember a young police constable describing a grisly crime site where a husband had stacked the dead bodies of his children and wife in the basement of their home. In my role as the Crown attorney, I asked the constable, "What did you do?" He hesitated and responded, "I threw up, I almost collapsed."

Moreover, I have also witnessed how the participants in the system from court staff through counsel, to jurors and judges take steps to sustain their health and well-being in the face of a traumatic case. Those steps can include seeking and finding help from a mentor, a professional counsellor, or just a shoulder to lean on.

In contrast to cases of violence and cruelty, I have also observed the amazing grace and compassion that individuals can bring to a situation. I speak in part about the ability of a victim to forgive the person who inflicted the harm. We occasionally read about these in the media. I recall the case of young men who uttered a racist epitaph as they pushed an innocent East Asian immigrant from the subway platform onto the subway tracks. That assault broke both of the victim's legs and, of course, exposed him to the greater peril of being struck by a train. Despite the racist brutality of the crime, the victim expressed the view that the youthful accused should not be given a severe sentence. He understood that justice is not simply about retribution or revenge.

Some cases are life-altering. I have known lawyers and judges who have been unable to resume their professional role after particular cases. I have known some lawyers who have taken their own lives; the events with which they dealt having played significant roles in their decisions to do so. Others have recognized the effects of the case and have sought help, or worked hard at sublimating the experience.

I have seen the effect of crime on many parts of the community; first and foremost the victims of crime, but also their families, police officers, medics, witnesses, court staff, the lawyers, the jurors and the judges and yes, even the families of the perpetrators. I have spoken to judges who previously unbeknownst to me had suffered deeply from the effects of a case or cases, be it the trauma flowing from the details of the crime, to the impact of having to view child pornography, to living in a smaller community where they found themselves always in the public eye.

The prosecution and the defence lawyer are not immune. I think of the two wonderful lawyers who initially represented Paul Bernardo and the fallout for them. One was charged criminally with obstruction. In my view, he was properly acquitted after a trial. The other, a very young person, left the practice of law. I do not suggest that such events are the norm. They are not. But these events occur.

Today our professional educators often present programs that help us prepare ourselves, and those in the courtroom, for the content of a particularly difficult trial. Potential jurors are sometimes forewarned before jury selection proceeds. Judges, court staff and, in many jurisdictions, jurors may be provided with counselling, if needed.

More Tough Crimes goes beyond the impact of cases on particular lawyers and coroners and judges. It provides a perspective on the conduct of a criminal or quasi-criminal proceeding. It is that framework that gives me solace about our justice system. We in Canada are the beneficiaries of a framework for justice in which I have faith. While in some instances justice is elusive at least for a time, for the most part our system functions well. To paraphrase Winston Churchill, our criminal justice system is a human one and not a perfect system. Nevertheless, even with its blemishes, when compared to others throughout the world, our system is remarkably sound and workable.

Over the years, I have experienced some interesting and almost always enjoyable public encounters. I recall on more than one occasion being stopped on a busy city street by people who I had either prosecuted when a Crown attorney, or whose criminal trial I presided over as a judge. Most cases had occurred decades earlier, and I was surprised the individuals recognized me. Each one had been sentenced to jail. In different ways, each person expressed their appreciation to me for the way I had handled the case or the sentence. Some also told me of their success in achieving rehabilitation after their sentence. One even told me that he was "proud of me" – he had followed my career. He said, "You were my lawyer." I reminded him that I had been the prosecutor not the defence lawyer. He responded that he knew and added "You were so fair." I am deeply touched by such encounters.

If I may, let me describe for the reader unfamiliar with

criminal proceedings, how our system works in a particular case. In proceedings such as a trial, a preliminary inquiry, or an inquest, lawyers will elicit evidence to describe what happened, as well as why, when, and how the event occurred. The description of events unfolds through the evidence: the testimony of witnesses and exhibits that may be filed. That evidence must be relevant to the issues in that case. That evidence then, subject to weight and credibility, forms the foundation for the ultimate decision: the verdict.

Not surprisingly, different witnesses can recall and describe a particular event in very different ways. Individual's memories and recollections of past events are most often in play. That is why we have so rightly come to be cautious about eye-witness evidence. While that sounds relatively straightforward, I share a comment from a judge regarding a case over which he was presiding. The case involved a large number of eyewitnesses to an event that occurred in broad daylight on a city street. As the judge related, "there were eleven dispassionate independent eyewitnesses who provided twelve different scenarios" of the event. He also observed that all the witnesses were doing their best to describe accurately what they had seen and what they had heard. These inconsistent perspectives occur because humans have different capacities to see or hear or recount events. They often do so in somewhat different ways and in different context, and sometimes because of different preconceptions.

That same divergence frequently arises in those instances when witnesses are permitted to put forward an opinion or a conclusion, as opposed to reciting simply what they saw, heard, or felt. Witnesses who are permitted to express an opinion or a conclusion from the facts are commonly referred to as 'experts'. Expert witnesses are often recognized as leaders in their field, frequently science based, who, through study and/or experience, are qualified to provide an opinion in a specific area. Their evidence is often said to be necessary because an ordinary person, be the judge or juror, would not on their own be capable of unravelling an opinion from the particular constellation of facts. Remarkably, experts not only frequently disagree, but not infrequently the evolution of science or the reexamination of the particular scientific fact has revealed their opinions to be faulty, wrong, unreliable and/or unfounded. Lawyers have often played a valuable role in this evolution.

In my early years as a judge, we did not have the benefit of 'specimen or standard jury charges' to provide guidance to judges in instructing a civil or criminal jury concerning how they approach their task. On one occasion, while working in Chatham, Ontario, I asked the long-serving local County Court Judge how he suggested I best explain the law to the jury in a civil case over which I was presiding. He replied "I usually tell the jury that the law is basically common sense as amended by statute." At the time, I was bemused by this comment but all these years later, I still reflect on his insightful wisdom.

That simple approach, however, cannot always be followed. The law today has become much more complex than basic common sense, and more so with forensic evidence. The reader of the enthralling stories in this book might well ask whether the criminal law, including the law concerning the admissibility of evidence, should be more reflective of common sense and more easily understood by all, rather than a multi-step complex incomprehensible analysis. As has been said, 'Law is not rocket science'.

Criminal laws are enacted to reflect societal views of what conduct will be a considered criminal. It is necessary therefore to ensure that our law is comprehensible. *The Criminal Code of Canada* was introduced in 1892. Its last substantial revision occurred in 1954. In the past sixty-three years, there have been a myriad of amendments, including hundreds of new sections and subsections. In my view, the *Code* has become more complex than it need or should be.

Is now the time for another substantial revision of the *Criminal Code*? Such a revision could make it less complicated, less convoluted and more intelligible. I sincerely believe that this would be for the benefit not only for lawyers and judges, but also for every one in this country whose law it is.

Congratulations to the publishers and editors. Most importantly, I thank the authors of *More Tough Crimes* who have shared with us their very personal experiences in this publication. This is an interesting, informative, and enjoyable read.

— *Honourable Patrick LeSage*

CONTENTS

Table of Contents Continued

Introduction

Few things in life are less efficient than a group of people trying to write a sentence. The advantage of this method is that you end up with something for which you will not be personally blamed.

— *Scott Adams*

THE FLIP EPIGRAPH above by Scott Adams, creator of the Dilbert cartoons, brings to mind two things that relate to this book. Firstly, Bill Trudell and I didn't manipulate our authors' writing in the least, rather our role was to nudge narrative, clarify details here and there, and stress deadlines. There is no hint of Dilbert-esque blame to assign, except if you wish to blame us for your possible neglect of everything else in your schedule once you pick up *More Tough Crimes*. If you can't put it down to the detriment of other tasks, you are in good company; we could hardly do so either and we place the entire blame upon the hardworking authors whose individualism and courage have amazed and even shocked us at times with their candour, passion, and riveting stories.

The second reason is that Bill Trudell, being the infinitely more lawyerly member of this book's editing team, has graciously allowed me a moment of solo personal expression within these introductory pages, a departure from the usual committee mentality of multi-editor book introductions. Writing here is a happy circumstance but one that comes with an immediate disclosure – I am not a judge or lawyer, nor have I been involved in the justice system, except as an editor and now publisher of Durvile's burgeoning True Cases Series. Notwithstanding the foregoing, a lawyerly phrase if there ever was one, I did represent myself recently in traffic court. I could have carved out my own chapter, as Bill enchantingly did with his story "Nice Job," but my victorious argument of section 161 of the *Alberta Traffic Safety Act* that featured interminable waiting in a stuffy Canmore courtroom; a hepped-up parade of high-speed drivers pleading for demerit reductions; the sharp-tongued Crown prosecutor replete with fearsome finger wagging skills; the accusatory traffic cop whose fondling of his gadgets verged on the erotic; and kindly Judge Danny Elliot who was gently instructive knowing I was a beginner at defending myself, does not hold a candle to the much more interesting cases in this book. Nevertheless, I had my day in court, just as all Canadians are entitled.

As a profound contrast to my banal courtroom experience, read, for example, Justice Raymond Wyant's heartbreaking story "The Scars that Never Heal." Even in early drafts, Judge Wyant's story of a terrifying crime in Manitoba that changed his life chilled us to our very souls. As the story bounced back and forth between Judge Wyant, Bill, and C.D. Evans, our editorial advisor, it became not just Raymond's personal story of coping with almost intolerable memories but grew to encompass the profound relationship between what we experience in life and how it shapes us as human beings.

Justice Faith Finnestad's story likewise brings thoughts and feelings to the forefront as she tells of a case in her career with the Ontario Court of Justice about a woman who nearly died for love. Many of our writers give credit to a mentor or influential muse who helped bring understanding to a situation they faced. In her tragic story that takes us to very the edge of doom, Justice Finnestad's inspiration leapt from William Shakespeare's *Sonnet 116*, which she included as an epigraph and wove into the title "Love is Not Love."

Justice Joseph Di Luca provides moments of levity in the book with his recounting of his role of duty counsel in the "Inmate Appeal Duty Program." He explains how appellants are often grateful, but also tells of a time where an indigent inmate told him that he had "screwed up," giving his duty counsel colleagues ample opportunity for a fine round of teasing. In a book rife with stories of murder and torment, Justice Di Luca gifts us with a laugh.

Justice James Ogle recounts a legendary 1980s Calgary crime case of self-defence that illustrates not only the powerful impulses of a man to protect his family at any cost, but the moral values of jurors who (spoiler alert) eventually found his client, Stephen Kesler, not guilty. I clearly remember the reactions of Calgarians at the time – those who generously donated to the 'Stephen Kesler Citizen's Defence Fund' versus those, such as *The Calgary Herald*, who proclaimed 'Kesler No Hero.'

Justice LeSage and Authors' Calls to Action

We have the great honour of welcoming into the pages of *More Tough Crimes*, The Honourable Justice Patrick LeSage. If you are the type of reader to progress through a book from front to back, you will have just read his wise and insightful Foreword where he articulates a few of his own life-altering memories throughout his career. Justice LeSage does not stop there. He steps up, in his Foreword's closing pages, with a plea for a less complicated and convoluted *Criminal Code of Canada*, quoting the sage advice of a mentor who described the law as "common sense as amended by statue." Justice LeSage advocates revising the *Code* so that it is not only intelligible to well-seasoned legal professionals but to ordinary Canadians whose laws these are.

Justice LeSage is not the only author in *More Tough Crimes* to take firm stands on issues of policy and contemporary practices. From the book's initial chapters, Donald Bayne in "Mike Duffy: Trial by Media in a Post Truth World" lambastes the media for its growing practice of reducing and portraying complex truths as 'infotainment' pandering to audience interests. Don Bayne's call to action? To make sure that in Canadian schools, students are taught about the precepts of the justice system, including the presumption of innocence.

In a further observation of our rights, David Bright, in "Justice Delayed: A Story of Complacency" recounts events that took place over a time frame of almost forty years from crime to decision. Bright's reminder to us is that both victims of crimes and the accused deserve a trial within a reasonable time frame.

Mona Duckett in her story "Two Troubled Youths and a Mr. Big Sting" illuminates the tragedy of ignoring another important precept of our justice system, the right of all accused persons to a defence. Ms. Duckett's young clients were not told of their rights to have a lawyer and were pressured into giving false confessions, a troubling contradiction to our guiding principles of common law.

Jonathan Rudin in his chapter "The Death of Reggie Bushie and the Eight-Year Inquest" speaks to the issue of racism against Indiginous people and the pernicious practices that get passed on across generations. He calls strongly on us to stand against racist behaviour and attitudes, writing that although there are limits to what the legal system can accomplish, as citizens it is possible and essential to take a stand against racism.

Further to Judge Ogle's observations about juries being triers of truth, Mr. Rudin's story also underlines the urgency of proper representation on a jury roll, as does Brian Beresh, in his chapter "A Penalty of Death for Dina Dranchuk." Mr. Beresh's chapter relates a case from the 1930s where an all-male, all WASP jury doled out a brutal and swift decision to an immigrant woman that ended with the dreaded line "... and may God have mercy on your soul." This historic case clearly shows that in the past, gender discrimination hindered quests for justice. Mr. Beresh asserts it still does.

James Lockyer's "The Wrongful Conviction of Steven Truscott" depicts immense pain and suffering caused by a jury which, in this cases, were not provided with the facts – the concealed, inconvenient evidence tantamount to, as Mr. Lockyer calls it, a 'noble-cause corruption'. Bill Trudell in "A Nice Job" tells of jurors who literally blocked the entrance of the courtroom seeking further validation of evidence of facts as presented in his jury address ... but I will not spoil Bill's fun by spilling the beans on his punchline.

Breese Davies' story "The Case of Ashley Smith: Insanity of Treating Mental Illness in a Prison" gives, arguably, the strongest call for action in the collection. She urgently demands the reform of a correctional system that operates under a cloud of secrecy and without oversight. As does Jonathan Rudin, Ms. Davies calls for public scrutiny and I invite all readers to take this task to heart.

The precepts of 'burden of truth' and 'reasonable doubt' are inextricably related in criminal cases because the burden of proving the accused's guilt is on the prosecution, and they must establish guilt beyond a reasonable doubt. The dynamics of these precepts appear in Alan D. Gold's story of "The Murder of a Criminal Lawyer" where he describes the unsolved Gilbank murders while simultaneously illuminating the fallibility of expert witnesses. In "Inauspicious Events in the Surrey Six Case," Brock Martland similarly pokes holes in the wisdom of trusting the word of witnesses who have been dealt, by the prosecution, "deals with the devil."

The True Cases Series

This is the third book in Durvile's True Cases series and serves as both a continuation and elaboration of the books that came before: the 2014 book *Tough Crimes: True Cases by Top Canadian Criminal Lawyers*, and the 2016 book *Shrunk: Crime and Disorders of the Mind*.

As a continuation, *More Tough Crimes* segues ideas from *Shrunk* primarily in Clayton Rice's chapter called "The Case of Kristen Budic: Too Crazy to be Insane" and Breese Davies' previously mentioned chapter about Ashley Smith. Mr. Rice eloquently relates the tale of Kristen Budic whose obsessive delusions caused him to kill a man in what he thought was act of self-defence. Ms. Davies' story about Ashley Smith calls into question the policies of Canadian correctional services. It also identifies the practices that must be implemented in order to manage inmates with mental disorders. Both Mr. Rice's and Ms. Davies' chapters help perpetuate the theme that we introduced in Shrunk of helping to solve problems that transpire at the intersection of mental disorders and criminal justice.

As a follow-up to *Tough Crimes*, the themes in this book exhibit the series' incremental development. In More Tough Crimes, the stories are more varied in thematic content than in the previous volume. The sixteen stories in this book found homes under the headings of 'Politics and Transborder Cases'; 'Covert Investigations'; 'Inquests'; 'Love and Despair'; 'Questionable Experts'; 'Self Defence'; and a final section called 'A Tough Fascinating Vocation'.

Many of the stories cross between these overarching themes, for example Brock Martland's story about the Surrey Six could just as easily come under 'Questionable Witnesses' as 'Covert Investigations', and Brian Beresh's story about Dina Dranchuk could be categorized under

'Self Defence'. (As an aside, Jonathan Rudin, Mona Duckett's, and David Bright's chapters could have formed their own sub-category of 'Mind-numbing Delays', or 'Complacency and Buck Passing', but perhaps we will save those section heads for another book down the line.)

Final Thoughts and Thanks

The only author in the book who has not been acknowledged in my Introduction so far is Mr. Brian H. Greenspan. I'd like to provide Mr. Greenspan with a special shout-out of thanks because of his role as an instigator of this entire True Cases series. I had the good fortune of accompanying my great friend and mentor, Christopher Dudley Evans to a dinner with Mr. Greenspan some years ago and the banter of stories that emerged during and after a splendid meal and a few glasses of wine seemed to me much too amazing to be withheld from interested readers, such as yourselves. I feel very fortunate to have Mr. Greenspan's story between these covers, alongside those of his equally remarkable colleagues. His chapter "The Eagle Has Landed: The Eagleson Transborder Resolution" is illustrative of the skills and strategies of not only a great criminal defence lawyer, but of an equally great storyteller.

Besides Mr. Greenspan and the one-of-a-kind Mr. C.D. Evans, I would also like to thank Lorraine McVean whose copyediting expertise reflects her talents as both reader and lawyer; my partner David Bunnell, a recent 'settler' into Canada from the US who so far has survived his head-first dive into Canadian laws and culture; and my co-editor William Trudell who is a most kind and generous collaborator. Cheers Bill, it has been an intense honour to team with you on this editorial jury and (spilling the beans on your punchline anyway) I will now have that B52.

— *Lorene Shyba, Co-editor*

PART ONE

Politics & Transborder Cases

Donald Bayne *is a partner with Bayne, Sellar, Boxall. He received his LL.B. from Queen's University, an L.L.M. from the London School of Economics and Political Science, and an M.B.A. from Queen's University. He has been designated a specialist in criminal litigation by the Law Society and has conducted trial and appellate advocacy at all levels of courts in Canada and at public inquiries (Somalia, Arar, Iacobucci). He has defended all manner of criminal charges including murder, complicated conspiracies, war crimes cases (in Canada, the Soviet Union, Ukraine) and charges against corporations. Mr. Bayne was the 2006 recipient of the G. Arthur Martin Award, the 2011 Ottawa Advocate Honoree awarded by the Advocates Society of Ontario, the 2016 Catzman Award for Professionalism and Civility, and the 2016 William Carrol Award for Case of the Year. Mr. Bayne is a Fellow of the American College of Trial Lawyers.*

Mr. Donald Bayne

Mike Duffy

Trial By Media in a Post-Truth World

THERE ARE GOOD JOURNALISTS who try to do a good job of getting the story and getting it right, and there are good and reliable media outlets too. However, they are up against the reality of a world in which print media is in general decline – advertising revenues are down and cutbacks are the order of the day. Television, the master of the superficial, of the 'sound bite', has accentuated the focus on the sensational and scandal-driven, pandering to celebrity. Television journalists themselves are accorded celebrity status. The goal today is less news and more 'infotainment' and 'audience engagement'.

Senator Mike Duffy's trial-by-media is an example of this new media reality – a case where I was involved as Duffy's lawyer. What will the world of criminal justice news coverage look like when the avowed goal is to pander to audience interests and engagement? In a post-truth world, does anyone care so long as it's entertaining?

Sensational Headlines

In July of 2014, headlines across Canada read, "Mounties Lower The Boom"; "Duffy Faces 31 Criminal Charges"; "Duffy Faces Charges of Fraud, Bribery." National media continuously featured caricatures of Senator Duffy as a greedy, corrupt, conniving politician. He was presented in print, on talk shows, in cartoon form, and even in a giant, thirty-foot inflated figure that toured Canada, as the grasping fraudster, a perfect and ready-made villain. Accompanying the blow-up depiction was a carnival barker hawking the following message: "Step right up ladies! Step right up gentlemen! Come and see the Senator who nearly ate a government! Two thousand, one hundred and fifty cubic feet of hot air, with a grossly inflated sense of his own self-importance and a giant bag of taxpayer money." One need only Google search "Mike Duffy cartoon" or "Duffy Blowup" to see examples of these sensational images.

Allegedly presumed innocent in a constitutionally protected democracy, Mike Duffy was convicted before trial in the media-led, and misinformed, court of public opinion.

Michael Dennis Duffy

Michael Dennis Duffy's relationship with the media, as is generally known, was not always as villainous outsider. Born in Charlottetown, Prince Edward Island, on May 27, 1946, Mike was the eldest of the five children of Wilfrid T. Duffy and Lillian Bernadette McCarron, both of Charlottetown. He was the grandson of Charles Gavin Duffy, Liberal Speaker of the PEI Legislative Assembly. The Duffy family had deep roots in PEI, dating from 1844. The young Duffy went to primary and secondary school in Charlottetown, but because he was committed to a high school news and record review column called 'Platter Chatter' rather than to academics, he became a 'Christmas graduate' of St. Dunstan's High School – was asked to leave halfway through Grade 11.

Although he landed a job as 'cub reporter' for the *Charlottetown Guardian*, later becoming a 'foreign correspondent' reporting from nearby Summerside, he briefly left this budding media career to become the road manager for a rock band called the Beavers, touring eastern Ontario and the Maritimes. When he didn't become the Phil Spector of small-town rock, Mike Duffy returned to the Maritimes to a short stint reading radio news but was fired after three months as he was told he lacked the right kind of voice. He persevered, and tried an Ottawa radio station but was told he should go back to PEI to sell ties. Returning to the Maritimes, he remained determined to work in the media and to cover Canadian politics. That determination ultimately led him back to Ottawa, to the CBC and CTV where he rose to become a nationally prominent political reporter. Despite the limitations that made a successful media career so unlikely, the persevering high school dropout made it as a media insider and part of the influential world that would ultimately turn on him.

Duffy's media career in Ottawa spanned the years 1971 to 2008, a thirty-seven-year period that, while it gave him media prominence, also featured the repeated onset of serious physical health issues – mainly, but not exclusively, heart-related. In 1988, he suffered from internal bleeding that led to two surgeries. A relationship blossomed with his VON nurse, Heather Collins. Three days before their planned 1992 wedding, Duffy suffered a serious heart attack and entered the Heart Institute in Ottawa, where the marriage ceremony took place. That same year, he was diagnosed with Type II Diabetes, requiring daily insulin injections. Thereafter, Duffy suffered from pernicious, unrelenting heart disease. Thus, by 1998 the Duffys began to look at Mike's retirement from the media job in Ottawa and a return to PEI. They purchased a Cavendish, PEI home that year, 10 Friendly Lane, intending it to be their retirement residence. Mike's media career ended in 2009 with his appointment as Senator for PEI and after he'd had 2006 open-heart bypass surgery.

Mike's folksy, gregarious, and publicly popular image was the key factor that led to both his Senate appointment and thereafter to his designated role in an intensely politically partisan institution. On behalf of the Prime Minister's Office (PMO) and Conservative parliamentary caucus, his job was to expand the pool of accessible voters and to fund-raise for an upcoming election, an election that eventually gave the Prime Minister a majority government. Duffy did those jobs so well and enthusiastically that only six months into the new job, on June 11, 2009 he was presented by the Prime Minister with a photograph autographed as follows: "To Duff, a great journalist and a great senator. Thanks for being one of my best, hardest-working appointments ever! Stephen Harper." Senator Mike Duffy remained in that light, on the right political side of the PMO, for the next three-and-a-half years, to early 2013 when he became a media problem for the Conservative government and was thrown under a sensation-seeking media bus.

The Issue of Living Expenses

The media momentum began in December 2012 with stories suggesting inappropriate living expense claims by Senator Duffy on the basis that he had designated his PEI residence (10 Friendly Lane) as his "primary residence in the province or territory that I represent." The stories argued that he had lived in Ottawa, working as a media journalist, for years before his appointment, so how could PEI be his primary residence? The media stories were ignorant of a critical fact, that is, that the primary residence designation required no element of time spent at the designated residences. Senator Duffy had been advised by the Senate leader's office upon his appointment that "residency is not defined … even if they live in Ottawa ninety-nine percent of the time."

Senator Duffy's designation was well within the Senate rules. This was evidenced by an email written to Senator Duffy on December 4, 2012 by Nigel Wright, the Prime Minister's Chief of Staff, in response to the scandal-suggestive media articles: "Mike, I am told that you have complied with all the applicable rules and that there would be several Senators with similar arrangements. I think that the Standing Committee might review those rules."

The real issue was, as Mr. Wright's email correctly identified, the state of Senate rules that permitted all Senators to claim taxpayer-funded living expenses for Ottawa-area residences. This was and remains a legitimate issue, but for the entire Senate, not just Mike Duffy. In Duffy's case, the Ottawa residence, a two-bedroom, row-house bungalow, was purchased in 2003, some five years after the PEI residence. However, Ottawa was, in the years before his appointment to Senate, where the Duffys spent more of their time. David Tkachuk, the Chair of the Senate Standing Committee, stated that "Duffy's expenses are entirely within the rules," and that "a lot of Senators stay here all winter long and then they go home for the summer."

A sensational story about an allegedly corrupt politician that ignored the truth of the Senate Administrative Rules proved more compelling for the media than an accurate, though complex and nuanced, version. For the media, Mike Duffy was a ripe target, especially as he had once laboured as one of them, but had gone to the 'dark side' to join a political class he once skewered.

Duffy as a PMO Asset

For two months after the Duffy story emerged in late 2012, the PMO and Senate leadership stood behind what they called their "asset," because they hoped the "classic" strategy, as Nigel Wright described it, of letting the story die would work and because there had been no violation of Senate rules, much less a crime. The media story, however, did not die. It resurfaced in February 2013 and created a political headache for the government – one the PMO characterized as "our agony" and "Chinese water torture." Because it was deemed too politically damaging for the government to continue supporting their star Tory senator and to try to justify the Senate rules to their voting base, a political damage-control strategy was hatched in the PMO to "staunch the bleeding," a mistake-repay script identified as the "Scenario for Repayment," as Chris Woodcock, the Prime Minister's Issues Manager, named it in an email to PMO insiders.

The 'Scenario' required Duffy to refrain from protesting his innocence publicly and to appear on television on February 22, 2013 to recite a PMO-scripted promise to repay all living expenses based on having made a mistake. Mike Duffy had not, in fact, made a mistake – he had made a decision after consulting Senate leadership and the same one that "a lot of other Senators," according to that leadership, had made. But Duffy was designated by the PMO to be the scapegoat for a systemic problem that was an ongoing political embarrassment to the Conservative Government of Stephen Harper.

Senator Duffy resisted the PMO damage-control 'Scenario' at first but, in the words of Nigel Wright (who said he told this directly to the Prime Minister) he was "basically forced" by the PMO to agree. As Mr. Wright would admit, "he [Duffy] thinks I've threatened to kick him out of caucus and force him to repay the money; he thinks his very existence as a Senator is at risk." Not only was a script provided by the PMO for Senator Duffy to parrot in an organized television appearance, but answers to prospective questions that might arise were scripted as well.

Moments before he went on television, Senator Duffy pleaded with PMO insider and confidante to the Prime Minister, Ray Novak, saying, "Ray, I did nothing wrong. If I take a dive for my leader when I am innocent, then I am totally at the mercy of the opposition." This plea fell on deaf PMO ears and insiders emailed one another with notes like, "I appreciate the work this team did on this. One down, two to go (and one out)," and "Yay this is fun," and "Sweet."

The media was conveniently delivered their villain. From that point, Mike Duffy was portrayed as a thief from the public – he was literally depicted in a political cartoon, along with similarly defamed Senators Pamela Wallin and Patrick Brazeau, as a masked, striped-prison-garb-wearing criminal making off with a bag of public funds. Mike Duffy wasn't even in the position of formally being 'presumed innocent' (because he wasn't accused by the authorities), yet he was already convicted and figuratively imprisoned by the national media.

The PMO's political damage-control 'Scenario' unravelled through March and April 2013. Behind the scenes, Nigel Wright approached Senator Irving Gerstein to arrange for the Conservative Fund of Canada to provide money for the staged Duffy 'repayment'. When that didn't produce the $90,000 required, Mr. Wright secretly provided the funds himself, but made it appear that the money, according to the phony scenario, had come from Mike Duffy. The media had been inquiring whether Duffy had repaid as promised in February, and so on April 19, 2013, the PMO scripted yet another 'Statement for Senator Duffy', asserting, misleadingly, that "I have repaid these expenses." Only three-and-a-half weeks later, however, it was revealed that Nigel Wright had, in fact, repaid and the political agony for the Harper government was compounded. The threat was that all the PMO manipulations would be exposed. To save political face, Wright had to go, and Duffy was told to resign from caucus or be kicked out. Duffy was forced to pay for the conduct of the Prime Minister's Office.

Senator Duffy, suffering from multiple serious health setbacks during this time and from the ongoing media onslaught, and rightly sensing a further political attack on him by the government-controlled Senate, sought to fight back, and so made two speeches in the Senate about the truth of the PMO-conceived scenario and how he was forced to comply. These were ridiculed by his political opponents, by the RCMP, by the Prime Minister, and in the media. The media reported, in the language of fact rather than allegation, that

> Cpl. [Greg] Horton [the RCMP investigator] says there is no evidence to support Duffy's claim that the PMO dreamed up and schooled him on a false story claiming he'd borrowed money from the Royal Bank to pay his debt; instead, Mr. Duffy's own account suggests there was no such plot. Noting Mr. Duffy's accusation that 'this monstrous fraud was the PMO's creation from start to finish', Cpl. Horton comments: 'The evidence that I have seen shows that the demands made by Senator Duffy in February were the start of the monstrous fraud'.

The RCMP allegation, in their publicity seeking Information to Obtain (ITO), was expressly that "the demands made by Senator Duffy in February were the start of a monstrous fraud."

That's it then: Duffy is the monster fraudster – the RCMP having conclusively so stated and the media so obligingly reported. The truth was, however, and the trial judge ruled, that the PMO was ordering Duffy and Senate leadership around "as if they were mere pawns on a chessboard", having them march "robotically" to "recite their provided scripted lines." The damning media version was simply untrue.

The Defence Team

By the Fall of 2013, after months of trial and conviction by media, we, as a defence team, made an attempt to stem the onrushing political and media tide. It was becoming clear that, though charged with nothing, Senator Duffy, along with Senators Pamela Wallin and Patrick Brazeau, would be further penalized politically by the PMO. They would be suspended from the Senate, without pay, without access to their offices or the Chamber, and without a hearing. We called a press conference and convened on Parliament Hill in a desperate attempt to counter the prevailing, erroneous media narrative and to get some critical facts and evidence into the public domain.

Press conferences, for criminal defence lawyers, are at best a risky proposition. Defence counsel are seen in the media, and thus by the public, as biased, hired guns paid to 'pretty up a pig'. That's why so much evidence was disclosed publicly during this press conference, including email evidence that a trial judge found compelling evidence to demonstrate that there was quite another side to the media stories. This was not merely the "not guilty ... will defend vigorously" defence counsel boiler plate public assertion on behalf of a client. Nevertheless, on all accounts, the press conference proved to be a complete failure. While the media reported the facts of the press conference and made reference to some of the email evidence, it was the sensational prospect of an ever-greater fraud, a bigger scandal involving the Prime Minister and his office – rather than the potential innocence of the much and long media-maligned Senator Duffy – that became the media takeaway. As a nationally syndicated columnist wrote: "Donald Bayne may not have succeeded, in the course of Monday's press conference, in lifting his client clear of the muck. But he has certainly dragged the rest of the Tory hierarchy down into it." For the media, Duffy remained a villain, but now one in deliciously deeper, muckier villainy.

The Prime Minister and RCMP responded promptly to the press conference, and their assurances of Mike Duffy's guilt were reported as "Harper blasted the three senators he wanted suspended from the upper chamber," saying that "It's beyond a shadow of a doubt that these senators in some cases have collected literally up to six figures worth of ineligible expenses. Did so willingly over a long period of time, … and that is clear." One week later, at the Conservative Party of Canada National Convention in Calgary, the media continued to play up the PM's repeated assurance of wrongdoing. The Sun chain reported that, in response to the press conference, "the Prime Minister, instead, attacked Duffy and portrayed him as a liar who has shown no remorse for his expense claim scandal." So now, before any charges are laid, before any trial, we have the national media (and political) message of guilt "beyond a shadow of a doubt."

Lowering of the Boom

In July 2014, the RCMP lowered the boom on Mike Duffy with thirty-one separate criminal charges of fraud, breach of trust and bribery, alleging deceitful frauds of the Senate and breaches of trust in respect of living expenses claims, travel claims, and awards of and payments pursuant to Senate consulting contracts and the Nigel Wright $90,000 'repayment'. The media trumpeted the laying of these charges, befitting their long narrative of Duffy's presumed guilt. It was difficult to understand how the police or prosecutors could have convinced themselves, without the year and a half of negative press coverage, that crimes had actually been committed or could be proven.

Initially, before things got hot politically for the PMO and before the media tidal wave of assumed guilt, both David Tkachuk, Chair of the Standing Committee, and Nigel Wright conceded that Duffy's living expense claims were all valid and within the rules and that his situation was not different from many other Senators. There was no 'prohibited act' required for a criminal conviction, not even a violation of administrative rules, much less a knowing, corrupt, deceitful criminal fraud or breach of trust. The audit firm Deloitte had concluded that, given the Senate rules, it could not be said that Duffy's living expense claims were even administratively inappropriate. The police and Crown offered no evidence of how other senators dealt with primary residence designations and claims. So how was a designation in conformity with the rules a crime and Duffy a headline criminal?

Similarly, the sixteen counts of alleged travel expenses frauds and breaches of trust seemed like an exercise in unrealistic overreach. These claims were all founded on allegations that Senator Duffy had billed for travel to engage in partisan activities or to visit with his children in Vancouver. But the Senate Rules expressly provided that travel expenses for partisan activities are not only not prohibited by the governing rules, they are "inherent" and "essential" parts of all senators' parliamentary functions. Further, Senate Rules define the "public business" of all senators as including "partisan business," for which the Senate may properly be billed.

Duffy's visits with his children in Vancouver were incidental to doing other valid Parliamentary business while in Vancouver. For example, Senator Duffy attended a non-partisan public event as the featured speaker to assist homeless veterans transitioning to civilian life and briefly saw his daughter who had just given birth. Senate Rules approve such personal, family contacts incidental to Parliamentary business where they don't create additional expense to the Senate. No such additional expense was ever created. There was no violation of travel rules and certainly no crime.

The Consulting Contracts and Bribery Charges

Senate consulting contracts are, according to the governing code of the Senate Rules, a matter of the sole and exclusive discretion of each Senator and are paid out of the annual office budget all Senators receive. Transactions that received particular media attention in Duffy's case, were for a consulting contract with Gerry Donohue who, the media reported, was unqualified and did little or no work; for what the media called a personal Mike Duffy make-up session; and for a consulting contract with a personal trainer.

The facts of the matter were that Mr. Donohue was a highly qualified consultant and did extensive work for modest pay. Whereas the media reported that Mr. Donohue was an uneducated high school dropout friend of Duffy's, evidence disclosed that he had almost thirty years' experience representing unions in national negotiations, consulting to CTV, and for the Calgary 1988 Winter Olympics. Yet the media persisted in seeking to cast aspersions on him, consistent with their pre-determined story line that he was just an unqualified pal of the corrupt Mike Duffy. Likewise, media portrayal of the three-hundred-dollar fee paid to Jacqueline Lambert was that it was for Senator Duffy's personal make up. She provided makeup services for Prime Minister Harper and Senator Duffy before a parliamentary function – a G-8 Conference – for which public funds were routinely paid. This was in no way a personal matter of Duffy's. As for the allegations that Mike Croskery's services were for personal training, the funds were used for consulting on a major project on which the Senator was working – the 'demographic time bomb' of aging seniors and their associated health care and social care costs.

In respect of the three bribery-related charges, the prosecution thesis, mirroring the media portrait of Duffy, was that Duffy had "demanded" a bribe to pay back his inappropriate/criminal expenses claims; he was the 'rat' making demands of the 'ethical' PMO and 'honest' Nigel Wright. This did not accord with the highly revealing email evidence.

Declining Health

Throughout this period, Mike Duffy's health continued in serious decline. Within a few weeks of his being suspended, Senator Duffy underwent intensive triple-bypass, open-heart surgery at the Heart Institute in Ottawa, in December 2013. Stress is obviously not recommended for severe heart disease. Seven months later, while still recovering, the 'boom' of thirty-one criminal charges was 'lowered' on him (and wife Heather and his children), a boom that the media echoed loudly. It was thereafter a time of even greater difficulty and stress for Mike Duffy and his family than when the battle was 'only' for his reputation and Senate seat.

The build-up to any trial is nerve-wracking for accused persons with little experience in the criminal courts. For the Duffys, it was a nightmare. The day before his trial began on April 7, 2015, in Courtroom 31 in the Ottawa courthouse, Senator Duffy was taken by counsel and helpful court staff to get the look and feel of the place. For many accused persons unfamiliar with criminal trials, that first day standing before a robed, sashed judge on a raised dais and being the focus of the full prosecutorial power of the state can be an overwhelming experience. This tour was a meagre attempt that didn't soften that blow. Instead, Mike Duffy became acutely short of breath, unable to talk, unsteady on his feet, and had to sit to try and compose himself. Ashen, he looked like he was having another heart attack. How would he ever endure what was coming, a lengthy, sensationalized trial and daily trips fighting through a hungry media horde with their extended microphones and constantly clicking lenses? Retreating from this courtroom preview, Mike and Heather were badly shaken, and we worried about more than their legal well-being.

Meanwhile, the media regarded the imminent Duffy trial as "the hottest ticket in Ottawa, a political *cause célèbre* that promised to lay bare the inner workings of one of the most secretive, media-wary governments in recent history." Media and politics fused in a cocktail toxic to calm, rational assessment and the measured pace of the adduction of the details of evidence in a criminal trial. The Duffy trial was seen by the media not so much as a criminal trial where the accused was presumed innocent, but instead as "some of the best political theatre in a generation," as put by Quito Maggi, President of Mainstreet Research. On day one, the Duffys had to navigate into the courthouse 'theatre' through what *Maclean's* called "an electrical storm of artificial lights, the boom microphones rising in unison." This pattern was repeated for a year.

Somehow, between the harrowing experience of the day-before courtroom preview and the next morning's trial start, Mike Duffy drew on his old perseverance reserves, pulled himself together, became a needed support to Heather, for whom the trial was a withering ordeal, and walked firmly toward his trial and judgment. This pattern too, was repeated for a year. And for that year, despite daily prodding by an insistent media mob, Duffy maintained a restrained, dignified public silence, doing his talking in the courtroom when called as a witness. This galled and frustrated the media who did not think "the biggest mouth in Ottawa would stay shut for long." About this, too, the media got it wrong.

During the trial, the justice system accommodated the media. Almost half of the public gallery of Courtroom 31 was made available to media members, plus a large overflow media room was created, replete with screens and audio so that the trial could unfold in real time while the national media could work, talk, compare notes and come and go at their own pace. Outside, a media platform was erected for constant and ongoing scrums. Exiting the courthouse was to walk into blinding headlights and an immediate 'performance venue'.

The pace and process of the criminal trial did not really fit the breathless, 'sound-bite' time line that characterizes so much of modern media. Thus, defence counsel was criticized by the print media for "hectoring innocent senate staff" about the details of the Senate rules and policies, practises, and procedures. *Maclean's* described this detailed examination of relevant documentary evidence as "awfully dull." That the devil truly was in these time-consuming details and buried in volumes of Senate documents did not matter to media who wanted faster action, some 'blood' to report, the spectacle of the Prime

Minister in the witness box. At one point, a group of senior media reporters corralled co-defence counsel Jon Doody and myself to point out, somewhat angrily but certainly in accusatorial fashion, that while we objected to Crown counsel 'leading' the witness, we ourselves constantly suggested answers and 'led' almost all the witnesses during the trial's first months. It was troubling to discern that these prominent, experienced and respected media journalists did not understand the basics of a criminal trial and critical difference between examination in chief and cross-examination. They were reporting the criminal trial "of a generation" to the Canadian public without understanding criminal trial fundamentals. To the media this was supposed to be 'theatre', and even as theatre it wasn't unfolding according to their pre-written script of obvious Duffy guilt.

And so, during the trial and despite the slowly mounting evidence, members of the media continued to cling to the portrait of Duffy culpability they had painted for over two pre-trial years. When one is blinded by pre-judgment, it colours what one sees before one's very eyes.

Mike Duffy on the Stand

While Mike Duffy took the stand for days in his own defence and sought to advance his own innocence, he described how he trusted that an independent criminal court, hearing and weighing all the evidence, would see things differently than the media and PMO-directed Senate. How they would, furthermore, find him not guilty so that he could return to sit as a Senator. His presumption and assertion of innocence became, according to the media, "an idle pipe dream," and a "delusion."

As is now well known, Justice Charles Vaillancourt found Senator Duffy not guilty of all thirty-one crimes alleged against him. The trial judge found Duffy to have been a "credible witness" who gave "straightforward evidence." Unlike the media who constantly referred to Mike Duffy's "inappropriate expense claims" and "expense-cadging," the trial judge found that no crime had been committed in respect of Senate living expenses. Unlike the media, the trial judge found that all impugned travel expenses incurred by Senator Duffy fell "within the valid expense provisions of the Senate Rules" and constituted no crime as alleged, no ill-gotten gains at all. Rather, "all of the travel claims before the court were appropriate." Unlike the media portrayal of consultant payments, the trial judge found, on the evidence, that all "met the criteria for Senate business" – the media-derided "makeup" payment had, in fact, he added, "no hint of criminality."

But it was in respect of the bribery-related charges that the judgment of Mr. Justice Vaillancourt was most damning of the media portraits of an honest and ethical PMO versus the obnoxious, delusional, demanding rat, Senator Duffy. And, it was perhaps the most damning judgment of any Prime Minister's Office in Canadian legal history.

Among the clauses in Justice Vaillancourt's 1241-paragraph, 308-page judgment of acquittal were these points made in a section called "Peering Through the Looking Glass."

> [1029] The email traffic that has been produced at this trial causes me to pause and ask myself, 'Did I actually have the opportunity to see the inner workings of the PMO?' [1030] Was Nigel Wright actually ordering senior members of the Senate around as if they were mere pawns on a chessboard? [1031] Were those same senior members of the Senate meekly acquiescing to Mr. Wright's orders? [1032] Were those same senior members of the Senate robotically marching forth to recite their provided scripted lines? [1034] Does the reading of these emails give the impression that Senator Duffy was going to do as he was told or face the consequences? [1035] The answers to the aforementioned questions are: YES; YES; YES; ... YES; and YES!!!!! [1038] However, in the context of a democratic society, the plotting as revealed in the emails can only be described as unacceptable. Putting aside the legalities with respect to some of the maneuvers undertaken and the intensity of the operations, a simple question comes to mind. Why is the PMO engaged in all of this activity when they believed that Senator Duffy's living expense claims might very well have been appropriate? [1039] Now, let us examine

whether Senator Duffy's conduct in the unfolding narrative amounted to criminality or whether Senator Duffy was just another piece on the chessboard when it came to Mr. Wright's $90,172.24 cheque. [1092] The Crown's theory with respect to the bribery count is very simple. Senator Duffy solicited funds and then voluntarily accepted Nigel Wright's money thereby elevating his conduct to the level of a criminal offence. [1093] In this case, the Crown seems to want to brush aside the particular facts of the case out of hand and turn a blind eye to Senator Duffy's particular circumstances in any possible 'Scenario'. [1098] I find that there is an overwhelming amount of evidence from the Crown witnesses, the emails and from Senator Duffy that the 'Scenario' theory put forward by the Defence was alive and well throughout this drama.[1099] I have included the emails earlier in this judgment to highlight the unbelievable lengths that Mr. Wright and his crew went to in order to deal with the 'Duffy Problem'. Could Hollywood match such creativity? [1102] The underlying message of, 'We're asking, basically forcing someone to repay money that, uh, that they probably didn't owe and I wanted the Prime Minister to know that, be comfortable with that:' keeps on resonating with me. [1111]I find based on all of the evidence that Senator Duffy was forced into accepting Nigel Wright's funds so that the government could rid itself of an embarrassing political fiasco that just was not going away. [1112] I find that Senator Duffy did not demonstrate a true acceptance of the funds and he did not accept them voluntarily. Throughout the entire 'Scenario", Senator Duffy was kicking and screaming to have the issues dealt with in an appropriate forum. However, as a result of the coordinated and threatening efforts of the PMO, his free will was overwhelmed and he capitulated. [1113] I find that there was no corrupt acceptance of the funds by Senator Duffy and he did not have the necessary elevated mental culpability or *mens rea* required to support a conviction on this count. [1114] I agree that this entire 'Scenario' was not for the benefit of Senator Duffy but rather, it was for the benefit of the government and the PMO. This was damage

> control at its finest. [1239] Mr. Neubauer stated that Senator Duffy's actions were driven by deceit, manipulations and carried out in a clandestine manner representing a serious and marked [departure from the] standard expected of a person in Senator Duffy's position of trust. I find that if one were to substitute the PMO, Nigel Wright and others for Senator Duffy in the aforementioned sentence that you would have a more accurate statement."

There was scandal all right, just not the one the media promoted for almost three years.

It was revealing that Justice Vaillancourt's judgment of acquittal began with a small, anecdotal preface. He wrote at the outset, "I would like to relate an interesting encounter that I experienced near the commencement of this trial that demonstrates the difference between the legal presumption of innocence and the application of that presumption by many citizens." The judge was well aware of the media massed in his courtroom and outside the courthouse. He, too, had to run a daily gauntlet. He had been stopped on the street early in the trial and was asked by a panhandler if he had any connection with the Duffy trial. Asked if he was one of the lawyers, he replied that no, he was the judge. "Without missing a beat, my new found friend enthusiastically stated, 'Throw him in jail.'" Two prior years of vilification and conviction by media had done their work. Most in the public believed what the media told them; the judge did not.

The national media reported the day after Justice Vaillancourt's judgment was released, "Duffy Vindicated", and repeated faithfully the judge's findings. That same day, however, a prominent columnist who had earlier branded Duffy an "obnoxious character" who had "royally jerked around" the "sympathetic" Nigel Wright, wrote that, "The media who made so much of this sorry mess weren't really after Mr. Duffy's scalp, of course (although he did make an undeniably attractive target)." Another columnist, who apparently took the verdict of acquittal personally, said "I cannot imagine how I could have borne the pleasure of Duffy and his lawyer Don Bayne, not to mention the self-satisfaction of Vaillancourt, had I been in the courtroom that day."

There was actually great, exhausted relief, rather than pleasure, for Mike Duffy and for us, his counsel, after so many draining years. Justice Vaillancourt, who presided over a lengthy and difficult trial in dignified and error-free fashion did his job impeccably well. The media did not.

The emails that formed the basis of the "Peering Through the Looking Glass" findings of the trial judge, had been compiled into a relatively easy-to-read, numbered, chronological booklet by Jon Doody and made available digitally to all media at the same time the booklet was filed during the trial. This booklet told the same story of PMO threats and manipulation that ultimately appeared – months later – expressly in the judgment, yet the media during the trial never connected the dots of the emails. The email story had never been told fully by the media until the judge told it for them in his judgment, although it was disclosed partially at our failed press conference two and a half years prior. Why did the media, with the same revealing evidence in hand as the trial judge, fail to see and report what was revealed?

Walter Lippmann and Carl Bernstein

The Duffy case is a graphic example of what prominent media commentators Walter Lippmann and Carl Bernstein have both described as a mass media devoted to sensation, scandal, oversimplification – a disservice to the education of the public.

Walter Lippmann has been described as the most influential journalist of the twentieth century and the father of modern journalism. He was awarded Pulitzer Prizes and was an informal adviser to several U.S. presidents. In 1922, he wrote his most notable book, *Public Opinion*, published by Harcourt Brace, in which he examined the impact of the media on democratic public opinion. Lippmann identified the tendency of journalists to generalize about other people based on fixed ideas.

Fixed ideas are what the Canadian media in 2013 to 2016 had about Mike Duffy. Lippmann argued that the media create pictures in their heads and convey those to the public who are more swayed by such pictorial symbols than by critical thinking. We are all familiar with the truism that 'a picture is worth a thousand words'. Mike Duffy was not merely depicted in print as a villainous, greedy thief, he was literally represented both in picture form and in tangible gigantic inflated form as an outright crook. This was before he'd had any form of hearing or trial. Lippmann lamented the failure of the media to do its real job, the 'intelligence work' of exposing the facts and transmitting them to the public who can then form their own opinion. Instead, Lippmann added, the media made up their minds before they fully knew or defined the facts, and so the public followed suit. It was because of this that the media represented an ineffective method of educating the public.

Carl Bernstein gained fame as the investigative journalist who, with Bob Woodward, exposed the complex truth of the 1972 Watergate break-in, leading to the downfall of President Nixon. Author of a number of books, in 1992 Bernstein assessed the state of the modern media in his cover story for *The New Republic* that he entitled "The Idiot Culture." Bernstein wrote that "the media – weekly, daily, hourly – break new ground in getting it wrong"; media coverage is "distorted by celebrity and the worship of celebrity; by the reduction of news to gossip, which is the lowest form of news; by sensationalism … and by a political and social discourse that we – the press, the media, the politicians and the people – are turning into a sewer." He continued, "The failures of the press have contributed immensely to the emergence of a talk-show nation in which public discourse is reduced to ranting and raving and posturing."

Lippmann's media assessment goes back to the start and middle of the twentieth century, Bernstein's closes the last century. *The Economist*, in September 2016, updated the Lippmann-Bernstein analysis, writing about the post-truth world of the early twenty-first century: "Post-truth … picks out the heart of what is new: that truth is not falsified, or contested, but of secondary importance …. Feelings, not facts are what matter." They continue, "Presented with evidence that contradicts a belief that is dearly held, people have a tendency to ditch the facts first."

The Canadian media, in the Duffy case, had a 'dearly held belief' in the sensational prospect of a Senator's grubby thieving, his inflated ego making criminal demands, and propagated that belief, even when it conflicted with disclosed evidence. Post-truth, as *The Economist* goes on to say, "damns complexity as the slight of hand experts use to bamboozle everyone else." So why get into the complexity of hundreds of emails or volumes of governing administrative rules when the simplistic picture of guilt has been predetermined?

Lessons Learned

There are some lessons from the Mike Duffy case media experience. The first is the confirmation of the reality of much of the modern media as the rush-to-judgment scandal and sensation-seeking instrument of audience entertainment, attraction and engagement. Complex truth suffers in service to simplistic pictures or fixed ideas/beliefs/feelings/biased pre-judgment. Criminal lawyers and the public should understand this reality, because it has consequences for both. The risk is that complex criminal cases can get portrayed in a way that causes the public to doubt the accuracy or integrity of the criminal justice system – experienced trial judges get portrayed as out of touch with common sense when they are actually and fully in touch with the evidence and evidence-based decision making. They are portrayed as smugly self-satisfied when in fact they have no personal stake in outcomes. This, in turn, weakens respect for rule of law, the foundation of western democracy.

A second lesson is that there is an education/communication gap between the justice system and the Canadian public. Even seasoned reporters and editorialists did not, apparently, during the Duffy trial, grasp the basic difference between examination-in-chief by the party calling the witness and cross-examination by counsel for the other side. Nor did they grasp the importance of the presumption of innocence. A case may be made that the Canadian education system should prioritize teaching certain fundamentals relating to our justice system, a system that distinguishes and protects Canada's democracy from autocracy and other forms of totalitarian government. A public that better understands the justice system will be less likely to misperceive it. Citing the Mike Duffy and Jian Gomeshi trials, a 2016 article in the Canadian Bar Association magazine, *CBA National* posited that "something has gone awry in the relationship between the media and the law" and "the system needs its own spokesperson – a judge whose role would be to act as a liaison between the courts, the media and the public. A press judge, in effect." There may be reasonable doubts that a public defender or 'press judge' would be seen, cynically, as anything more than a vested-interest mouthpiece for the system. Formal education about the system, the fundamentals of how it works, and why it is important to democracy and the rule of law would arguably be better explanation and justification.

A third lesson of the Duffy case is the importance of an independent judiciary. Justice Charles Vaillancourt presided over a political *cause célèbre* who was covered daily in a near-frenzy by all major media outlets. The litigation was lengthy and complex, involving issues of parliamentary privilege, the admissibility of expert evidence, forensic audit evidence and volumes and volumes of documents. It was also high-stakes and was heated and conducted in the constant and jaded glare of the national political media. With professional calm and dignity, with wit and wisdom, Justice Vaillancourt maintained gentle but firm and artful control of the entire process – the adversary lawyers, witnesses, evidence flow, media concerns – and rendered a thorough, well-explained, well-reasoned, evidence-based judgment beyond appeal reproach. He was alive to media pre-judgment, and therefore pressure to convict, and never yielded even slightly to it. In a post-truth world, he represented the very finest of judicial independence and his judicial professionalism is the most positive takeaway of the entire Duffy case. Post-truthism is pervasive but need not prevail, not when subjected to rational, evidence-based analysis and thoughtful judgment.

***Brian H. Greenspan** received his B.A. from the University of Toronto, LL.B. from Osgoode Hall Law School, LL.M. from the London School of Economics. He received the G. Arthur Martin Medal in 2010 for contributions to criminal justice in Canada, and in 2012 and was recognized by The Law Society of Upper Canada with an honorary Doctor of Laws degree. In 2013, he was awarded the Alumni Gold Key for achievement by Osgoode Hall Law School and was selected as one of the Alumni of Influence of University College at the University of Toronto. Brian is the Past President of the Criminal Lawyers' Association (Ontario) and the founding Chair of the Canadian Council of Criminal Defence Lawyers. He has been twice named as one of the 25 Most Influential Lawyers in Canada by Canadian Lawyer Magazine.*

Mr. Brian H. Greenspan

The Eagle Has Landed

The Eagleson Transborder Resolution

SOLICITOR-CLIENT RELATIONSHIPS in criminal defence practices seldom engender personal friendships and from a practical and ethical perspective are justifiably discouraged. In the more than four decades in which I have been engaged exclusively on the defence side of the courtroom, the number of close personal friendships I have developed with clients can be counted on less than one hand. Alan Eagleson is a close personal friend. I met him as a client in March of 1992 and almost from the outset, his charismatic personality, his devotion to family, to friends and to his community, as well as his candour and love of Canada inspired my respect and admiration for one of Canada's most controversial iconoclasts.

As a result, I caution the reader not to expect objectivity or a neutral legal analysis of the factors which ultimately resulted in the Eagleson resolution. This is a personal account which will likely please Eagleson loyalists and be condemned by his detractors.

My Introduction to Eagleson

In mid-March 1992, our receptionist came to my office door, interrupting a meeting, to advise me that "a John Sopinka was on the line" and urgently wished to speak to me. I left the room, picked up the phone and with some trepidation simply said "M' Lord." Mr. Justice Sopinka of the Supreme Court of Canada, in his forthright manner, responded: "Brian, in the next ten minutes you will be receiving a call from my closest and dearest friend in the world. I would be grateful if you would take on his matter." Thus began my odyssey with R. Alan Eagleson.

When I first met Alan, he possessed one of the most formidable resumés in the country. He was called to the Bar of Ontario in 1959, had been a member of the Legislative Assembly of Ontario from 1963 to 1967, and was president of the Ontario Progressive Conservative Association from 1968 to 1976. In 1967 he had directed the formation of the National Hockey League Players' Association, the first major professional sports 'union' and had been its Executive Director for twenty-five years. He had been a founding member and on the Board of Directors of Hockey Canada since 1967 and was the architect, chairman and organizer of the USSR/Canada Summit Series in 1972. He had received the Vanier Award in 1968, was appointed Queen's Counsel in 1971, received the Lester B. Pearson Peace Award in 1987, was elected to Canada's Sports Hall of Fame in 1988, and the Hockey Hall of Fame in 1989, when he was also named an Officer of the Order of Canada. His memoir, which was published by McClelland & Stewart in 1991 with celebrated sports journalist Scott Young, was suitably titled *Power Play: Memoirs of Hockey Czar Alan Eagleson*.

In March, 1992, although there were nascent investigations at the Law Society of Upper Canada and in the United States, no charges had yet been initiated in either country.

The Investigations

The rumblings of discontent had initially been aired by a number of players and by rival agent Ritch Winter in June 1989 in a move to displace Eagleson as Executive Director of the NHLPA, a position he vacated in 1992. Almost contemporaneously, the Law Society of Upper Canada received a fifty-one-page complaint from Winter who represented a number of professional hockey players under the auspices of 'The Sports Corporation' in Edmonton. It is perhaps ironic that almost twenty years later, in 2007, Winter was also instrumental in forcing the resignation of Ted Saskin as head of the NHLPA.

However, the most effective and ultimately destructive investigation was conducted by Russ Conway, the sports editor of *The Eagle-Tribune* published in Lawrence, a suburb of Boston, with a modest circulation and readership. Conway, who had known and developed a twenty-year friendship with Bobby Orr, Eagleson's chief antagonist, began his investigation in June 1990. It was Conway who became the conduit for every rumour and innuendo interspersed with a modicum of reliable information which was funneled to the FBI. By early 1991, the FBI had initiated its probe of Conway's allegations and the complaints of players who Conway had interviewed. The public announcement of the investigation and the service of subpoenas did not take place until December of 1992.

In the interim, in mid-1991, Assistant U.S. Attorney Paul V. Kelly, who headed the Public Corruption Unit in Boston, was asked to lead the Eagleson investigation. A Boston Bruin and Bobby Orr zealot, Kelly was accused by Eagleson admirers of tunnel-vision and conducting a less-than-objective inquiry. In another bizarre and ironic twist, Paul Kelly replaced Ted Saskin as Executive Director of the NHLPA in October 2007, and was then dismissed by the Board less than two years later, the shortest tenure of any Executive Director.

The Eagle-Tribune published Conway's first series of articles in September, 1991. The introductory article was entitled: "Big Time Hockey: A Study in Conflicts of Interest. Did Union Chief Alan Eagleson Help the Players or Himself?" The central theme of Conway's accusations was that Eagleson had persistently placed himself in a position of conflict of interest, in some circumstances favouring the league and team owners. It is interesting to consider the historical context of these allegations. Following the ultimate resolution of the charges against Eagleson both in Canada and in the United States, Barbara Amiel, in a column in *Maclean's* on March 30, 1998, noted:

> The much praised book, *Game Misconduct* by Russ Conway, may be accurate in its details but brings an inaccurate sensibility to the story. Eagleson built up his hockey edifice in a different culture to that of today. Heaven knows one may not like that culture, with its *laissez-faire* attitude to expense accounts and disclosure, but even according to Conway's own account, Eagleson generally had most of his cards out on the table.
>
> It is a separate matter that the players didn't look at those

> cards. Conway provides many examples of players saying they didn't know what was going on when they signed forms and letters of agreement. Today's sensibilities were not those of the embryonic culture of showbiz hockey in the 1960s and 1970s. Eagleson's ethos then was shared by his associates and the players. An aspect of justice is the need to judge according to the times in which a man lived. Where would the players be if there had been no Alan Eagleson? Who created their mega-salaries and the world in which they now live?

Until February of 1993, it had been assumed that the RCMP were merely cooperating or providing assistance to the FBI in its criminal investigation. However, following an announcement by Hockey Canada that they were cooperating with a joint FBI-RCMP probe of Eagleson, the RCMP announced on January 28, 1993 that it had commenced an independent investigation of Alan Eagleson's activities.

Preparing for the Inevitable

Alan enjoyed the benefit of the advice and counsel of Edgar Sexton of the Osler law firm. He was a superb and elegant litigator who in 1998 accepted an appointment to the Federal Court of Appeal. Shortly after my retention, Edgar travelled with Alan to Boston to interview a group of prominent Boston criminal lawyers in order to retain local counsel to monitor the ongoing grand jury investigation and to strategize with Canadian counsel, should criminal charges be initiated. This rather select 'selection committee' retained a remarkable and legendary criminal lawyer, Jeremiah T. O'Sullivan, who had recently moved to the defence side at the prestigious Boston firm, Choate, Hall & Stewart. 'Jerry', as a prosecutor, had headed the New England Organized Crime Strike Force and briefly, in 1989, had been the acting United States Attorney for the State of Massachusetts and was Paul Kelly's boss. He was a charming and persuasive advocate assisted most ably by Sarah Chapin Colombia, a *magna cum laude* Harvard Law graduate. A number of years after his death in 2006, Jerry re-emerged in the media as the prosecutor who was alleged to have made the immunity deal with the notorious gangster, Whitey Bulger. Not surprisingly, the court found Bulger not to be credible.

Indicted in the U.S

On March 3, 1994, Paul Kelly released a 32-count indictment in Boston charging Alan Eagleson with embezzlement, fraud, racketeering and obstruction of justice. With what one observer had described as "the determination of a bulldog," Kelly had persuaded the federal grand jury to hold Eagleson responsible for the theft of millions of dollars from NHL players between 1975 and 1992, despite the fact that the majority of the alleged misconduct had taken place in Canada. It was the breadth, the unsustainability and the overreach of these allegations which dictated the defence strategy for the ensuing two and a half years.

Jerry O'Sullivan immediately issued a statement that Alan Eagleson was "innocent of all charges…and looked forward to an opportunity to clear his name and have his day in court." But the immediacy of the desire to respond had to be tempered by the reality of a parallel Canadian RCMP investigation reviewing the same subject matter and potentially arriving at either redundant or contradictory conclusions. In addition, the Americans had included a charge under RICO (Racketeer Influenced and Corrupt Organizations Act) which many academics have characterized as a form of legalized state extortion. Once charged under RICO, an accused can have all his assets forfeited before trial. Even attorney fees paid by the client may be subsequently forfeited. RICO reverses onuses and presumptions, and in addition to forfeiture of assets, penalties may include fines and up to twenty years imprisonment. Initially enacted to address Mafia activities, RICO was regularly misused to force a person accused of a financial crime to the bargaining table.

As a result, later in March 1994, Edgar Sexton and I convened a press conference in which we announced that Eagleson would not voluntarily appear for arraignment in Boston and that we would await a request for extradition to the United States. We were not going to permit Eagleson to enter a trial by ambush.

The Canadian Charges

Although the RCMP had belatedly undertaken the investigation of Eagleson's alleged misconduct, they were engaged in what they claimed was a thorough analysis, much of which revisited the complaints investigated by the FBI. It was also clear that with access to far more comprehensive documentation, as a result of the execution of search warrants in Canada, there were additional areas of concern, particularly relating to the financing of the Canada Cup and World Cup tournaments while Alan was chairman, between 1976 and 1991.

In the meantime, no request by the United States for extradition appeared to be forthcoming. There were rumours, never substantiated, that Canada, through diplomatic channels, had advised the Americans to postpone any request until the conclusion of the RCMP investigation. It was clearly in Eagleson's best interests to patiently await the outcome of the criminal investigation in Canada and anticipate, that should criminal charges be initiated in Canada, they would be, in large measure, redundant with the American allegations. Far better to be prosecuted in Canada and whether convicted or acquitted, to be insulated from extradition to the United States on the allegations which formed the basis of a prosecution in Canada.

Throughout the RCMP investigation, we had attempted to cooperate and facilitate evidence gathering from all Eagleson related entities. We had encouraged Alan's business associates to assist the police by providing full and frank disclosure. Late in the fall of 1996, we were informally advised that the RCMP were concluding their work and that charges should be expected. As a result, prior to the formal announcement of eight charges of fraud and theft on December 3, 1996, we were able to agree to a voluntary surrender that morning and a release later that day.

The Motivation to Settle

By early 1997, the stage had been set for a sober analysis of the challenge which the complex array of trans-border allegations presented. We were comforted by the fact that there was some overlap between the American and Canadian charges which would ultimately preclude a subsequent extradition to the United States based upon the matters which would be dealt with in Canada. At the same time, we were concerned that a significant number of the American charges, including the demonic RICO counts, had no parallel in the Canadian allegations. We, therefore, faced the potential of a preliminary hearing and trial in Toronto, followed by an extradition hearing and then potentially a trial in Boston. This reality, from the defence perspective, had to be addressed in a practical and meaningful way.

On the other side of the equation, the American bloodlust had been frustrated by the charges in Canada. Their worst fear, that an extraordinary delay in the trial which would diminish its public prominence, its media exposure and its career building potential had been realized.

The public fervour against Eagleson led by Russ Conway and his cadre of supporters, most vociferously Carl Brewer and Bobby Orr, had always been offset by a subdued and more private list of Eagleson loyalists and admirers including Bob Gainey, Bobby Clarke, Marcel Dionne, as well as a distinguished group of former politicians and judges. I had always felt confident that my list of All-Stars would eventually outperform and outlast their All-Stars. Following the announcement of the Canadian charges, Paul Kelly was inundated with demands for speedy justice. At the same time, I was bombarded with protestations of Alan's innocence and demands for his ultimate vindication.

These competing and ostensibly irreconcilable objectives were superseded by a visit to my office by Alan and Nancy Eagleson on April 24, 1997. It was Alan's 64th birthday. Alan and Nancy were always a devoted and inseparable couple dedicated to their family and friends. They arrived at my office that day with a thoughtful and focused inquiry: "If we fight this to the bitter end in both countries – with every appropriate motion and appeal pursued – no stone left unturned, how long will it take and how much will it cost?" They were convinced that although they might find justice in Canada, justice in America would always remain elusive. I paused while trying to calculate the incalculable but I knew Alan required a fair and balanced estimate of time and cost. He hadn't asked about the risks, as he was prepared to accept the risks if he and Nancy and their family could endure the cost and the disruption in their lives. I responded with some misgivings with an estimate of seven to eight years until the entire process would be completed and $3-million to $4-million in fees and disbursements. In unison and without hesitation they responded: "We don't have the time and we certainly can't afford the cost. Settle it." Alan then added: "Too much pain and too much expense." Those instructions were clear and were unwavering. I contacted my American counterpart, Jerry O'Sullivan, and we began to strategize as to how we might bring about a resolution.

The Negotiations

From the outset, the condition precedent to any resolution was that any period of incarceration would be served in Canada and that any bargain struck would only result in a financial or probationary penalty in the United States. We were not prepared to expose Alan to what, at that time, prior to a subsequent determination of unconstitutionality, was an almost slavish adherence to the U.S. Sentencing Guidelines. Any meaningful downward departure from the draconian Guidelines would have to be creatively based on an agreement to some period of incarceration in Canada. As to a financial penalty in the United States, Alan and his family had an interest in two condominiums, one located in New York City and the other in Florida. Conveniently, their total equity in the two properties was approximately $700,000 U.S. which converted to a more politically acceptable sounding sum of $1-million CDN.

It is my belief that it was the meeting with the Eaglesons on April 24, 1997 that triggered the initiation of meaningful discussions with the American prosecutor and Canadian Crown. Approximately two weeks later, Paul Kelly and a delegation of associates met with Jerry O'Sullivan, Edgar Sexton and me at my offices in Toronto in an attempt to structure a resolution.

However, in a letter to the editor of *The Toronto Star* dated June 2, 1998, Paul Kelly had a different recollection as to both the commencement and the motivation for our discussions. In responding to a May 23, 1998 column by sports writer, Mary Ormsby, in which she referred to the U.S. investigators and prosecutors as "dummies" and "foreign dolts," Mr. Kelly claimed that "it was the U.S. that started the plea discussions that led to Eagleson's convictions in both countries." Ormsby had stated that "the U.S. attorney's office failed to make their … indictment stick and had to bargain down, hat in hand to three counts." Kelly, in response, claimed that they had commenced the negotiating process "for two reasons: first, because we knew that Eagleson would never be indicted to face trial on the most serious U.S. charges since our request was never even passed on to a Canadian judge; and second, because it made sense to seek some closure, not only for the victims … but for the game of hockey itself." In addressing Ormsby's position that the U.S. "failed to negotiate a plea bargain that any of them … could understand," Kelly stated that the U.S. had "recognized the potential for Eagleson to be granted work release or parole." Finally, Kelly challenged the assertion of a former member of the RCMP that "the Americans backed themselves into a corner with a precipitous indictment" and asserted that, in fact, "the U.S. stepped in only after the RCMP initially refused to investigate, and had carried out its efforts despite Canadian roadblocks."

It is my view that Mr. Kelly's remarks, penned after his departure from the U.S. Attorney's office and while facing criticism from some quarters that he had bargained badly, is simply historical revisionism. To the displeasure of the Americans, the Canadian investigation had progressed slowly and they had become extremely impatient. The problem came into greater focus when the anticipated Canadian charges became a reality in December 1997. The Americans had been told that they had to wait, initially for the outcome of the Canadian investigation and subsequently for the outcome of a Canadian trial. There was never, nor could there have been, a Canadian outcome that precluded an extradition to the United States on the allegations not addressed in the Canadian charges. Consistent with our prediction when Alan had asked us how long to the "bitter end," I had warned Paul Kelly that absent a resolution, the Canadian trial, subsequent extradition hearing and possible appeals would delay the commencement of a trial in Boston for at least five years. For the consideration of an ambitious U.S. prosecutor ready to transition to a private and more lucrative practice, I viewed delay as one of our major bargaining chips.

Mr. Kelly's response to the Ormsby article had also included a claim that prior to the U.S. Indictment "as a courtesy to Eagleson's lawyers, we granted a request that we not arrest Eagleson on the promise he would voluntarily surrender in Boston. Regrettably, that promise was breached." Sarah Chapin Columbia, on behalf of the defence team, responded by letter to *The Toronto Star* published on June 24, 1998. After citing the alleged promise, she stated: "This is not true and Kelly knows it is not true. Eagleson's lawyers neither requested special courtesy from the U.S. government in connection with Eagleson's impending arrest nor promised that Eagleson would appear voluntarily in Boston. Nor would we have done so."

While the discussions with the U.S. prosecutor were ongoing, a number of contemporaneous meetings took place with Susan Ficek and Anthony Graburn, two senior and very capable members of the Crown Law Office in Toronto who had been assigned carriage of the Eagleson prosecution in Canada. These candid, focused and productive discussions were conducted in conjunction with senior RCMP investigators who appreciated both the strengths and weaknesses of their case. It was clear that if we were unable to consummate a cross-border agreement which would resolve all outstanding charges in both countries, no deal was possible.

The Resolution

Regardless of the competing interpretations of the factors that ultimately resulted in a plea resolution, a letter of agreement executed by R. Alan Eagleson on October 24, 1997 incorporated the negotiated settlement of the Eagleson saga. It was historic, at least in the sense that it was unprecedented, that an accused charged in both the United States and Canada would enter into an agreement, the terms of which required that both parties in both countries live up to their end of the bargain. The resolution contained the following provisions:

(i) that the 32-count U.S. Indictment would be substituted by an Information alleging three counts of mail fraud relating to international hockey events, personal expenses from NHLPA funds and a disability claim;

(ii) that Eagleson would voluntarily enter the United States and plead guilty to that Information;

(iii) that Eagleson would be placed on unsupervised probation for a period of one year (the U.S. Attorney agreeing to defer the custody component of the sentence to the Canadian authorities and the related prosecution in Canada);

(iv) that Eagleson would pay restitution in the United States in the amount of $1-million (Cdn.) prior to the time of plea and sentencing;

(v) that the non-custodial resolution in the United States be conditional upon Eagleson's agreement to plead guilty to related criminal charges in Canada and to advocate and receive "… a sentence of not less than eighteen months of incarceration to be served in a penal institution and not in a halfway house, home confinement, or community service, such sentence to be implemented in accordance with Canadian law."

In order to effect the terms of the agreement, it was necessary, from an American perspective, to extensively and expressly address the mandatory provisions of the United States Sentencing Guidelines. The agreement recited the circumstances which were not adequately taken into consideration by the Commission in formulating the sentencing guidelines and which warranted a departure from the otherwise applicable sentencing provisions. The agreement further specified that if the U.S. Attorney determined that Eagleson had failed to comply with any provision of the agreement or had committed any crime prior to the commencement of his term of his imprisonment in Canada, the U.S. Attorney would, at his option, be released from his commitments under the agreement and pursue all remedies available under the law. The agreement was executed by James B. Farmer, Chief of the Criminal Division, on behalf of Donald K. Stern, the United States Attorney for Massachusetts.

The Plea in Boston: January 6, 1998

On Monday, January 5, 1998, Alan, his son Allen and I flew to Boston for the first phase of implementing the settlement. We met for dinner with our American counterparts who walked Alan through the protocol and the manner in which the proceedings would unfold before District Court Judge Nathaniel Gorton and the formalities of the plea inquiries and acknowledgements which would take place in open court the next day. A comprehensive 22-page Pre-sentence Investigation Report had been prepared by Probation Services in Boston. The report expressly detailed and acknowledged the recommendation of the government to a downward departure to a probationary sentence "because of circumstances of a kind, and to a degree, not adequately taken into consideration by the United States Sentencing Commission in formulating the sentencing guidelines."

After dinner, we returned to the hotel and met to discuss further details. The phone rang. Alan answered, had a brief conversation, turned and advised me that: "Bud Estey wants to talk to you." The legendary Willard Zebedee Estey, former Chief Justice of Ontario and a retired member of the Supreme Court of Canada, spoke with clear, unequivocal and memorable 'instructions' in language more colourful than I will repeat: "This proceeding is a miscarriage of justice. I don't think that Alan should participate in a plea of convenience. They are applying today's thinking against common practices at the time when these so-called misdeeds occurred and when I was Chairman of Hockey Canada." I acknowledged and expressed my appreciation for his advice and concern. I looked at the two Alans and asked whether we were going to the airport. Eagleson smiled and simply said, "Don't worry, I'll take the heat with Bud – it's got to get done."

The next morning we proceeded, in accordance with the plan, to the FBI building for surrender. It had been agreed that Alan would be processed, taken by elevator to the underground parking lot, transported to the court house underground parking lot, and be brought directly to Judge Gorton's courtroom. We were aware that protocol required that he be handcuffed while in FBI custody. As he was led to the elevator en route to the FBI parking garage, Alan instinctively felt that the agents were not going to adhere to the plan. He had taken off his top coat and was able to place it over his handcuffed wrists as the officers led him out the front door at ground level to provide Russ Conway's photographers from the *Eagle-Tribune* with an opportunity for an exclusive of the Eagleson surrender.

The plea, the recitation of facts, the plea inquiry and the submissions of Paul Kelly and Jerry O'Sullivan were then presented uneventfully under the watchful eyes of Bobby Orr, Carl Brewer, and Russ Conway. I personally regret only one lapse on our part, which was seized upon by the media as indicative of arrogance and a lack of remorse. Members of the Order of Canada almost instinctively display their lapel pin and Alan was accustomed to the pin being part of his wardrobe. He had not considered the optics of wearing it in a Boston criminal courtroom, and likewise, I had failed to advert to this oversight. A difficult lesson learned.

The Plea in Toronto: January 7, 1998

We returned to Toronto on the evening of January 6th and were virtually assaulted at the airport by a media maelstrom. Microphones and photographers descended upon us in droves. Although Alan was no stranger to media attention, it had been an exhausting emotional experience in Boston and he was facing yet another challenging day in Toronto, after which he would commence an eighteen-month sentence at Mimico Correctional. With limited success, I attempted to respond to timing and technical inquiries to divert attention, while Alan made a rather hasty exit to the taxi stand.

The next morning, in accordance with the terms of the resolution and its timetable, we appeared in what is now the Superior Court of Justice in Toronto before Chief Justice Patrick LeSage for plea, submissions, and sentence. The carefully crafted statement of fact was based upon admissions to three counts of fraud in relation to rink board advertising in the 1984, 1987, and 1991 Canada Cup Series. One count named Hockey Canada as the victim while the other two alleged that one of the corporate sponsors, Labatt Brewery, had been deprived of advertising revenue. The agreed facts relied upon Eagleson's 'creative' negotiations and 'wheeling and dealing' with sponsors of the tournament to support the fraud convictions. The amount of the fraud and the benefit to Eagleson remained unresolved and in dispute. It was only conceded that the loss was "clearly in the hundreds of thousands of dollars" but any actual financial benefit to Alan, if any, could not be ascertained.

We had met with Chief Justice LeSage on December 22, 1997 in a pre-trial conference and had canvassed the proposed eighteen-month disposition. He had assured us that he would give "great weight" to the joint submission. In adopting that recommendation on January 7th, Chief Justice LeSage observed:

> You are a nationally recognized person. You have fallen from a great height… it should have been known to you a long time ago, that you could not wear all of those hats and conduct all of those different businesses, in representing these different persons, each in conflict with each other, without something like this happening.

When asked whether he had anything to say before the imposition of sentence, Alan briefly responded: "I sincerely apologize for any harm I might have caused and I hope I will have the opportunity in the future to make a positive contribution to our community and to our country." He was then unceremoniously taken into custody to commence his sentence.

Mimico Correctional

There was a tragic irony in the fact that Alan served his sentence at Mimico Correctional Centre, located in Etobicoke-Lakeshore, the constituency which he had represented as a member of the Legislative Assembly of Ontario from 1963 to 1967. Although he was almost immediately eligible for conditional release programs, the Ministry of Corrections and the administration at the jail resisted early release and incorrectly maintained that Eagleson was somehow bound to remain in custody pursuant to our agreement with the United States. In fact, one of the critical aspects of the resolution was that the "sentence [was] to be implemented in accordance with Canadian law." Alan was belatedly granted limited work passes and received full parole on his first eligibility date, having served six months' imprisonment.

The Aftermath

Shortly after his release on parole in July 1998, the first 'Eagleson Freedom Lunch' was convened at the Senator Restaurant in Toronto where a group of distinguished Canadians assembled to wish Alan well. Former Prime Minister John Turner announced that "whatever debt Al Eagleson owed to society, if any, has been paid in full." Bud Estey then observed: "Eagleson is the only person to escape from both world super powers. He escaped from the Soviets in 1972 and from the Americans in 1998." Alan then rose to express his gratitude to those who had been so incredibly supportive during his ordeal. He began his remarks by noting that: "What has sustained me during this difficult period of my life are the three F's." The assembled group braced itself for what was anticipated to be the rather graphic language often associated with Eagleson. He then simply said: "Friends, Family, and Faith." Those three words and the sentiments which they embrace best describe the true Alan Eagleson.

Alan is now eighty-four years old and quietly resides with Nancy, to whom he has been married for fifty-seven years, in Collingwood, Ontario. His two children have prospered both in business and in the legal profession and he is devoted to his three grandchildren. He continues to sponsor an annual fundraiser for the cardiac unit at the Hospital for Sick Children in Toronto, where one of his grandsons underwent the 'Dr. Mustard procedure' at birth. The Eagleson Freedom Lunch, which is now referred to as the 'Old Boys' Lunch', still attracts the extraordinary group of friends to whom he paid tribute upon his release from custody. As the youngest member of the group, I am honoured to be invited and frequently listen to sage advice in uncharacteristic silence.

And even after twenty years, I occasionally reflect upon the resolution and regret that we didn't 'fight the good fight'. We could have won.

***David Bright Q.C.** is a partner and practices in the areas of criminal law, military law, and police discipline. He has a Martindale Hubbell Peer Review Rating of AV: Preeminent 5 out of 5, reflecting his abilities in the practice of law as judged by his peers. David has been included in the Best Lawyers annual publication, The Best Lawyers in Canada, since 2006. David served as a Naval Air Crewman in the Royal Canadian Navy, flying a tracker aircraft from HMCS Bonaventure, Canada's last aircraft carrier, and the USS Essex. He is presently a board member of the Canadian Council of Criminal Defence Lawyers, a special advisor to the Board of Directors of the Royal Nova Scotia International Tattoo, and is the former Honorary Consul to the Kingdom of Lesotho, South Africa.*

Mr. David Bright

Justice Delayed

A Story of Complacency

PERSONS CHARGED WITH A CRIME in Canada, are presumably entitled to a trial within a reasonable time frame. It is actually one of the specified rights (referred to as 11b) enshrined in the *Canadian Charter of Rights and Freedoms*. This story is an saga of exceptional delays and complacency, commencing with a 1998 telephone call from a colleague of mine leading to a chain of events that had happened twenty years previously. As a result of that notorious call, I inherited a case that spanned almost forty years from alleged crime to decision by the courts, leaving me with a lifetime of disturbing memories.

The Beginning, 1998

Did Alexander Graham Bell have any idea of the potential consequences of his invention of the telephone? In early 1998 the phone rang in my Halifax office. It was a regulatory lawyer, Ron Lunau, calling from Ottawa. He told me that his client who was living in India at the time, one Ernest Fenwick MacIntosh ('Fen'), had received a letter from the Canadian High Commission stating that his passport was being cancelled because the Crown was re-visiting a previously dormant prosecution. The letter from the High Commission did not specify who or what the offence concerned, or when it had occurred. Ron's request was straightforward: Would I write to the Crown prosecution office and obtain the particulars of the alleged offence? So, on April 2, 1998 I wrote to the Crown office requesting disclosure of all relevant evidence in their possession.

The Crown office was located in Port Hawkesbury, Nova Scotia; a small, industrial town located on the Cape Breton side of the Canso Causeway which links the Nova Scotia mainland and Cape Breton Island. At one time, Port Hawkesbury had been a busy and prosperous town with a refinery, heavy water plant, and paper mill. At the time of the MacIntosh matter, the paper mill remained as the main industry. The Senior Crown Attorney at the time was Richard MacKinnon, now Judge MacKinnon of the Provincial Court of Nova Scotia. A polite and affable person, he was running a busy office that was short-staffed, and not equipped to handle a large and potentially complex criminal trial.

On May 25, 1998 I received some basic disclosure from the Crown office relating to an Information dating back to 1995. An 'Information' is typically a charge sheet setting out the alleged offence, in other words a criminal charge which begins a criminal proceeding in the courts. This particular Information alleged "gross indecency" and "indecent assault" by MacIntosh against a person who was publicly identified as 'DRS'. These sexual assaults allegedly happened in Port Hawksbury, dating back twenty years – to the mid 1970s. Mr. MacIntosh would have been in his mid-thirties at the time the alleged assaults occurred.

The background of this matter is of some interest. MacIntosh worked in the marine electronics and telecommunications field, a craft that he had learned in the Canadian Forces. MacIntosh moved to Port Hawkesbury from Halifax in 1971. He bought a rooming house, 'The Farquhar House', together with his business partner, Marcie MacQuarrie in July of 1973. MacQuarrie and MacIntosh lived in the Farquhar House, along with Vince Burke, a Crown Attorney, Mary MacDonald, the housekeeper, and several Straits Pirates Junior B hockey team players, who boarded in hockey season. Farquhar House was named by a number of the complainants as a location where many of the assaults and indecent acts had taken place.

Ernest Fenwick MacIntosh had been a candidate in the Nova Scotia provincial election of 1974. During the time of the election, a boy, who will be referred to in this story as 'DRS', and his family lived outside of Port Hawkesbury. The story unfolded that the family of DRS would not permit contact between DRS and MacIntosh because of rumours that MacIntosh was a child molester. MacIntosh remained in Port Hawkesbury living in the Farquhar House, but in 1975, MacQuarrie purchased a home of his own and moved out of Farquhar House. Vince Burke moved to Ontario. In 1976, the hockey players stopped boarding at Farquhar House. MacIntosh decided to convert Farquhar House into apartments.

The Charges: Allegations from 1995

The main accuser in this matter was the boy referred to as 'DRS', the boy whose parents had responded to rumours about MacIntosh's reputation. It seems that 'DRS' had contact with MacIntosh in the mid 1970s. In January 1995, DRS spoke with his father to "check some dates" and spoke with his cousin 'JAH' who lived in Port Hawkesbury.

By this time, in 1995, DRS was living in British Columbia. He went to the RCMP in B.C. and gave a statement alleging sexual abuse against Ernest Fenwick MacIntosh. Eventually, that statement and the allegations contained were forwarded to the Port Hawkesbury Detachment of the RCMP, where Cst. Deveau was assigned as the Chief Investigator. The allegations from DRS were that MacIntosh performed oral sex on him between two dozen and seventy-five times. Based upon the allegations of DRS, Cst. Joseph Deveau had reasonable grounds to charge MacIntosh in relation to that complaint as of February of 1995. In February of 1995, at the urging of DRS, Cst. Deveau contacted JAH, the cousin, who also made a complaint, actually in his own handwriting.

He alleged MacIntosh had performed oral sex on him on one occasion at a hotel near Halifax. In his statement, he confirmed that there was no sexual activity at the Farquhar House. Deveau had reasonable grounds to charge MacIntosh in relation to the DRS complaint, as of February 1995. He did not do so until December 1995 – almost a year – with no real explanation provided for the delay. Interestingly, there appeared to be no questioning by Deveau as to whether or not DRS and JAH had discussed the matter in any detail, or at all. It is obvious that if DRS suggested Deveau speak with JAH, there had been some sort of discussion.

Deveau referred the JAH complaint to Halifax Regional Police, as it was not within his jurisdiction. The Halifax Regional Police investigated, confirmed that Ernest Fenwick MacIntosh was living overseas in India, and they attempted to arrange a meeting with JAH. He showed no interest in meeting with the police in this matter. As a consequence, the Halifax Police deemed it was not appropriate to lay charges, and advised JAH and Deveau that they would not be proceeding.

The Indian Connection

In early 1995 Cst. Deveau obtained MacIntosh's telephone number and address in India from MacIntosh's relatives. It was not until August of 1996 – almost another year – that Deveau called MacIntosh in India. Years later, under examinations at trial, each of the relatives had conflicting recollections as to what was said to Cst. Deveau. In any event, Deveau said that he spoke with MacIntosh in India and gave him details of the charges, asking him if he planned to return to Canada. He remembered MacIntosh indicated he would not return. MacIntosh, however, said that he was asked if he had any immediate plans to return to Canada, and indicated that he did not. MacIntosh also said that he was never told the nature of the charge. The call was interrupted, Deveau never called back and MacIntosh heard nothing further for years.

Incidentally while Cst. Deveau was pursuing MacIntosh, the Canadian High Commission passport office, after a gentle nudge from the Federal Court directing that the passport office substantiate its decision, withdrew its application to cancel MacIntosh's passport. In May of 1997, nine months before the 1998 call, MacIntosh renewed his passport, providing his updated contact information. To the knowledge of the RCMP and the Crown, MacIntosh travelled back and forth to Montreal from India, using that passport.

Although some disclosure had been provided by the Provincial Crown, it was apparent that there was likely much more material around. Obviously, the Federal Department of Justice was involved. I wrote to them seeking copies of materials that they had in their possession. The quick response was that these Federal Justice materials were 'State to State' communications between India and Canada and were considered to be privileged and need not be produced. Materials received from the Provincial Crown however, indicated that there was to be an attempt to extradite MacIntosh from India back to Canada. This would require the affidavit of DRS.

Obviously, a sworn statement by the complainant would be relevant and helpful to the defence and provide for cross-examination, especially if it contained inconsistencies. Additionally, the Provincial Crown advised that they were told by the Federal Department of Justice that affidavits identifying the accused were required.

This was in November of 1998. In January of 1999 it was revealed by disclosure that a photo line-up of MacIntosh and other persons had been prepared.

DRS was shown the photo array, but was unable to identify MacIntosh. The Crown said this was because the photographs were of poor quality. It was interesting to note that the first statement from DRS was in January of 1995. Not until January of 1999 was he shown a photo line-up, which had totally been within the control of the RCMP. Four years is a long time in which to conduct the initial phase of any investigation. The *Charter* clock was ticking.

In the meantime, new allegations had surfaced against MacIntosh. In January of 1999 one 'RM' disclosed an allegation of sexual abuse. In March of 2000, similarly 'CM' alleged abuse, but he was unable to identify MacIntosh from a photo line-up, which now contained a photocopy of MacIntosh's passport photo. In July 2000, the RCMP travelled to Edmonton and received a statement from one 'WMR' alleging sexual abuse. He could not identify MacIntosh from the photo line-up. The RCMP then travelled to Vancouver, where DRS was then able to identify MacIntosh from a photo line-up.

In September 2000, an allegation of abuse was received from one 'AM'. In October, a further allegation was received from one 'GB'. In March 2001, one 'DB' provided the RCMP in Winnipeg with a statement alleging abuse by MacIntosh, and in August 2001, the RCMP in Port Hawkesbury received a fax statement from 'BS'; the brother of 'DRS', who was residing in Florida. In October 2001, an Information was sworn charging MacIntosh in relation to offences disclosed in the statement of 'WMR'. Shockingly, there appears to have been no effort by the RCMP to ascertain whether or not there was any collusion between these various complainants, as many of the names and contact information came from DRS.

After a four-year investigation on the allegation of essentially one person, DRS, eight more complainants came forward in three years, making a total of nine complaints. The task of the defence became more difficult.

Extradition ... After Eleven Years

Nothing was done with respect to the 1997 request by the Canadian Federal Government for MacIntosh's extradition from India to Canada. Finally in July 2006 – over eleven years from the initial complaint by DRS – a formal request for extradition was forwarded to the Government of India. On April 5, 2007, MacIntosh was arrested in New Delhi and taken before the presiding Justice. Surprisingly, only four of the nine complaints were before the Indian Court. Moreover, the request for extradition was not supported by evidence as required by the treaty. The argument, therefore, was that the Crown in Nova Scotia could not proceed with all nine complaints, as it would be prohibited by the Rule of Specialty when only four complaints were before the Indian court. The Rule of Specialty, I learned, was an international law of extradition which applies with equal force whether extradition occurs by treaty or by courtesy between nations.

When MacIntosh was taken before the presiding Justice in India, he indicated that he was not contesting his return to Canada, but needed time to wind up his affairs. He had been living in India for many years and had a household of furnishings that required disposal, as well a duty to his employer to turn over the office to a successor.

Indeed he was given time, but he was accompanied everywhere by armed Indian police. During the nights and non-business times, he was housed in the infamous Tihar Jail, which is a vast penal colony in Delhi. It is equipped to handle some 5,200 prisoners, however, at the time of MacIntosh's incarceration, some 10,500 were housed there.

Conditions were abhorrent. MacIntosh slept and sat on a wet, concrete floor, with a variety of other prisoners incarcerated for serious crimes. He had to purchase his own food. The so-called dormitory area was visited by rodents and vermin, and snakes were a common sight. Finally, on April 25, 2007 an Indian Court recommended the extradition of MacIntosh, although that court was vague on which charges they had considered, made no reference to some of the difficulties in the charges, and made no mention of the failure to apply the treaty. The RCMP then dispatched officers to India to take MacIntosh into custody and return him to Canada.

Nine years since the prophetic phone call came in from my colleague in Ottawa in June of 2007, MacIntosh made his first appearance before the Provincial Court of Nova Scotia in Port Hawkesbury. The presiding judge, Laurie Halfpenny MacQuarrie, is a courteous, no-nonsense judge who was a Crown Attorney prior to her appointment. The matter was set for bail hearing in June of 2007 and on June 18, 2007, bail was denied and MacIntosh's incarceration continued. No further disclosure was provided to the defence, apart from the initial provision in May of 1998.

The Clock Continued to Tick

In some cases with a number of complainants, disclosure can often be somewhat delayed or provided piecemeal. This may be understandable. This matter, however, was unique in that the Crown was aware from day one for the need for disclosure and had been pushed in that direction by the RCMP. Four years prior to the request for extradition from India was submitted, the RCMP and Crown were well aware of their need to fulfill their disclosure obligation. Indeed, in June 2002 the RCMP reviewed the Crown's file. That file did not contain copies of video or audio statements, photo line-ups, or other relevant material. The RCMP ironically noted "the present disclosure falls far short of what is required by Stinchcombe." It is to be remembered in the famous Supreme Court of Canada decision in *R. v. Stinchcombe*, the importance of timely disclosure was established, including the recognition that it should occur prior to election. That is because the defence needs disclosure before the accused elects trial either by the Provincial Court, judge alone, or judge and jury.

The RCMP then proceeded to prepare disclosure. The RCMP delivered two disclosure packages to the Crown office in August 2002 consisting of binders with videocassettes with extra copies to facilitate production to the defence. In October 2007 – five years after the binders had been assembled – the defence had still not received any of the video or audio tapes referenced in the binders, nor any pertinent information respecting the complainants and potential witnesses. No explanation was given for the failure of the Crown to provide this relevant information.

Action at Last

The request for the video/audio tapes was repeated in November 2007, January 2008, and early February 2008. These statements and tapes were finally provided to the defence on February 22, 2008. The request for DRS' affidavit and other materials was not provided until May 2008. The final disclosure was provided on May 2, 2008, and the accused disclosure election took place almost immediately thereafter, on May 7, 2008.

This significant delay in disclosure resulted in our application to the Nova Scotia Supreme Court for an Order of Prohibition, stopping the Preliminary Inquiry from proceeding (sort of suggesting that 'enough is enough'). The Application for Prohibition took place before Justice Frank Edwards, a seasoned jurist who, prior to his appointment, had been a member of the Crown office in Sydney, Nova Scotia. The Application for Prohibition was dismissed. On appeal to the Nova Scotia Court of Appeal, the appeal was dismissed by the decision of Justice Thomas Cromwell, who later was named to the Supreme Court of Canada.

As discussed earlier, the Supreme Court of Canada in *R. v. Stinchcombe* makes it clear that full and timely disclosure is essential for the proper running of the Criminal Justice System. It is fair to suggest that in this matter, the concept of full and timely disclosure was forgotten or ignored by the Provincial prosecution services, and adequate explanation was simply not provided. The victims of a crime, and the accused, are entitled to have a trial within a reasonable period of time. Obviously, for matters that are complex, it will take longer. However, that does not relieve the authorities of attempting to bring an accused person to justice as quickly as possible.

Upon his return to Canada, we, MacIntosh's counsel, immediately asked for disclosure. However, the Crown did not disclose the bulk of materials, which comprised 147 files, for some six months. Besides that, the video and audio recordings of some of the complainants were not disclosed for nine months, an affidavit from the primary complainant was not disclosed for twelve months, and a package of affidavits sent to the Canadian government (to ground the extradition request) was likewise not disclosed for twelve months. On the other hand, MacIntosh made his election five days after receiving the affidavit and the further materials. He moved without delay. It seemed like time was suspended, and of no importance to the prosecution.

A Trial at Last

The defence team was composed of myself along with colleague Brian Casey QC, who carried much of the burden of this case. Additionally, we were joined by our associate, Jan Murray. Interestingly enough, in this day of suggesting that preliminary inquiries are worthless, the Crown called no evidence with respect to some of the complainants, which resulted, of course, in their trials and their matters not proceeding. By consent, the final Information was severed into two Informations, each alleging distinct counts.

Before Justice Simon MacDonald of the Nova Scotia Supreme Court, DRS, his brother, and cousin JAH were on one Information as alleged victims, whilst the remaining complainants were on the other. As the trials were set to commence, I suffered a heart attack. I don't want to suggest that the slow agonizing pace of these proceedings, such as they were, caused my heart attack, but it didn't help. Lawyers, like everyone else, suffer from stress over time. MacIntosh, however, did not ask for a delay in the trial, rather he wanted the matter to proceed. Clearly no delay can be laid at his feet.

Brian proceeded with the first trial. DRS was driven around the Port Hawkesbury area by the RCMP and pointed out various sites where the alleged 'indecent assaults' had occurred, including his home, where he said he had a specific recall of being assaulted in the downstairs family TV room. During the trial, it came out in cross-examination that this could not have been true, as the TV room had not been completed until some years after DRS had moved away from the family home. Nevertheless, the eventual outcome of that trial was MacIntosh being found guilty in relation to a number of the offences.

The Second Trial

The second trial took place before Chief Justice Joseph Phillip Kennedy, again with myself, back on my feet, and Jan Murray. The atmosphere between counsel was most collegial, which fortunately is quite typical of criminal trials in Nova Scotia. However, during this trial, the Crown suggested that we meet during a break, as they had something they wished to discuss. Ever the eternal optimist, I thought perhaps there would be a resolution to the trial. Such was not the case. The Crown had received a letter from a police department out west suggesting that one of complainants intended to kill Fen MacIntosh, and suggested that he would kill Jan and me on his way to complete the execution. I must say that I thought it rather odd that the police would write this in a letter and not pick up the telephone. In any event, as a consequence, court did not proceed on that day, and Jan and I relocated our hotel from one in Port Hawkesbury to one in Antigonish. The RCMP assured us that they would have a patrol car in the immediate area patrolling and looking out for this gentleman. Nothing transpired, we moved back to our original hotel, and the trial proceeded along.

Heart attacks are thankfully not the norm for defence counsel, but sadly death threats are. Over my career, I have not been immune, but this was Jan's first.

Sentences Imposed

At the conclusion of that trial, MacIntosh was convicted of some of the charges and acquitted of others. The Chief Justice deemed that the sentence imposed should be consecutive to the one imposed by Justice MacDonald. I must admit to still being puzzled by that judicial approach.

The matter moved to the Nova Scotia Court of Appeal. In a decision written by Justice Duncan Beveridge and concurred with by the other two judges, a detailed analysis of the time line was set out, including the concept of prejudice, failure to disclose, potential witness contamination, and a misapprehension of much of the evidence by the trial judge.

The Nova Scotia Court of Appeal unanimously ordered a judicial stay, which was entered with respect to both my trial and the one conducted by Brian.

One would reasonably think that this outcome would be the end of the matter. Not so quick, the endless clock continued to tick. The Crown sought leave to appeal to the Supreme Court of Canada from the unanimous decision of the Nova Scotia Court of Appeal. Leave was granted.

Off Brian and I went to Ottawa. The Crown was represented by Mark Scott, a proficient and fair-minded Crown. The Crown stood and addressed the questions from the panel, chaired by the Chief Justice. I always remember the comment by Justice Michael Moldaver directed to the Crown. "As I see it," he said, "in Nova Scotia you can have a speedy trial or full disclosure; but you can't have both."

As we prepared to stand and defend, the Chief Justice indicated that there was no need to hear from Brian and me. This is music to the ears of defence counsel, not a disappointment, as those who have appeared before this court will attest.

The End

Finally, the matter was over. The media had no sympathy for MacIntosh, even though it was clear that he had not been fairly treated. Some of the complainants were demanding a public inquiry. Justice officials were apologizing. No one seemed to give a thought for the man who had lost his job, exhausted his savings, and been subjected to a lengthy period of incarceration whilst awaiting his trial.

It is against a backdrop of cases like this that the recent decision of the Supreme Court of Canada, in *R. v. Jordan*, set out trial time lines. As of writing, there is now a ceiling of eighteen months on the length of a criminal case in Provincial courts, from the charge to the end of trial, and a ceiling of thirty months on criminal cases in superior courts, or cases tried in provincial courts after a preliminary inquiry. Persons victimized by crime are fully entitled to have trial within these reasonable time frames and accused persons likewise. This is a case that took an astounding eighteen years from the laying of the charge in 1995 until the decision of the Supreme Court of Canada in April of 2013. To put this eighteen years in context, when the phone rang in 1998, William Jefferson Clinton was President of the United States, Joseph Jacques Jean Chrétien was Prime Minister of Canada, Anthony (Tony) Charles Lynton Blair was Prime Minister of the United Kingdom, and Antonio Lamer was Chief Justice of Canada. There were certainly no iPhones.

It is highly unlikely that such as this will ever occur again. Nonetheless, it is instructive in realizing that an atmosphere of complacency, and a slow ticking *Charter* clock, are not the friend of the justice system.

PART TWO

Covert Investigations

Mona Duckett QC *served as a Bencher with the Law Society of Alberta from 2000 to 2006, finishing her tenure there as its president. She has been a Fellow of the American College of Trial Lawyers since 2003, and is a current member and past president of the Criminal Trial Lawyers Association. She lectures regularly for continuing legal education programs for lawyers, judges, and police. She is currently a sessional instructor in Advocacy at the University of Alberta Law School and has also taught Professional Responsibility and Advanced Criminal Law. She served for approximately fifteen years as a member of the Faculty of the Federation of Canadian Law Societies, National Criminal Law Program. Ms. Duckett has produced numerous criminal law papers over the course of her career, and is a co-author of the 2010 criminal text,* Trial of Sexual Offences.

Ms. Mona Duckett

Two Troubled Youths and a Mr. Big Sting

JUST AFTER 5:00 P.M. on May 31, 2009, two fourteen-year-old boys ran away from Bosco Homes Ranch, a youth facility in a rural area outside of Sherwood Park, near Edmonton, Alberta. By 2:30 the next morning, they were in police custody for driving erratically in a truck they had admittedly stolen. Police had trouble finding the registered owner of the truck, but at 5:40 a.m. the man's body was found on his rural acreage, twelve kilometers from Bosco Homes Ranch. The truck's owner and his female tenant had been brutally murdered. RCMP members met to brief the double homicide at 8:00 a.m. on June 1, and by 8:30 a.m. they decided to arrest both boys for the killings. This is a story of tunnel vision, false confessions, 'Mr. Big' stings, police exploitation of the highly vulnerable, and the development of the common law. In its wake remains an unsolved double homicide and one or perhaps two profoundly impacted young men who were exploited by the state.

The Boys and Their Escapade

When the fourteen-year-old boys, referred to in this story as Nate and Alan, ran away from the youth facility on an evening in May 2009, they took nothing with them. They walked down country roads and through fields for about an hour before coming to an acreage where they took a fire extinguisher from a tractor and finished off a few ounces of vodka they found in some near-empty bottles. They wandered to a travel trailer storage lot, called the Double Dutch, where they damaged a vehicle windshield, broke into thirteen RVs, and damaged and stole various property including two CO2 pellet guns and pellets. The damaged vehicle with a fire extinguisher on the front seat was discovered at 7:30 p.m.

From the storage lot, the boys walked to an apparently abandoned house, found nothing worth taking and continued walking to a property where there were two house trailers. The land, and one of the trailers, was owned by Baldur Boenke. His friend Susan Trudel was the tenant of his trailer. The other trailer was owned by Leroy Martin, who lived there with a roommate by the name of Robert Lerner.

About twenty meters from the house trailers was a clearing where several other vehicles were stored. The boys arrived to the property in that area and tried unsuccessfully to start the vehicles with keys they found. They smoked some cigarette butts and shot pellets at some of the cars and at the barking dog that approached from the area of the trailers. It was cold and getting dark. They headed toward the trailers to see if the residents could give them a ride into Edmonton, or at least provide them with some coats to wear.

No one answered when they knocked on the door of the first trailer so they walked right in. No one was home. They shot some pellets at the TV and grabbed a couple of jackets. They found some car keys that they hoped would start the little red car in front of the trailer. The keys fit, but the car seemed out of gas. They decided to look around the property for gasoline.

When Alan left the red car, he noticed a white truck parked nearby. There were keys on the front seat. When the keys started the engine, he called to Nate. The boys jumped into the truck and drove off the property.

They drove the short distance into Edmonton and caused some mischief by randomly shooting the pellet guns. At about 11:00 p.m., they broke into a group home where Nate had previously been placed and they stole some money. By 1:08 a.m. they were at the home of a drug-dealing friend whose mother sent them away after they rang the bell. Just after 2:30 a.m., Edmonton Police responded to a complaint by a citizen of erratic driving by a white truck and arrested both boys as they walked out of a 7-Eleven store.

Immediately, Alan admitted to stealing and driving the vehicle and of driving it. He had some keys as well as a pellet gun and a CO2 cartridge. He also had broken glass in his pocket that had come from a trailer at Double Dutch. Eventually his DNA was found in blood at that trailer. Nate had a set of keys on him as well as three CO2 cartridges. The boys were detained in cells by the Edmonton Police Service.

The Truck's Owner Turns Up Dead

The registered owner of the white truck, Baldur Boenke, lived in the jurisdiction of the RCMP. After the boys were detained, they had trouble locating him. They finally went to one of his acreage properties at 5:40 a.m. where they found his body on the lawn between two house trailers. Susan Trudel's body was found in the kitchen of her trailer. It was a bloody scene, both people having been shot and beaten.

The intensive forensic investigation of the scene, including a bloodstain pattern analysis, showed that Mr. Boenke was killed where he was found. He suffered three gunshot wounds; two to the head and one to the back of the shoulder. There was no stippling around the wounds, causing the Medical Examiner to believe that the shots were fired from more than two to three feet away. He had a significant injury to the back of his head. The skull bone beneath the two-inch-long wound was fractured. Nearby blood spatters showed that he received a high-energy impact such as a gunshot or a blow with an object at the site.

Ms. Trudel's body was on the floor of her trailer kitchen. She suffered four gunshot wounds; two to her head, one to her shoulder and one to her finger. The two head-shots penetrated soft tissue but did not damage bone or brain. The ME believed that those wounds could have incapacitated her, but saw no medical reason that she would have lost consciousness. Again, there was no stippling around those wounds. But the cause of Ms. Trudel's death was blunt cranial trauma. There was a two-inch-long wound to the centre of her scalp at the top of her head below which the skull was fractured. There was a thin scrape-like line down the front of her chest below which were fractures to four ribs. The most significant injury was to the right side of her face and head over the ear, below which was a depressed skull fracture and a serious injury to the brain. She had been struck repeatedly with an object with a severe degree of force.

The scene, particularly in the kitchen, was a bloody mess. Ms. Trudel's blood was found outside the trailer, in a transfer stain on the back of Mr. Boenke's jacket, and also in drops on a lawn chair near Mr. Boenke's body. A trail of her blood droplets led into the trailer. There was blood on the smashed window of the kitchen door and broken glass on the kitchen floor. Ms. Trudel's body was lying on the kitchen floor with a mixing bowl beneath her head. Blood had collected in the bowl. There was a large quantity of blood on her clothing, the floor around her, and the kitchen cupboards nearby. Blood spatter stains, caused by blood spraying when something impacts a wet blood source, were found as high as the kitchen ceiling. There were blood stains on an axe found beside Ms. Trudel's body which showed that the axe was not the murder weapon.

One area of the kitchen floor close to Ms. Trudel's body had very little blood staining compared to the rest of the surrounding area. The expert who examined the scene believed the void in staining occurred because a person or an object was in that area at the time. He expected there would be blood spatter stains on the person who had stood there. There were no bloody footprints in the kitchen.

Expert firearms evidence established that four gunshots hit the exterior wall of the trailer. Nine expended cartridges were found on the ground outside and one on the floor of the inside porch. Three bullets were recovered during the autopsies, one from Trudel and two from Boenke. All the recovered bullets and expended casings were .22 calibre. A .22 calibre rifle was found on the freezer in Ms. Trudel's trailer. Although some of the expended cartridges police found had been fired by that rifle, seven had not. Those seven shots had all been fired by the same gun – a firearm that could have been either a rifle, or a handgun. Ms. Trudel's DNA was found on all seven of those expended shell casings. The gun used in this crime to kill Ms. Trudel and Mr. Boenke has never been found.

Mr. Boenke had last been seen at about 6:00 p.m. on May 31st, 2009. He had failed to return home shortly thereafter, as had been expected by his spouse. Similarly, Ms. Trudel spoke to her brother on the telephone that same afternoon at 5:16 p.m. for thirteen minutes. However, a call to her at 7:00 p.m. went to voicemail.

Arrested for the Murders

RCMP took custody of Nate and Alan from the Edmonton City Police on the morning of June 1st and transported them back to their Strathcona Detachment in Sherwood Park. Alan was arrested for the murders of Baldur Boenke and Susan Trudel at 10:04 a.m. and Nate was likewise under arrest by 11:40 a.m.

Police tested for gunshot residue on both boys' hands, faces, and glasses. The testing showed no evidence that either had fired a firearm or was in the proximity of a firearm. No DNA from either of the homicide victims was found on the clothing of the boys. No DNA from either boy was found at the scene of the killings. No blood from either homicide victim was found in Mr. Boenke's stolen truck.

Alan was interviewed briefly by the RCMP that morning. He described activities and events from the time that he and Nate ran away from Bosco Homes Ranch until the time they were arrested coming out of the 7-Eleven in Edmonton. He admitted stealing the truck but denied that he ever saw Mr. Boenke or Ms. Trudel, dead or alive.

Nate had turned fourteen just three weeks earlier. He had been a ward of the Province since the age of seven so police contacted his social worker who he had identified as being his legal guardian. When asked about his medical condition, Nate told police that he took medication for ADHD but hadn't taken it for twenty-four hours. He was read his legal rights, and was asked whether he wanted to contact a lawyer. He said he had never had a lawyer.

Nate's social worker, her supervisor Lise Durand (whom Nate had never met), and a legal aid staff lawyer met with Nate at the detachment for an hour and twenty minutes that afternoon. Most of the meeting was private between the lawyer and Nate. For the balance of the day, Nate remained alone in a cell. At 8:12 p.m., Sgt. Patrick Kennedy began a formal interview with Nate. Ms. Durand returned to the detachment to be present for the interview. She told Sgt. Kennedy before the interview began that she "didn't think [Nate] fully comprehends" what the lawyer said and that he was "in shock." The interview began with the Sergeant reading some legal forms to Nate, which he signed without question.

At the beginning of the interview, Nate calmly and politely answered the Sergeant's questions about his background, his placement at Bosco

Homes Ranch and running away with Alan. He repeatedly denied any knowledge of the murders and became irritated when pressed on the point. At 10:19 p.m., the adults left the room for forty minutes, the first break in the interview. Nate's frustration was evident as he remained alone in the interview room. The video recording captured him talking to himself and saying "Oh my god hurry up….Fuck you man, just want to get out of this shit. Fucken done talking man…I'm so fucking tired man. This guy talks forever… I need a break. I swear these fucking guys I didn't do shit…"

When the adults returned to the room at 10:56 p.m. Nate immediately asked, "How long do we have to talk for?" His continued denial of knowledge about the murders was again challenged. Ultimately Nate told police that he saw and heard something at the acreage. He later testified in court that he lied in the police interview when he said he saw Alan kill the people.

Sgt. Kennedy suggested to Nate that they "push the pace… because you're tired we've been up all day… give me the whole goods here." Nate asked, "What am I supposed to say?" After a second break at 11:41 p.m., Sgt. Kennedy returned, seeking information about the gun that was used to kill the two deceased and "guarantee[d] then we're done." Nate provided information about a weapon. The interview ended at 12:07 a.m.

Charged with the Murders

Ultimately, both boys were charged with both murders. Each had his own lawyer representing him in court. The legal aid staff lawyer who had attended the detachment to speak with Nate but had left before he'd given his statement, initially represented Nate in court. He soon found himself in a conflict of interest and unable to continue to represent the young man.

It was under these circumstances that I took over as Nate's lawyer, late in 2009. By this time, both boys were co-accused on two charges of first degree murder. As there was no forensic evidence linking them to the bloody homicide scene, I knew that the initial focus of the defence would be the admissibility of Nate's statement to the police. He had been interrogated by an experienced RCMP member after having been abandoned by the lawyer his guardian called after his arrest. Nate was a fourteen-year-old caught in a system he knew nothing about with no understanding of his legal rights. Police were aggressive in their questioning and clearly pressured him to provide information, having decided very quickly that the boys would be the focus of their homicide investigation.

A three-week preliminary inquiry was held in youth court in the summer of 2010 to determine if there was enough evidence for a trial. As required, both boys were present throughout those proceedings to hear all the witnesses testify and to see all the evidence gathered during the RCMP investigation, including four hundred photographs, expert evidence, and a video of the crime scene. In May of 2011, a joint trial began in Edmonton Court of Queen's Bench for Alan and Nate on two counts of second degree murder. The trial began with a *voir dire* to determine whether the statement Nate gave to Sgt. Kennedy was admissible in evidence.

The Youth Criminal Justice Act requires that any statement made by a youth to the police be made in the presence of legal counsel unless the youth does not want a lawyer present. Police are required to inform the young person of this right in language the youth can understand and ensure that any waiver of that right is recorded. Additionally, all statements to a person in authority, whether by an adult or a youth, must be proven by the prosecution to have been made voluntarily before being admissible in evidence. These were the issues facing the first trial judge on the hearing to determine whether Nate's statement could be used as evidence.

Justice John Gill of the Alberta Court of Queen's Bench heard testimony from Sgt. Kennedy, Ms. Durand, and Nate before ruling that Nate's statement could not be admitted as evidence in the trial. He found that Nate was not properly informed of his right to have a lawyer present and that he did not waive that right: 2011 ABQB 356. He also ruled that the statement was not a voluntary one on Nate's part, relying heavily on Sgt. Kennedy's concession during his testimony that "it was in his mind at the time that this was crossing over to a stress compliant" statement. A stress compliant confession is one in which the interpersonal pressures of the interrogation become so intolerable that the suspect just complies to end the interview. Nate testified that he lied in order to end the interview. He gave no information in that interview which could only have come from the actual killer.

This ruling lead the Crown Prosecutors to enter a stay of proceedings on the two murder charges against both boys. Such a stay temporarily ends the prosecution and places the matter in legal limbo for a year. If the charges are not re-activated within the year, they are deemed "never to have commenced" but they cannot be re-laid after that time. The entry of this 'stay' is solely within the discretion of the Attorney General's agents and cannot be objected to or contested by the defence. The Crown Prosecutors were clearly concerned about the strength of their remaining case without the statement as evidence.

So in July of 2011, Nate and Alan, both sixteen years of age and both still wards of the Province, were released after twenty-six months in jail.

The Mr. Big Operation

Within months, the RCMP went ahead with a major crime undercover operation colloquially known as a 'Mr. Big'.

The Mr. Big sting, an invention of Canadian law enforcement, has been highly developed over the last couple of decades and used often with great success. It lures a suspect into a fake criminal organization with promised and delivered benefits on the understanding that true membership, and the consequential windfall, will only be granted by the crime boss, Mr. Big. The suspect is persuaded to convince Mr. Big of his or her organizational worthiness by confessing their involvement in the crime that police are secretly investigating.

The operation involves various 'scenarios' employing undercover RCMP members who play different roles. The estimated length and cost of the project on these homicides was five-and-a-half months and $205,551.12, mostly RCMP member overtime costs. In fact, it took only four months for police to capture the evidence they thought they needed from Nate. The actual total cost, no one professed to know. Police targeted both boys, who by then were living in different cities and had no contact with each other. The stings ran concurrently.

The evolution of the twenty-nine scenarios conducted to lure Nate into Mr. Big's trap is detailed in the reasons for judgment of Mr. Justice Brian Burrows, the second trial judge, who ruled the evidence police obtained through the Mr. Big to be inadmissible at Nate's trial in 2013: 2013 ABQB 288. Nate confessed to the double homicides multiple times to the Mr. Big undercover operators, causing the Crown prosecutor to re-activate his charges within a year of the stay. Alan's charges were never re-activated because he told Mr. Big that he witnessed Nate commit the homicides. Alan testified during Nate's trial as a Crown witness and said that he lied to Mr. Big about what he saw and heard. He lied to avoid being kicked out of the criminal organization which would have made him homeless once again. And he only did so after first telling the truth to Mr. Big. That truth was met with repeated challenges and indirect reminders that full time work with the organization was at stake.

The Edmonton sting involving Nate began mid December 2011. At the time, sixteen-year-old Nate was staying with an aunt and having little contact with his social worker. He had no high school education and he wasn't in school. He had no driver's licence or even photo identification. He had no job, no experience and no stable supportive family. The RCMP knew all of that either before the sting began or shortly into it because between November 2011 and January 2012, they intercepted almost fourteen-thousand pieces of his private communications. None of them were of evidentiary value on the homicide but the information police learned was used to more effectively plan the sting. As Mr. Justice Burrows observed, the RCMP "carefully charged their trap with bait especially attractive to Nate given his particular needs and vulnerabilities."

The RCMP also used information in the planning of the Mr. Big that came from those who had responsibility to protect Nate. One such source was a police interview Nate gave in October 2011 reporting his sexual victimization by an uncle. Others included a probation officer and a social worker. Police became aware before the sting started that Nate was then in a sexual relationship with a married thirty-year-old youth worker who had been employed at the secure child welfare placement that was his home after his release from jail in July of 2011. They decided not to arrest and charge her, which might have terminated the relationship – one which the law deems exploitive because she was in a position of trust over the sixteen year old. Instead, the undercover operators pretended to be impressed as Nate bragged to them about his sexual escapades with the woman.

Police knew that Nate was a troubled youth and some of the operators took on that history for themselves to strengthen their bond with Nate. The operators played characters with comfortable and exciting lifestyles that a sixteen year old would see as cool. The crime organization was set up to provide the family Nate never had. He was regularly paid cash for simple work like cleaning a warehouse. He was taken to restaurants which would be high on the 'best places to eat list' of a sixteen year old. The undercover operators took him to his first rock concert, his first semi-professional hockey game at Rexall Place, and his first snowboarding trip to Jasper, Alberta. He was repeatedly given access to beer, purchased for him at the hockey game. He was given unsupervised access to hotel rooms and to a condo stocked with food in which he was free to entertain his friends so long as they behaved reasonably. He was told to wash the sheets if he used the bedroom for sexual encounters.

Nate developed a bond with the operators who offered to "have his back and respect him" as others had failed to do and not "judge him." In Nate's trial testimony he described the operator he hugged on a couple of occasions as "like a brother, a friend I never had."

The police operators in these covert Mr. Big stings carefully note, when they testify later in court, that a suspect can technically walk away from the sting at any time. However, as Justice Burrows concluded, "Nate would have reasonably believed that without hardly any effort on his part, he had arrived in heaven. Who in their right mind would risk returning to the hell represented by Nate's life away from the Mr. Big operation?"

The RCMP also knew or could easily discover that Nate was a young man extremely vulnerable to the manipulation that is inherent in a Mr. Big operation. Nate had been apprehended at age seven from a home environment marked by adult substance abuse and domestic violence. He had been sexually abused by his uncle when living with his aunt. He had been diagnosed with a long list of psychological conditions including ADHD and Tourette disorder. The psychologist who testified at his 2013 trial had assessed him in 2010, while he was in custody before the stay. Dr. Val Massey observed then that his complex neurodevelopmental needs had never really been addressed. Asked at the 2013 trial how she would expect him to respond to the Mr. Big operations, she called him a "social chameleon" who had been rejected and socially isolated much of his life. He experienced significant abuse and neglect and was used to being left behind. As such, he would "do and say pretty well anything to maintain what looks like a social affiliation with people who would be supportive of him, uncritical and non-judgmental" and would supply him with money he was otherwise unable to earn.

Dr. Massey expressed the opinion that the Mr. Big operation would have a future psychological impact on Nate, "further entrenching his feelings of abandonment and rejection and lack of trust." When Nate testified at the 2013 trial, he spoke about discovering that the organization he called family was a fraud. The realization of the deception brought up his childhood issues including the abuse he had been subjected to by older males.

The Legal Framework for "Mr. Big" Stings

Challenging the admissibility of evidence obtained through Mr. Big stings has been very difficult for defence counsel over the years. These operations were structured to slither untouched between existing legal restrictions on obtaining confessions from suspects. The Supreme Court finally re-wrote the law in 2014 making these operations inadmissible unless the Crown can prove the confessions' reliability: *R. v. Hart,* 2014 SCC 52. But Nate's 2013 trial was held before that change in the common law.

Challenging Mr. Big stings was difficult at the time of this trial because the normal requirement that a suspect's statement to authorities must be voluntary didn't apply. Mr. Big wasn't a "person in authority" in the traditional sense. A suspect's 'right to remain silent' didn't apply as the suspect wasn't in the custody of the authorities at the time s/he spoke to Mr. Big. Although the law allows judges to exclude evidence obtained through an 'abuse of process', that test requires the judge to find that the police tactic would 'shock the community'. No Canadian case can be found where a Judge has ever excluded a Mr. Big confession for that reason.

By the time of Nate's trial, the law had developed however, largely through the Hart case from the Newfoundland Court of Appeal which reached the Supreme Court in 2014, changing the common law.

Though a suspect's right to silence traditionally only applies when the person is in police custody, the law around 'Mr. Bigs' was developing such that the snare created to lure the suspect might be seen as 'functionally equivalent' to police detention. Where the suspect was effectively in the control of the state, subject to state coercion and in an adversarial relationship with the state, it could be argued that there was a real risk of the confession being unreliable such that its use would raise a real possibility of abusive conduct. Ultimately, that was the finding of Justice Brian Burrows who excluded Nate's confessions to Mr. Big from the double murder trial. The case then collapsed, as without those confessions, there was simply no evidence. Nate was found not guilty in May 2003 and released from jail again.

Sherwood Park RCMP released a statement after the 2013 trial indicating that they were "satisfied that we conducted a thorough investigation in this case," and officials said they would not be seeking further suspects on the matter.

Although I was clearly pleased that Nate was finally aquitted, I had hoped that this might be one case in which a court finally condemned the RCMP conduct as an abuse that would shock the conscience of the community. Justice Burrows called that legal test "a subjective test dressed in the costume of an objective test." I had argued strongly that the susceptibilities of this particular youth, who was in the protection of the state at all relevant times, combined with the police failure to take any steps to minimize the harm to him that they should have foreseen, met that very high objective threshold.

Canada, and many other countries, have historically had different legal frameworks for youths in conflict with the criminal law. We recognize that youths have heightened vulnerability, less maturity and reduced capacity for moral decision-making. The Youth Criminal

Justice Act is the last in a long history of laws recognizing youths' distinct vulnerability and diminished responsibility. The preamble to the YCJA specifically recognizes society's responsibility to address the developmental challenges and needs of young people, our need to guide them into adulthood, and it encourages guidance and support to seek their effective rehabilitation and reintegration.

Not only was Nate a young person, but he had been in the care of the state as a permanent ward since the age of seven. His known personal circumstances were such that he clearly had no means of independent survival. RCMP baited this trap using information obtained from adults charged with protecting him. They stood by and watched while another adult sexually exploited him.

At the time of the Nate sting, there were no RCMP policies governing these covert operations. How the operation unfolded was in the discretion of the planners and operators. The "Investigation and Planning Report" prepared for this operation stated that one of the goals was to "seek the truth." But that simply became an easy mantra for the planners to repeat as they attempted to cloak the operation with credibility when they testified. The mantra rang hollow here, as no steps were taken to ensure that actual truth would be captured. No mid-sting assessment was done of the quality of the confessions being obtained which might have led police to terminate the operation and reduce the harm to Nate. Instead, the planners forged ahead, reckless about the risk that only ridiculously unreliable information was being obtained. For example, in his first confession to Mr. Big, Nate said he was asked by another person to "make this hit" and did it for no fee. He wore a "bunny suit" like the cops wear when they do "forensic shit." He purchased it at a store. He dragged the woman into the house and shot her in the chest there. The frying pan he hit her with was left in the house. He dragged the dead man to the trailer door and put the man's hand print on it. He made sure there was no blood around the woman's body and used bleach to clean up. All of that was false.

The tunnel vision of the main investigator on the double homicide was evident when he included in the Report's synopsis a statement that "During break-ins [at Double Dutch] … they armed themselves with… a small calibre firearm." Thorough investigation had turned up no evidence of any firearm missing from any of the Double Dutch trailers or any other property in the area. The investigator included this statement as one of 'fact' in the approval document on the basis that he believed there was "a strong possibility" it could be true. But that was one of the lies Nate told Sgt. Kennedy on June 1st, 2009 after Kennedy promised to end the interview if Nate gave some more information about the weapon. No other evidence supported it.

The operators were allowed to remain ignorant of facts that might have led them to realize the futility of continuing the charade in which they were participating. For example, the ruling excluding Nate's statement to Sgt. Kennedy from evidence in the first trial was never given to the operator who played Mr. Big. Although that officer knew that a statement had been excluded from evidence, no one told him that Justice John Gill described Nate as "a pleaser with a learning disability who was in a special program at school." He didn't know that the statement was excluded from evidence because it was involuntary and likely stress compliant. The cover person who planned the sting operation didn't even read the court ruling himself, but gained his knowledge about it from media reports that the statement had been excluded by the Judge!

The RCMP were also aware that both Alan and Nate had 'confessed' to a couple of dozen youths while in the youth jail before their 2011 trial. They were aware that many of those confessions were provably false and were contradicted by the forensic evidence.

They became aware from the first 'confession' made by Nate in the sting that he was lying about many aspects of what he was telling the operators. He had sat through the entire preliminary inquiry and heard and saw all the evidence. Yet his confessions changed from scenario to scenario. They contained information that the forensic investigation proved wrong. When Mr. Big finally 'cross-examined' Nate in the last scenario to try to find some explanation for Ms. Trudel's DNA on the casings, Nate finally abandoned his story that the gun used to kill these people had been stolen from a trailer at Double Dutch.

Despite suspicious activity by certain others whose names surfaced in the investigation (lying, refusing to provide bank records, phone records, police statements) these boys were the target of investigators within thirty minutes of the first police briefing of the case and remained so throughout the prosecution. Despite a judicial ruling that shed light on the quality of Nate's initial 'confession', and clear evidence that the boys were both lying to other prisoners, police forged ahead with an expensive and time-consuming sting. Those actions must surely have revived the hopes of two grieving families that someone would finally be brought to justice as responsible for killing their loved ones. How false those hopes were proven to be.

Those police actions also profoundly affected Nate who still finds himself enmeshed in 'the system'. One can only guess that they also had an impact on Alan who himself spent twenty-six months in jail, gained an institutional reputation as a 'Bosco boy', was manipulated by police and was required to finally testify about all that happened when he stole a truck four years earlier. At Nate's 2013 trial, Alan described the boys' activities the night of May 31, 2009 just as he had in his statement to the RCMP on June 1. Yet the RCMP gave no credence to it at the time as it didn't fit with their initial (and apparently only) theory that the boys were responsible for the killings.

The special laws around youths' statements to police exist for a reason. Yet they were effectively ignored when Nate was not properly told of his right to have a lawyer present for the interview and when he was pressured into that first false confession. By then the RCMP entered into a tunnel that forever constrained their investigation. That tunnel lead down a four-year path of lies, charades, ignored information, wasted resources, and the wrongful imprisonment of two kids the state was charged with protecting. In the end, there was justice for no one.

***Brock Martland** is a criminal lawyer with Martland & Saulnier in Vancouver. His practice covers virtually all criminal allegations, with a particular emphasis on trial and appellate work, murder, extradition, youth criminal justice law and police disciplinary cases. Brock has served as associate commission counsel for two public inquiries. Brock is a graduate of the University of Victoria (LL.B.) and Queen's University (B.A. Hon.), and clerked for the Honourable Mr. Justice John C. Major CC QC at the Supreme Court of Canada.*

Mr. Brock Martland

Inauspicious Events in the Surrey Six Case

IT WAS A MASS KILLING that shook British Columbia. Six men shot dead inside a high-rise apartment in Surrey, a suburban city in the Vancouver region. Four of the deceased were involved in the drug trade, but two were innocent victims caught in the web of time and place. The killings took place in 2007 at a time when criminal gangs were battling for control of the drug trade and employing violence in pursuit of their aims. The RCMP quickly surmised that the Red Scorpions gang was responsible – a notorious drug dealing organization originally formed in a B.C. young-offenders' facility.

Eventually, three men were charged and brought to trial together. And three defence teams were created. Two of those teams knew that something was afoot on an inauspicious day in the middle of the trial when lawyers for the third accused person didn't show up.

It was November 25, 2013. We were two months into the Surrey Six trial, and I was one of three lawyers acting for accused killer Matthew Johnston. The trial was underway inside the best courtroom in the province, Courtroom 20 at the Vancouver Law Courts. The courtroom was known as the Air India Courtroom because it had been built for that mega-trial in 2003-2004. It was a large, spacious, modern room, kitted out with technology and screens and bulletproof glass to house the participants. It was also furnished with an unusual feature: a set of anterooms for the parties to use as chambers. The three defence teams in the Surrey Six trial each had their own backstage anteroom just beside the courtroom itself, as well as a large common boardroom linked up with video feed of the trial in progress.

The case had already seen its share of twists and turns, which I'll step back to describe shortly. By the time the trial was underway, before Madam Justice Catherine Wedge, there were three defendants on the direct indictment: Matt Johnston (our client), Cody Haevischer, and Mike Le. It was the Le lawyers who were so glaringly absent from court the morning of Monday, November 25, 2013.

Our ritual had been to make abundant use of the shared defence boardroom. The defence lawyers would strategize there, brainstorming about the case and discussing the witnesses and the progress of the trial. The common space allowed us to share our thoughts in a fairly intimate setting. In the morning before the start of court, there would always be at least one of the Mike Le lawyers there, and often two of their ranks.

That day in November was an important day in the trial. We had been at it for two months already; viewing and analysing extensive crime scene and forensic evidence, hearing civilian witnesses whose accounts the Crown tendered to build the case against the three accused, and establishing a timeline of events. Before November 25th, we had heard from experts on blood-stain patterns, pathology, firearms, and DNA. We had also heard testimony from people who had interacted with the deceased men that day, from people who had found the bodies, and from others who described three men arriving at the apartment building in a black BMW and subsequently leaving. But November 25th was the first day that we would hear the evidence of a gang insider.

Not Hard to Piece Together

The first key witness was K.M. She had been Cody Haevischer's girlfriend at the time of the crime. They had lived together at a Surrey apartment building that was just a five-minute drive from where the killings had taken place. In her account, Haevischer, Johnston and a third man, who became known as Person X, used her apartment as the staging site, preparing for the murder there, and returning to that base afterward.

So, we were finally moving into the critical phase of the trial when we would hear the evidence of the key witnesses who were insiders. (The lawyers called these 'Vetrovec witnesses,' referring to a 1982 Supreme Court of Canada case and serving as shorthand for an unsavoury and inherently unreliable witness.) But we were missing one defence team. And as we learned minutes later, we were also missing one of the accused: Mike Le had not been transported to court by the Sheriff service.

It was not hard to piece it together: Mike Le had cut a deal, mid-trial.

We soon heard as much in a short tense meeting in our boardroom, backstage from the courtroom. Le's lawyers and Crown counsel came in together to brief us about the surprise development. We came to learn that Le had made a sweetheart deal. He would plead guilty and be sentenced, but not for murder and a life sentence. He would instead plead guilty to conspiracy to commit murder. There would be a joint sentencing submission for twelve years. The court would hear only a highly sanitized account, under which he reluctantly tolerated a murder plot rather than ordering it. With double credit for his time in remand custody, he would be sentenced to just three years, despite being the founder and leader of the Red Scorpions, the gang alleged to be the moving force behind the plot. Besides this, Le had a criminal record that included an earlier manslaughter.

In *Thunder Road*, Bruce Springsteen sang about "that long walk from your front porch to my front seat." Mike Le's long walk was from the prisoner's dock to the witness box – a distance of only thirty feet but a far-longer journey. The Mike Le deal saw an accused killer walk away from a first degree murder charge with its attendant sentence of life imprisonment and receive only a minimal sentence. In exchange, Le would testify for the Crown and place blame squarely at the feet of his co-accused for the Surrey Six killings. He would do so after having studied the voluminous disclosure in the case for years. He also benefitted from a large team of lawyers, and as a result of this, he knew exactly what the Crown's trial strategy was. With these ingredients, perhaps he would serve up the perfect dish for the Crown.

In an ordinary murder trial, if there is such a thing, one twist like this would be more than enough. In the Surrey Six trial, we came to expect the unexpected. I should add a disclaimer here. My client, Matt Johnston, was convicted of six counts of first degree murder, as well as one count of conspiracy to commit murder. He has filed an appeal against conviction that we have not yet argued as I write this. I am, of necessity, restricted in what I can say about the case and my client. Despite this, I can describe the killings, the trial, and the strange twists and turns that continually arose in this engrossing case.

The Killings and the Investigation

October 19, 2007 was a Friday. Ed Schellenberg was working at a Surrey apartment complex called the Balmoral Tower, doing routine servicing of the gas fireplaces. A building manager took Schellenberg to the 15th floor at about 1:35 p.m. In short order, Schellenberg went into Suite 1505. That apartment was being used by Corey Lal and three associates to prepare crack cocaine and to deal drugs.

At about 2:00 p.m., across the hallway in Suite 1504, Christopher Mohan spoke by phone with his mother, Eileen Mohan. That was the last time she spoke with him.

A little before 4:30 p.m., after being unable to summon Schellenberg by radio or by using the PA system, a building manager went into Suite 1505. He found six men dead on the ground, including Schellenberg and Mohan; two entirely innocent victims. Initially it was thought there had been a gas leak, but first responders determined this was not so. In fact all six men had been shot repeatedly, mostly in the head and neck area. The trial judge found they had been shot while lying on the ground. Two handguns were found in the apartment. They were the murder weapons.

As criminal lawyers we get a different type of tension and drama than some of our desk-bound colleagues, but it is detached from the immediacy and unpredictability of the crime itself. We study the evidence and analyze photographs from the crime scene and autopsy. They can be disturbing. But our analysis is all after-the-fact and second-hand. It does not have the same intensity as being there. In the Surrey Six case, veteran RCMP Staff Sergeant Dave Teboul described the crime scene as horrific, even for seasoned homicide investigators.

In the Lower Mainland region of B.C., the RCMP and a handful of municipal police departments work together to investigate murders, through the Integrated Homicide Investigation Team (IHIT). The Surrey Six investigation was given to IHIT investigators, and they were quick to make headway in identifying suspects.

The police had an eyewitness (there for Bible study, no less) from the Balmoral Tower who described three mean-looking men wearing hoodies entering the building through the parking garage, using a building key fob. Another witness saw these same men departing quickly about twenty minutes later. The car was a black BMW 745 sedan. By sheer chance, a drug unit with the Surrey RCMP had been conducting ongoing surveillance at the nearby apartment building where K.M. and Cody Haevischer lived, and they had some surreptitious video clips showing men in hoodies coming and going from that building at times that connected with the evidence from the Balmoral. This evidence provided a link that moved the case from generic; that is, a few men in hoodies in a certain type of car, to specific; that is three particular men who could be identified as being at the Balmoral at that time. Later on at trial, this type of evidence supplied the scaffolding of corroboration to some evidence from key Crown witnesses.

Within just a few days after the shootings took place on October 19, 2007, the police identified suspects including Haevischer and Johnston. But they did not have enough evidence to charge anyone. In short order they saw the black BMW being taken to a car-detailing service. The police sprung into view by seizing the car to search for evidence before the vehicle was cleaned up. The police likewise obtained phone records with a view to situating people at certain places at relevant times. They searched the apartment that Haevischer shared with K.M. and they aggressively arrested Johnston by smashing into his car, although he was released not long afterward.

The investigation continued but did not furnish any lead capable of supporting charges, until Person Y came into view. Person Y was a long-standing criminal who had been immersed in violence and gangs for many years. As the year 2007 drew to a close, he suddenly did the unthinkable and went to the police, reaching out to senior homicide investigators he knew from his own murder prosecution some years before. He soon made himself a police agent, and set out to capture confessions on audio or video wiretap from the suspects. Person Y's involvement turned the case, and built up a body of evidence supporting murder charges at last.

The final piece, for the Crown, involved a different gang member, Person X. It was understood that Person X was one of the killers, who had shot three of the victims at the Balmoral apartment in October of 2007. In April of 2009, Person X suddenly pleaded guilty to three counts of second degree murder. He became the central witness against the accused, and they were arrested the same day that X pleaded and was sentenced to life with no parole eligibility for fifteen years.

Charges are Brought, and Case Set for Trial

On April 3, 2009, the police arrested four men on the same indictment for the Surrey Six murders: Matt Johnston, Cody Haevischer, Mike Le, and Jamie Bacon, who was a leader of the Red Scorpions gang.

As often occurs, the accused took some time to settle on counsel, and had to address funding for the upcoming case. Ultimately, Matt Johnston retained Michael Tammen QC, Jonathan Desbarats, and me. I knew Michael Tammen well, first from the Air India trial, and then through work we did together on a public inquiry dealing with the death of a homeless First Nations man in Vancouver. Tammen is a tenacious and experienced barrister – someone well placed to take on the most difficult gangster witnesses. Jonathan Desbarats brought the most detailed knowledge of the evidence and a strong analytical and writing background – in fact he had worked previously as a journalist. We all got along and worked well together. This was a great plus given the many impending challenges we would face.

To complete the roll call, Cody Haevischer had, as trial counsel, Simon Buck, Dagmar Dlab, and Alex Willms, while Mike Le had Chris Johnson QC, Mark Jetté, Shelley Sugarman, Georgia Docolas, Paul Ferguson, and Andrew Nelson. The Crown, meanwhile, had a large roster of counsel, Mark Levitz QC, Catherine Murray QC, Geoff Baragar QC, Louise Kenworthy, Alex Henderson, Matt Stacey, Kathleen McIntosh, Dan Loucks, Chris Karlsson, Lindsay Pearce, Heather Guinn, and Shirley Pederson.

While there were inevitable moments of chippiness and tension between the various lawyers, I was happily surprised by how well counsel got along and collectively moved the case forward. A case like this, with such high stakes and such difficult issues, could easily have descended into acrimony or paralysis or both, and we avoided that.

We brought a series of pre-trial motions, dealing with a host of issues such as disclosure, challenging privilege claims, and admissibility of evidence. We fought hard on publication bans, and took the somewhat unusual step of siding squarely with the media and asserting our client's constitutional right to a public trial with full reporting on the evidence. (There were no less than two publication-ban rulings which sparked applications by witnesses to get leave to appeal to the Supreme Court of Canada – we opposed the cases going to Ottawa and neither of them did get leave.)

As we worked our way through pre-trial applications in August 2012, to our surprise we were told that the Crown had elected to separate the four accused from each other. They would proceed separately against Jamie Bacon, and would prosecute Haevischer, Johnston, and Le together. The reasons the Crown gave were unhelpful, referring vaguely to distinct issues relating to Bacon. The Crown's decision was a surprise because on virtually every element of the test for severance, that is whether to prosecute jointly or separately, it was obvious to us that this was a case that ought to be prosecuted once, and with all accused present. The disappearance of Bacon from our indictment was unexpected. His case has moved at a snail's pace, and is set to commence in March of 2018, eleven years after the killings, and nine years after he was arrested and charged.

The privilege issue proved to be the wellspring for the single most important application in the case. In criminal cases, it is customary to receive the entirety of the police investigative materials as 'disclosure' to the defence, to prepare for trial. The law allows the prosecution to withhold disclosure if the material is protected by a legal privilege or rule of secrecy. We challenged a number of privilege claims made by the Crown in relation to disclosure that they refused to give us. For some of these claims, the Crown insisted they would have to appear before our trial judge in the absence of both the accused and defence counsel and hold a secret hearing in a closed courtroom, at which time the privilege claim would be assessed. Because of this unhappy but necessary feature (nobody wants to miss out on their own trial), we had sought the appointment of *amicus curiae*, a 'friend of the court', to provide an adversarial context and to advance the defendants' position in those closed hearings. We selected the best possible *amicus*, Anil Kapoor from Toronto, whose name appears on many leading privilege cases and who has a wealth of experience in these tricky and sensitive waters.

Many of our privilege challenges were dismissed: the Crown's arguments prevailed, and their privilege claims were upheld. One claim, however, took on a life of its own. It involved an informer coded as E5. We challenged E5's status as an informer. The E5 litigation moved into a closed hearing at which the Crown and *amicus* appeared for roughly forty days of court time before our trial judge, all in our absence. At one point, we brought a further application at which I made submissions referring not to caselaw, but to a 1970s FM radio song, Marvin Gaye's 'What's Going On?' We were quite perplexed that this challenge had sprawled to almost forty days, with Informer E5 having his or her own senior counsel, Paul Stern from Toronto.

The biggest surprise of the case came in late August 2013, just before the trial was set to start in September. Our 'What's Going On' application was still fresh in the air when we learned that Justice Wedge was releasing a ruling. We read and then re-read that ruling. We called each other to see if we had read it correctly. It told us that Person X, the shooter of three, gang insider, and the most critical of the Crown's witnesses, would not testify. We were told only that Person X's evidence was inadmissible for reasons set out in a sealed ruling that we could not see.

At this moment in the proceedings, lesser prosecutors might have thrown in the towel or pushed the case off by a year to re-think it. Led by Mark Levitz QC, the Crown was admirably tough-minded in reframing its case and pressing on. The development led to a slight delay in the trial but the Crown adapted and carried on. The trial started in late September, 2013.

The Trial

The Surrey Six trial took place over eighty days of testimony, involving some seventy-three witnesses, as well as many more days for pre- and mid-trial applications involving legal argument. Neither Johnston nor Haevischer led evidence or testified. The case took place before Justice Catherine Wedge with no jury. Her extensive reasons for conviction are reported as 2014 BCSC 1863 and give a much more detailed recounting of the evidence. My sketch here is highly selective, to give a flavour of what transpired.

Person Y's evidence was the most compelling piece of human theatre I have ever witnessed. It was mesmerizing – at times compelling, at times ridiculous, wild, unpredictable, and emotional. We had been told by Crown, before he testified, that Person Y might need to stop and start in his testimony for health reasons, but as he got going he seemed able to carry on. If I were casting the movie (and could time travel) I would choose Philip Seymour Hoffman to play Person Y; he could have captured the intensity and the strangeness of this man.

Person Y was himself a repeat killer. He had killed by shooting, by strangling, and by stabbing. He had shot and killed his own best friend, a man whose name he had tattooed on his body. Justice Wedge referred to him as a "career gangster." He referred to himself as "despicable" and "a monster." Person Y had volunteered to kill Corey Lal, the target in the plot that led to the six killings, but on the condition he do it alone, such as by luring him into a parking lot.

One of the handguns used for the killings had been in Person Y's possession just before the killings. He had stuffed it in his pants and had worn it at the gym. Perhaps because of this sweaty (and unsafe) storage mechanism, the gun was found to have his DNA on it when it was located at the crime scene. Person Y testified he gave the gun to Person X, one of the shooters. No other DNA was found on either gun.

Person Y lost his temper at questions from my colleague Mike Tammen at one point during his cross-examination. Seething with fury, he said he had to stop because he was "seeing red." But at other times, Person Y spoke casually about violence and killing and acts of enormity. His testimony was dramatic and fantastical and rambling – and totally engrossing.

Person Y's evidence came at a huge cost to the public purse. The police paid him substantial benefits for his cooperation and testimony, and even purchased him a high-end Mercedes sedan. The tally we had at trial for payouts was over $1.3-million. Amazingly, Person Y was allowed to leave Canada and travel to Brazil, all before testifying or proving his worth to the prosecution. And yet, he came back, put his head down, and pleaded guilty to two other murders.

There were moments in the trial that had a near-comic aspect. In presenting evidence about the Red Scorpions gang, the Crown relied to a surprising degree on a handwritten document they called "The Rules," which were said to spell out what Red Scorpions members had to do. Some of the rules were serious-sounding, for instance a requirement to come immediately if beckoned and to be ready to fight. But other rules were unintentionally hilarious, like the rule banning drug use but excepting OxyContin and marijuana. Some drug prohibition that was! Our favourite was the rule stipulating that honesty was important, giving the explanatory note that not admitting to farting was the start of shadiness. As much as the Crown hoped the Rules would show this gang to be highly organized and terrifying, the abundant typos and the content were more reminiscent of Spanky and Buckwheat's *Little Rascals* gang than *The Godfather*.

Another moment of entertainment came when Person Y tried to resist the proposition that he had been on a crime spree. He insisted it wasn't a spree. He said it would not meet "the legal definition" of a spree. Finally, he had to accept that he was caught red-handed by the police on his way to carrying out the latest in a series of home-invasion robberies – so yes, maybe it was a spree after all.

Mike Le testified relatively late in the Crown's case at trial, which made sense given his late addition to the witness list. We argued that his evidence was tailor-made to blame his co-accused and minimize any responsibility for himself. Ultimately Justice Wedge disbelieved him and found him untruthful.

Closing Remarks

We made our closing submissions in the summer of 2014, and Justice Wedge adjourned to October 2, 2014 to give her decision. She convicted both Johnston and Haevischer. We then sought a judicial stay of proceedings, that is, an end to the case, on the basis that there had been an abuse of process. Our abuse arguments focused on two sorts of misconduct that arose for our clients. First, our clients had been held in solitary confinement for excessive periods, in what we said were inhumane conditions, at the direction of the police. Second, amazingly, senior male IHIT investigators had allegedly, in the course of the Surrey Six investigation, committed misconduct including by having sexual relationships with gang-affiliated women whom they had been charged with protecting. Four RCMP officers face criminal charges as a result; their case has yet to go to trial.

Madam Justice Wedge declined to enter a stay of proceedings and dismissed our application, and we then moved to a hearing at which the Court imposed life sentences on both accused men. As noted, we are challenging the convictions at the Court of Appeal for British Columbia.

Reflections on the Case

The Surrey Six trial was a wild ride. The only certainty was uncertainty. The Crown cut a sweetheart deal with a gang leader, only to have his evidence firmly rejected by the trial judge. The Crown and police, likewise, made a deal with a trigger-man, Person X, but never got the benefit of his evidence. His evidence was excluded for reasons that remain a great mystery to the accused men who are now serving life sentences, and to the public. As an outsider to that process, it seems that something must have been deeply and fundamentally wrong – so much so that the Crown lost its one eyewitness to the killings, himself responsible for shooting three of the victims on his own account. But the defence must ask the next question: if something was so far amiss, why was the prosecution allowed to continue at all? That is a question we will be addressing in the appeal.

One remarkable feature of the case was the willingness on the part of the Crown and police to make a deal with a murderer. In British Columbia, historically, the Crown has made deals with accomplices and conspirators but not with the actual killers. There has been, in recent years, a significant shift. What was once considered *verboten* now occurs with some regularity in serious homicide prosecutions. I assume the Crown would say this is necessary: these cases are just so hard to prove, and so important, that the public interest requires prosecutors to hold their noses and cut these deals. I question whether this is true. On the facts of this case, the deal was made to obtain the evidence of Person X, but he never did testify. Likewise, the deal with Mike Le gave the Crown his evidence, but it was firmly rejected and proven to be of no value. But in reliance on Person Y's evidence, the Crown was able to take the case to convictions at the trial level. In other words, and appreciating that hindsight is always 20-20, these 'deals with the devils' did not help the prosecution's case.

As a policy matter, should the Crown make deals with actual killers? Should this type of deal-making be reserved for cases that are otherwise impossible? Or should we shift back to the old approach, under which such outcomes were just not in the cards?

As a final comment, the mystery surrounding Person X continues to keep the accused and their lawyers up at night, wondering. If experienced Crown and police took such care to cultivate this person as a witness and structure a deal with him, how in the world did they not anticipate and address whatever privilege issues arose that rendered Person X incapable of testifying? It is impossible to know what happened in this piece of litigation because the defence was kept in the dark. Matt Johnston and Cody Haevischer are in the same position as Huck Finn and Tom Sawyer, sneaking into the church to watch their own funeral, except in our case they weren't even allowed in. What remains troubling is that two men are now serving life sentences for six murders, in circumstances where something of signal importance happened in their trial. And they have never been allowed to know what it is.

PART THREE

Inquests

***Breese Davies** received her B.A., M.A. (Criminology) and LL.B. degrees from the University of Toronto. She started her legal career as an associate with Ruby & Edwardh, was a partner at Di Luca Copeland Davies, and she is now at Simcoe Chambers. Breese is an adjunct professor at the University of Toronto in the Criminology program and at Osgoode Hall Law School and is currently a Vice President of the Criminal Lawyers' Association. Throughout her term on the CLA board, she has worked on retaining women in defence practice, improving the professional experience of female lawyers, and promoting diversity in the criminal defence bar. Breese has done volunteer legal work in Nigeria through Avocats Sans Frontières Canada and is a current member of the Board of Regents at Victoria University, University of Toronto. She is the 2017 recipient of The Law Society of Upper Canada's Laura Legge Award.*

Ms. Breese Davies

The Case of Ashley Smith

Insanity of Treating Mental Illness in a Prison

On the morning of October 19, 2007, Ashley Smith died alone, naked except for an anti-suicide 'gown', in a segregation cell at the Grand Valley Institute for Women. Technically, Ashley had self-asphyxiated by tying a piece of cloth around her neck. She had 'tied up' dozens and dozens of times before – too many times to count. She would cut or tear a piece of cloth from anything available to her. She was incredibly skilled at acquiring pieces of glass or metal and hiding them on (or in) her. She even peeled up her floor tiles. She used these sharp fragments to cut her blanket, her mattress, even her 'tear proof' gown into strips of fabric she would tie around her neck, often so tightly that she passed out. Time after time, the correctional officers rushed into her cell to cut off the ligature. And the deadly game would start again.

But on October 19, 2007, when Ashley tied yet another ligature, the correctional officers did not rush in and remove it. For weeks, the front-line correctional officers charged with supervising Ashley had been harshly criticized by Grand Valley's managers and the deputy warden for being too quick to respond when she engaged in self-harming behaviour. Disciplinary proceedings had been commenced against a number of them in the days and weeks before Ashley's death for using 'force' too frequently in their efforts to save her life.

At the same time, the correctional officers were being told by prison psychologists that engaging with Ashley would just encourage her to continue to act out. In fact, they were told to "withdraw warmth" from Ashley when she was acting out.

Eventually, the correctional officers were ordered not to enter Ashley's cell as long as she was still breathing, and so on October 19, 2007, they didn't immediately respond when Ashley once again tied a ligature around her neck. Instead, they watched and waited for close to fifteen minutes, listened as her breath become increasingly laboured, finally entering her cell to remove the ligature. Ultimately, they had waited too long. They waited and watched as she took her last breath. And as per Correctional Service of Canada policy, they videotaped it all.

Ashley's Unpredicable Behaviour

Ashley had been diagnosed as suffering from anti-social personality disorder with traits of Borderline Personality Disorder (BPD), a mental disorder characterized by an intense fear of abandonment, unstable relationships, impulsive and self-harming behaviour, extreme emotional swings, chronic feelings of emptiness, and explosive anger. Borderline Personality Disorder cannot be treated or managed with psychiatric medication which is the mainstay of mental health care in federal prisons. Rather, BPD is a complex cluster of behavioural traits that requires intensive, long-term intervention by a team of highly trained, trusted mental health professionals focused on teaching people skills to regulate their intense emotions, reduce self-harming behaviour, and how to manage their distress. This is what Ashley desperately needed.

Instead, what she got was months, and months, and months of detention in segregation with very little in the way of human interaction or meaningful activity. In fact, Ashley was in segregation her whole time in CSC custody with the exception of a few days.

But Ashley was much more than a self-harming, aggressive nineteen-year-old. In the moments when she was more settled, she was engaging, with a quick sense of humour and a mischievous, impish smile. She would joke around with the correctional officers, often the same correctional officers who ultimately watched her die, and talk with them about her family.

Because of Ashley's unpredictable behaviour and the number of times force was used to remove ligatures from around her neck, directions had been given to correctional officers to videotape Ashley. They would videotape her in her cell. They would videotape her if she was being moved from one part of an institution to another. They would videotape her if she was being transferred from one institution to another. CSC had hours and hours of videotape of Ashley. Some of those videos captured Ashley when she was distressed and acting out in a violent or self-destructive manner. Others captured shocking images of Ashley being physically restrained, with duct tape in one video, or being forcibly injected with anti-psychotic medication.

Other videos captured Ashley's funny, outgoing, self-deprecating side. Some would show Ashley acting like a regular teenager, talking about boys or shopping. It was that side of Ashley that I felt needed to be seen and defended throughout the Coroner's Inquest that was called to examine the circumstances of her death.

Ashley's Journey through the Correctional System

Ashley was first charged criminally when she was fourteeen years old with a number of public nuisance offences. She was also exhibiting disruptive behaviour at school. She was given one-year probation and enrolled in an intensive support program. In April 2003, at the age of fifteen, Ashley was sentenced to a short term of imprisonment for breaching her probation, assault, and causing a disturbance. While in youth custody, Ashley started demonstrating aggressive and self-harming behaviour. Between October 2003 and February 2005, she was in and out of youth custody, charged with breaching her probation (for throwing an apple at a postal worker), pulling a fire alarm in a public building, and stealing a CD from a local store. While in custody, Ashley accumulated hundreds of 'institutional charges' for violating various rules, which resulted in her being held for extended periods of time in segregation, or 'therapeutic quiet' as they euphemistically call it in youth corrections. She was often physically restrained as well. She accumulated dozens of additional criminal charges for assaulting prison staff, largely in response to their efforts to prevent her self-harming behaviour, and damaging property in the youth detention centre.

In January 2006, while still serving her youth sentence, Ashley turned eighteen. She was no longer considered a youth by the criminal justice system. Shortly after her eighteenth birthday, Ashley was again charged with assaulting a correctional officer and, in October 2006, given her first adult sentence. The Superintendent of the New Brunswick Youth Centre brought an application to have Ashley's entire sentence converted into an adult sentence and to have her transferred to the adult correctional system. Ashley was afraid. She knew she was incapable of controlling her emotional outbursts and she was scared of how she would be treated in the adult system. The judge who heard the transfer application ignored her concerns about the transfer.

By the time Ashley entered the federal correctional system on October 31, 2006, she had three years and forty-two days left to serve on her sentence. It had become clear that she was struggling with a mental illness or mental disorder. However you label it, Ashley was in significant distress much of the time she was in the custody of the Correctional Service of Canada. She communicated her distress through self-injurious, defiant, and disruptive behaviour – by tying pieces of fabric tightly around her neck, by lashing out at correctional officers who tried to remove them, and by physically resisting attempts to search her person or her cell for ligatures or anything she may use as a make them.

The Correctional Service of Canada quickly labeled Ashley as a behavioural problem that needed to be controlled, rather than a health issue that needed to be treated. They tried to control and modify her behaviour by placing her in segregation and depriving her of all personal belongings, meaningful activities, normal human contact and regular communication with her family. They set up a system by which Ashley had to earn, through good behaviour, even the most basic human amenities, like clothing, a blanket, a mattress, or even a roll of toilet paper. Staff were directed not to engage with Ashley when she was misbehaving, but to instead ignore her like she was a naughty toddler. They also used physical and chemical restraints on Ashley to control her self-harming behaviour.

I recognize that it was incredibly challenging for correctional staff to work with Ashley, particularly towards the end of her life. She was determined and ingenious, and would use anything she could get her hands on to make a ligature to tie around her neck. She would also cover the surveillance camera in her cell to frustrate staff efforts to monitor her. This resulted in the staff sitting directly outside her cell for hours on end, watching her through the meal slot in her cell door. It was a mind-numbing task, punctuated by moments of acute danger. Ashley's self-harming and aggressive behaviour pushed many correctional staff to their breaking point. She confounded the system because of her unpredictability, her ingenuity and her apparent compulsion to harm herself.

When Ashley's self-harming, defiant, aggressive behaviour became too much for the correctional staff at one institution to handle, Ashley would be abruptly transferred to another institution, often moving her further away from her family in Nova Scotia. In total, Ashley was transferred seventeen times between seven different institutions in four different provinces during the eleven months she was in the custody of the Correctional Service of Canada.

The working diagnosis for Ashley's mental disorder was Anti-Social Personality Disorder with Borderline Personality Disorder traits but meaningful treatment was not implemented. She never underwent a full psychological assessment while she was in the custody of the CSC, although she was transferred to three different psychiatric facilities. Ashley would often not cooperate with the assessment process or she would withdraw her consent to treatment. She would refuse to even speak to certain psychologists.

To me, it is hardly surprising that Ashley refused to cooperate with the psychiatrists and psychologists. She was never in one institution for long enough to develop a trusting relationship with the psychologists or psychiatrist. The psychologists and psychiatrists in most correctional institutions did not have the time or expertise that was needed to build a therapeutic alliance with Ashley. Most prisons do not have a psychiatrist on staff. Instead, they bring in a contract psychiatrist for a mere two to four hours per week. The psychiatrist's primary role is to diagnose and monitor the psychiatric medications prescribed to the inmate population. The staff psychologists simply do not have the time or capacity to develop treatment plans for severely ill women.

The latest statistics suggest that close to thirty percent of women entering prison have been diagnosed with a mental illness and half of the women in prison have a history of self-harm. With that number of patients, the medical staff were not able to devote enough time and resources to finding ways to help Ashley.

The Inquest Process

The Coroner's Inquest into Ashley's death started in January 2013. I was counsel for the Canadian Association of Elizabeth Fry Societies (CAEFS), a national organization that works with and for criminalized women and girls.

In Ontario, Coroner's Inquests have five-person juries who are charged with answering five questions: who died, where the deceased died, when the deceased died, how the deceased died and 'by what means' the deceased died. There are five possible answers to the 'by what means' question: homicide, suicide, natural, accidental, or undetermined. Unlike in a criminal trial, where intention (or *mens rea*) must be proven, a homicide verdict at a Coroner's Inquest is simply a finding that the death in question was caused by another person or group of people.

Coroner's Inquests are not fault-finding exercises. The jury is prohibited from making findings of criminal or civil liability. Nevertheless, in addition to answering the five questions, the jury is permitted to make recommendations aimed at preventing deaths in similar circumstances.

People, groups or institutions with an interest in the outcome of the Inquest can apply for the right to participate in the Inquest. At the Inquest into Ashley's death, there were more than ten parties, including Ashley's family, the Correctional Service of Canada, the Union of Correctional Officers, the physicians who provided medical care to Ashley, the Canadian Civil Liberties Association, and CAEFS. Not surprisingly, each party to the Inquest, including CAEFS, had its own agenda.

Many of the parties at the Inquest wanted to focus on how aggressive and unpredictable Ashley's behaviour had become. Instead, CAEFS wanted the Inquest to focus on the humanity behind her distress, the illness behind her behaviour, and the numerous ways the correctional system failed to treat her or protect her.

Other parties at the Inquest hoped to show that there was nothing the Correctional Service of Canada could have done to prevent Ashley's death, that Ashley was suicidal and determined to kill herself. Others still wanted to characterize her death as a tragic accident. In my mind, neither of these verdicts would reflect the truth of what happened to Ashley behind the walls of Grand Valley Institution.

Ashley was not suicidal. Minutes before Ashley tied that last ligature around her neck, she talked with one of the correctional officers with whom she had a good rapport. She told him about a bad dream she had in which her mother died before she was released from prison. She was upset and confided in the officer that she felt like tying something around her neck. When the officer asked her not to, Ashley responded "just let me do it, I won't die. I know what I'm doing." Those were Ashley's last words: "I won't die." She trusted the officers to save her. She expected them to intervene, like they had done so many times before. Little did she know that they had been ordered to engage her in a deadly game of chicken.

CAEFS was determined to show the order to 'not enter Ashley's cell until she stopped breathing' was the real cause of her death. Not surprisingly, the Inquest was never able to conclusively determine the origin of the order. No one admitted to having conceived of the order, or even to having communicated it to the correctional officers. But each of the correctional officers who had stood by and watched Ashley die testified that they received the order and understood they would be disciplined if they didn't follow it.

So, as Counsel for CAEFS, I had two very clear directives for the Inquest: 1. Ensure the jury did not classify Ashley's death as a suicide or accident, and 2. Ensure the jury recommendations focused on getting mentally ill women out of segregation and out of prisons entirely. To advance our agenda, I had to form strategic partnerships with some parties and maneuver around others who were working against us.

The jury, composed of five women, heard ten months of evidence from employees of the Correctional Service of Canada (CSC) at all levels, from forensic psychiatrists and psychologists, and from experts in the area of penal reform. The evidence the jury heard was powerful and, at times, disturbing. But there was no avoiding the harsh reality of the last months of Ashley's life and how she was 'managed' by the Correctional Service of Canada.

In December 2013 the jury concluded that Ashley's death was a homicide. With that verdict, the jury clearly rejected the fatalistic picture of Ashley that some parties had tried to paint. The jury, with a single word, found that it was the CSC policy not to enter Ashley's cell while she was still breathing that caused her death. The jury found that Ashley's death was not inevitable or unavoidable.

The jury also made 104 recommendations directed mostly at the Correctional Service of Canada, each of which was designed to ensure nobody else would ever suffer the indignities Ashley suffered in the last eleven months of her life. In particular, the jury recommended that "female inmates with serious mental health issues and/or self-injurious behaviours serve their federal terms of imprisonment in a federally operated treatment facility, not a security-focused, prison-like environment." For Ashley, this would have meant being detained in a hospital environment with expertise in treating complex personality disorders, close to her family who could provide her with ongoing support.

The jury also recommended an absolute prohibition on the practice of keeping female inmates in segregation for longer than fifteen days at a time and no more than sixty days in a calendar year. For Ashley, this would have forced the CSC to find more creative, productive ways to address her disruptive, self-harming behaviours than warehousing her in segregation.

I cannot bring myself to describe the outcome of the Inquest as a 'victory'. We were, after all, examining the death of a spirited, clever teenager who was also incredibly vulnerable and mentally ill. But the verdict and the comprehensive recommendations did provide a clear blueprint to the Canadian government on the astonishing failures in our correctional system and the need for immediate and extensive reform.

A Flawed and Rigid System

As the Inquest unfolded, it became clear that the CSC was not equipped to provide Ashley with the sort of therapeutic care she needed to overcome her compulsion to self-harm. And Ashley was not alone.

Unfortunately, there are many other women in CSC custody who are also struggling with serious mental illness and self-harming behaviour. At the time of the Inquest, there were at least eight other women who were considered, like Ashley, at high risk of self-harm and in need of acute mental health services. Two of those women have since died in CSC custody.

It also became clear that prisons will never be equipped to provide the sort of patient, understanding, committed therapeutic interventions needed by women who are seriously mentally ill. Prisons are not therapeutic. They are a complex morass of rules, regulations and administrative decisions. The 'Commissioner's Directives' that are used to run the institutions leave little room for discretion or common sense. They cover matters as diverse as when and how CSC monitors an inmate's written and telephone communications, what clothing and other possessions an inmate is entitled to have, and when correctional officers are justified in using force on an inmate. There are rules on searching cells for contraband. There are rules regarding the way in which an inmate's security level is determined. There are rules about transferring an inmate from one institution to another. There are rules about the use of administrative segregation. There are policies on the provision of programs within the institutions. Every aspect of the operation of a prison is regulated and controlled. Detainees are expected to comply with all the rules and if they don't, they can be charged with an institutional offence and punished.

CSC's paramount focus is the security of its institutions, its staff and its detainees. To maintain this security, order and obedience are required. Compliance is achieved through the threat, or use, of disciplinary charges and the withdrawal of privileges. Every inmate is subject to the same rules and expectations. Uniformity is a major priority in prisons. Correctional institutions run most efficiently when the rules are applied consistently to everyone and the inmates comply or respond to incentive systems.

It is not only the detainees who are subject to strict rules. Commissioners Directives and CSC policies are equally directed at staff and how they are to carry out their various functions.

Unfortunately, mental illness generally, and self-harming

behaviour in particular, cannot be controlled through rules or threats. You can't discipline someone out of self-harming behaviour. Mental illness can cause people to act in unpredictable ways, or predictable ways that don't fit with the security model created in prisons. People with severe mental illness do not always respond to apparently 'rational' incentive systems. When someone is in distress, withholding care or human interaction or meaningful activity or privileges as a punishment will not solve the problem. Mental illness cannot be treated through isolation.

Women like Ashley who engage in self-harming behaviour need human connection. They need individualized, persistent care in a therapeutic environment, designed exclusively to improve the patient health. The goal of a therapeutic environment is to reduce stressors for patients, provide positive distractions and enable social and other forms of support. These goals are completely inconsistent with the security model of a correctional institution. The structures that make for effective penal control; consistent application of rules, rigid systems of discipline premised on deprivation and continuous, intrusive surveillance, are not and will never be conducive to the effective provision of mental health services. This is exactly why CEAFS was focused on recommendations to keep severely mentally ill women out of prison entirely. It is not a funding issue. It is not a staffing issue. It is about the fundamental incompatibility between providing health care and providing correctional services.

Public Scrutiny

The Inquest also highlighted for me the importance of public scrutiny of our prison complex. Shedding light on the practices in prisons is a real challenge. By definition, prisons operate behind perimeter fences and locked doors. The security apparatus that keeps detainees in also functions to keep the public out. Inquests allow the public to glimpse what is occurring in the shadows and to scrutinize how Canada is treating its most vulnerable population. Sadly, this only occurs in the wake of some horrific event.

The Inquest into Ashley's death highlighted the risk of allowing

CSC to continue to operate under a cloud of secrecy. Institutions that operate without oversight are at risk of losing their collective moral compass. How else can we understand the order that was given not to enter Ashley's cell while she was still breathing, or the fact that the guards were prepared to follow it. There is no other way to explain how the managers and medical staff came to design and put into effect such an absurd order or how ordinary correctional officers could act on it. CSC, as an institution, and individual employees clearly lost their ability to differentiate between right and wrong. There is also no other way to explain why Ashley was left in a segregation cell without any personal belongings, meaningful activity or human contact for months and months.

Canada has a very strong moral compass that binds all government institutions. It has been enshrined in our *Charter of Rights and Freedoms*. Ashley had rights that were completely ignored by management as they struggled to control her destructive behaviour – her right to life, her right to security of the person (including her right to access necessarily medical treatment), her right to be free from cruel and unusual punishment, and her right not to be arbitrarily or indefinitely detained in segregation. These rights should have protected Ashley. But without independent oversight, Ashley's rights and her humanity gave way to institutional needs and priorities.

Imagine for a moment what would have happened if someone from Grand Valley Institution had asked a judge or an independent oversight body for permission to issue an order to its officers to 'not to enter Ashley's cell when she was engaged in potentially lethal self-harming behaviour until she stops breathing'. First, it's unlikely the request ever would have been made. No doubt, someone would have seen exactly how ludicrous it was before daring to place it before a judge. More importantly, no truly independent oversight process would allow such an illegal, ill-founded order to be made. But there is no mechanism for independent review of most of the decisions made by CSC. Nobody outside the walls of the institutions was fully aware of Ashley's circumstances or truly able to monitor what was happening to her.

Ashley's Gift

We are coming up on the tenth anniversary of Ashley's death and very little has changed in that time. Years have passed with little progress being made on implementing the jury's recommendations.

Just writing about Ashley brings back the awful images from the video of her death and the videos of her being restrained and forcibly medicated. But it also brings back memories of watching her playfully tease the correctional officer and crack childish jokes with some of the same correctional officers who watched her die. Although I never met Ashley, it was those images that shaped my approach at the Inquest; they drove me to fight for a just verdict for Ashley and for powerful, practical recommendations for imprisoned women in the future.

The images of Ashley smiling and laughing continue to compel me to advocate for profound changes to our correctional system – a system that would have recognized Ashley's humanity and her struggles, a system that will not incarcerate severely ill people, a system that will welcome oversight and public accountability, a system that would have protected Ashley Smith.

Jonathan Rudin *received his LL.B. and LL.M. from Osgoode Hall Law School. In 1990 he was hired to establish Aboriginal Legal Services and is currently ALS Program Director. He has appeared before all levels of court, including the Supreme Court of Canada including representing ALS before the Supreme Court in R. v. Ipeelee (among other cases). At ALS he helped establish the Community Council – the first urban Aboriginal justice program in Canada in 1992, and in 2001 helped establish the Gladue (Aboriginal Persons) Court at the Old City Hall Courts in Toronto. Mr. Rudin also teaches on a part-time basis in the Department of Liberal Arts and Professional Studies at Osgoode Hall Law School at York University, and also at Ryerson University. Last but not least, he plays the mandolin and sings with Gordon's Acoustic Living Room, a group that plays regularly in Toronto and has a number of videos on YouTube.*

Mr. Jonathan Rudin

The Death of Reggie Bushie and the Eight-Year Inquest

On Thursday, November 1, 2007, the body of Reggie Bushie was recovered from the McIntyre River by Ontario Provincial Police divers. Reggie, aged fifteen, had last been seen the previous Friday evening near the river by his older brother, Ricky Strang. Later that same Friday evening, Ricky had arrived alone back at the boarding home where they both resided, soaking wet. Reggie had only been living in Thunder Bay for about a month prior to his death.

Reggie and Ricky were born and raised in the Poplar Hill First Nation, a fly-in community approximately 700 kilometres northwest of Thunder Bay, Ontario. The boys came to the city because there was no high school in or near the Poplar Hill First Nation. The best option available to First Nations' youth in Northern Ontario who want to further their education is to attend high school in Thunder Bay and live in boarding homes, away from friends and family.

Reggie attended the Dennis Franklin Cromarty High School (DFC). The school was operated by the Northern Nishnawbe Education Council (NNEC), a body set up in 1978 to provide educational opportunities for First Nations students in northwestern Ontario who did not have access to secondary school education in their communities.

At the time, Reggie's death was the fifth death since 2000 of a young person who had left their First Nation for high school in Thunder Bay. It would not be the last.

After Reggie's death, his mother Rhoda King and stepfather Berenson King wanted to know what had happened to their son, so they pressed for an inquest to be called into his death. Their campaign was supported by the Chief of their community as well as by the Deputy Chief of Nishnawbe Aski Nation (NAN), Alvin Fiddler. Their persistence paid off. An inquest was called into Reggie's death by the Ontario Coroner's Office, to be presided over by Dr. David Eden. The inquest was set to start in June 2009. It didn't happen then.

The Long Road and Huge Challenges

It took another five and half years for the inquest into Reggie's death to get underway and by then the inquest had expanded to look into the deaths of seven young people from fly-in First Nations, all of whom died while attending high school in Thunder Bay. The inquest took nine months, involved twenty-seven lawyers representing twelve parties, and 165 witnesses were called. The inquest jury made 145 recommendations.

Christa Big Canoe, my colleague at Aboriginal Legal Services, and I represented six of the seven families at the inquest (the seventh family chose not to participate). My direct involvement with the case began just after Labour Day in 2010.

The twists and turns in the story leading up to the inquest and of the inquest itself graphically illustrate the difficult and massively unequal relationships between Indigenous and non-Indigenous people in Canada, and particularly the precarious situation of those living in remote First Nation communities. This story shows there is reason for hope but also that there are huge challenges that the country must be willing to confront.

To understand why it took over five years for Reggie's inquest to begin, we have to look at another inquest into the deaths of two young First Nations men, Ricardo Wesley and Jamie Goodwin, who had lived in the Kasechewan First Nation, another remote fly-in community in northern Ontario. On the evening of January 8, 2006 both men were arrested in Kasechewan for being drunk and were placed in the jail on the reserve. Later that night, a fire started in Ricardo's cell. The jail had no smoke detectors, no sprinkler system and no master key for the cell doors. Both Ricardo Wesley and Jamie Goodwin died of smoke inhalation.

Kim Murray, then of Aboriginal Legal Services (ALS), was one of the counsel for the Wesley family. One of her concerns was to have a jury composed of at least some individuals with knowledge of the realities of life on a remote First Nation in Northern Ontario. In order to see if this was possible she asked about the presence of First Nations residents on the jury rolls in the Kenora District of Northern Ontario, the eastern counterpart to Thunder Bay. In September 2008, in response to her inquiries, an affidavit was prepared by Rolanda Peacock, the Acting Supervisor of Court Operations in Kenora. The information in the Peacock affidavit surprised Kim, threw the entire jury system in Ontario into turmoil for years, led to cases being argued at the Ontario Court of Appeal and the Supreme Court of Canada and the calling of a Commission of Inquiry, chaired by former Justice of the Supreme Court of Canada, Frank Iacoubucci.

The Peacock affidavit stated that it was problematic getting Northern Ontario First Nations on-reserve residents on the jury roll. Jury rolls in Ontario are constructed by using the names on municipal assessment rolls. Since First Nations are not municipalities, residents are not included on those rolls. The Juries Act explicitly allowed the province to obtain names of on-reserve First Nations residents through other sources and until 2000, that had been done by writing Indian and Northern Affairs Canada (INAC). The ministry has gone through many name changes over the years but it has returned to the INAC acronym, although it now stands for Indigenous rather than Indian. In 2000 INAC wrote the Province and said they would no longer provide lists of band members.

In the Kenora district, where on-reserve First Nations members make up approximately thirty percent of the population, this caused a problem. The Peacock affidavit revealed that in 2007 less than eight percent of jury notices sent to on-reserve First Nations residents were completed and returned, as compared to fifty-six percent in the rest of the district. The memo revealed that 2007 was not an anomalous year, but rather the continuation of a trend that had been observed since 2000.

Because Kim Murray was representing Reggie Bushie's family, the issue of on-reserve First Nations representation on juries in the western part of Northern Ontario was front and centre for her. At the same time,

Mandy Wesley, another ALS lawyer, was preparing for a February 2009 inquest into the death of a young Indiginous man named Jacy Pierre, who had been found dead in the Thunder Bay District Jail.

Both Kim and Mandy wanted to know whether the problems in the Kenora district extended to Thunder Bay. Despite their many inquiries and requests for information from the Crown attorneys who were acting as counsel for the coroners, they were met with bland assertions that there were no problems, although no supporting documentation was provided. Kim and Mandy sometimes received no response from them at all. When they asked to examine Robert Gordon, the man responsible for court operations in both the Kenora and Thunder Bay Districts for the Ministry of the Attorney General, they were told by Mr. Gordon that they would have to obtain a subpoena from the coroner first. The coroners were not prepared to issue those subpoenas.

Concerned that a lack of a representative jury roll would impact the fairness of the inquest, in January 2009 Kim asked Dr. David Eden to postpone Reggie's inquest until guidance could be sought from the courts with respect to requiring Robert Gordon to testify. Dr. Eden agreed. Mandy made a similar request of Dr. Shelagh McRae, the coroner who was conducting the Jacy Pierre inquest, but she refused. The Pierre inquest began, the family walked out and the matter eventually made its way to the Ontario Court of Appeal.

The hearing of the appeal into both inquests was scheduled for September 14, 2010. By this time, Kim had left ALS to take a position with the Truth and Reconciliation Commission, as Executive Director, and so Mandy was set to argue the case. Sadly, on September 5, Mandy's mother, Coleen Tenona Beardy, a residential school survivor from Northern Ontario, passed away. Mandy asked me to fill in at the Court of Appeal, which is how I got involved in the case.

Evident Lack of Understanding

In a decision released in March 2011, the Court of Appeal accepted our arguments. We, along with counsel for Nishnawbe Aski Nation, contended that the concerns regarding First Nations residents on jury rolls in Northern Ontario was a legitimate issue, and that the coroners should allow questioning on those issues with the relevant witnesses being produced. Since the Pierre inquest had already been held, the Court took the unusual step of ordering a new inquest. Before Reggie's inquest could start, or Jacy Pierre's could restart, we had to determine what the situation was like in Thunder Bay. In the summer of 2011, I went up there to discover what was or was not happening.

The hearing on the Thunder Bay jury roll was conducted by Dr. David Eden as part of the now-resumed inquest into Reggie's death. On behalf of the Pierre family, who ALS also represented, we agreed that findings with respect to Reggie's case would also apply to Jacy's inquest, whenever that started.

The evidence that came out over three days showed that low response rates from on-reserve First Nations residents to jury questionnaires was also the case in the Thunder Bay District, just as in Kenora. The evidence also revealed a deep lack of understanding of the basic realities of First Nations life. For example, witnesses called from the Ministry of the Attorney General's Court Services Division, people who were responsible for compiling the jury roll in the Thunder Bay area, did not even know what lists First Nations kept of their members.

For example, none of the staff was aware that the electoral list of First Nations peoples included the names of members who did not live on the reserve. In 2000, the Supreme Court of Canada decided that First Nations electoral lists have to include all of their members, wherever located. Somehow the significance of that decision had not been understood by anyone in the Ministry of the Attorney General responsible for obtaining names of on-reserve First Nations members for inclusion on the jury roll.

It got worse. Robert Gordon, the man responsible for court operations for the Ministry of the Attorney General, testified under cross-examination by counsel for Nishnawbe Aski Nation that the position he had taken requiring a subpoena to have him testify was dictated to him by senior staff at the Ministry and went against his instincts. He went on to say that had he been able to decide this question on his own, he would have provided the information that we requested. When given the opportunity at the hearing, he apologized to Reggie and Jacy's family for the hardship and delay that his position had caused. While the Kings were unable to be present for the hearing, Marlene Pierre, Jacy's grandmother, was there to hear the apology.

Testimony at the hearing concluded on July 28, 2011 and Dr. Eden indicated he would release his decision in the autumn of that year. Whatever decision he arrived at, it was clear that the Ministry did not have a handle on on-reserve First Nations residents participating in the jury process in the province. On August 11, before Dr. Eden released his decision, the Ontario Attorney General announced that he had retained former Supreme Court Justice Frank Iacobucci to conduct an investigation into First Nations representation on Ontario juries. Justice Iacobucci's report would be made public and was due in August 2012 but, to no one's surprise, given the complexity of the issues, it was delayed.

Proper Representation Demanded

Dr. David Eden released his decision on the Thunder Bay jury roll on September 9, 2011. He found that the problems with the jury roll there were similar with the problems in Kenora and felt that an inquest could not be called until First Nations on-reserve residents were properly represented on the jury rolls. While this was a victory in one sense, it also meant the inquest into Reggie's death was going to be delayed even further. Since the time of Reggie's death in 2007, two more students from remote First Nations had died while attending high school in Thunder Bay.

Following the release of Dr. Eden's decision, we participated in a press conference along with representatives from Nishnawbe Aski Nation urging that the province call a public inquiry into the deaths of the students. There were now two major hurdles with respect to Reggie's inquest. The first was that it was not clear when it would ever be held, given the problems with the jury roll. The second issue was that an inquest solely into Reggie's death would not necessarily get at the larger issues surrounding the deaths of the seven students. It was hoped that a public inquiry would be able to overcome those hurdles.

What followed was a period of discussion and negotiation that concluded with the Office of the Chief Coroner announcing, on May

31, 2012, that the inquest into Reggie's death would now be expanded to look at the deaths of the seven young people. The inquest would not actually get under way for another three and half years.

An inquest of this scope and size had not previously been undertaken in Ontario and getting it off the ground took more work and time than anyone had anticipated. Because the Ontario Provincial Police had to provide a brief of evidence into all of the deaths, all files had to be examined and witnesses had to be contacted and interviewed.

When the expanded inquest was announced, the families of the other students who were now part of the inquest process also needed the opportunity to obtain counsel. In the end, the families of five other students asked us to represent them along with Reggie. We were now representing the families of: Jethro Anderson, who died on November 11, 2000; Paul Panacheese, who died on November 11, 2006; Robyn Harper, who died on January 13, 2007; Kyle Morrisseau, who died on November 10, 2009; and Jordan Wabasse who died on May 10, 2011. The family of Curran Strang, who died September on 26, 2005, decided that they did not want to participate in the process.

A Report Worth the Wait

As this work proceeded, Justice Iacobucci was also conducting his inquiry that included a number of trips to Northern First Nations as well as consultations in the rest of the province. Justice Iacobucci's report, *First Nations Representation on Ontario's Juries* was finally released in February 2013.

The report was worth the wait. It made seventeen wide-ranging and comprehensive recommendations. On the day it was released, Hon. John Gerretsen, then the Attorney General, promised that the province would implement all of the recommendations.

One of the first recommendations in the report was that the province create a new position in the Attorney General's office – an Assistant Deputy Attorney General responsible for Indigenous Issues. The person hired for this position was Kim Murray.

Another recommendation was that the Province consider the idea of allowing on-reserve First Nations residents to volunteer to be on inquest juries. This too was implemented and was in place by the time the inquest into the deaths of the seven First Nations youths began in Thunder Bay on October 5, 2015. In fact, one of the five members on the inquest jury was selected through that process.

The jury had much to deal with. First, of course, were the circumstances of the deaths of the seven youths. Paul died in the kitchen of his home in Thunder Bay and there was no immediate cause of death. Robyn, the only young woman of the seven, died of alcohol poisoning on the floor of the boarding home where she had been living for just a few days since her arrival from the Keewaywin First Nation. As in the case of Reggie; Jethro, Curran, Kyle, and Jordan were all found in the rivers of Thunder Bay and had gone missing between late September and February (although Jordan's body was not found until May, he went missing in early February and it is assumed that he died very soon after he was last seen).

In addition to looking at the deaths themselves, the jury also needed to learn about the state of education on First Nations; why students had to leave home if they wanted a high school education; the way DFC and the Matawa Learning Centre (MLC), the other high school for on-reserve students in Thunder Bay, were operated and funded; the police investigations surrounding the deaths; and, of course, the broader circumstances of the realities of First Nations people in the North, including the legacy of residential schools.

The number of issues that were to be canvassed also meant there were many parties who felt that they had a need for legal representation at the inquest. In addition to the families, standing to call and examine witnesses was given to Nishnawbe Aski Nation (NAN); Northern Nishnawbe Education Council (NNEC); Matawa Learning Centre (MLC); Keewaytinook Omikanak Council; Ontario First Nations Young Peoples Council of the Chiefs of Ontario; the City of Thunder Bay; The Thunder Bay Police Board; the Chief and Deputy Chief and the Thunder Bay Police Services; the Thunder Bay Police Association; the Office of the Provincial Advocate for Children and Youth; the Province of Ontario; and Canada. Dr. Eden had his own counsel as well who were responsible for calling witnesses, scheduling and trying to keep things on track.

What all of this meant was that there were many issues to cover at the inquest and a lot of lawyers as well. Funding had been secured to ensure all the families could attend the opening of the inquest, closing submissions, and the final recommendations of the jury. Funding was also available to bring families in when the deaths of their loved ones were examined.

Unfortunately, things did not go well when the inquest began. Although a brand new courthouse had just been constructed in Thunder Bay with a number of large courtrooms, the one that was chosen for the inquest was too small to accommodate the family members who wanted to be there. The hearing was delayed on the first day as people tried to find chairs and make room for family members. After that very rough beginning, a courtroom was found that was large enough to accommodate the lawyers and the families.

Falling Finally into a Rhythm

Once all the bugs were worked out, the proceedings fell into a rhythm that often belied the challenges faced by the families. While it had been four years since the last death had occurred, and fifteen since the first, the families had generally not received much information regarding the deaths of their loved ones. For that reason alone, the process was very difficult for family members.

In Reggie's case, his family had never really heard about the circumstances surrounding his death; they just knew he had drowned. Making it all the more difficult, the last person to have seen him alive was his older brother Ricky. During the portion of the inquest focusing on Reggie's death, coroner's counsel called Ricky as a witness. As counsel for the family, I had to cross examine him. It was a very tough time for Ricky and his family.

The evidence was clear that on that Friday evening, the two brothers had been drinking by the river with a number of other students from Dennis Franklin Cromarty High School (DFC). Since alcohol consumption was not permitted by the school and could result in students being sent home, the students drank by the river because it was a concealed spot and they were out of sight of bystanders. The drinking that evening was, in part, to say goodbye to a student who was being sent home for consuming alcohol. Ricky and Reggie and the other students were too young to purchase alcohol and they relied on a runner – an older person – to go to the liquor store in the mall by the river to buy the booze. While the recollections of the people present that evening were clouded by the passage of time and the amount of alcohol consumed, it was clear that around 9 or 10:00 p.m., Reggie and Ricky were the last ones by the river. The witnesses testified that Reggie was very drunk.

Ricky testified that he remembered being with Reggie. He then thinks he passed out and when regained consciousness he was in the McIntyre River. He got out of the river and made it back to his boarding home, cold and soaking wet. He did not recall seeing Reggie when he left but he had fleeting memories of trying to pull something out of the water. He also thought he might have been pushed in the water, but again he had no precise memories of anything other than coming to consciousness in the water.

The other river deaths followed generally similar themes – there was alcohol consumption and there were other people present for some period of time, although precisely how any of the students ended up in water was never clear because no one saw them go in. In the case of Jordan Wabasse, the last student to die, he was last seen exiting a Thunder Bay bus near his boarding home and was not near the water at all.

Five Possible Verdicts

One of the purposes of an inquest is to determine the cause of death. At an inquest, there are five possible verdicts with respect to cause of death: natural causes; accident; suicide; homicide; or undetermined. As there was no evidence that any of the deaths were self-inflicted, there was never any consideration of suicide as a cause of death. In the coroner's context, homicide has a wider definition than in criminal law and includes a death caused by the actions of another person whether criminal or not. In all of the seven deaths, cause of death was a live and disputed issue.

With respect to Paul, who died at home at the age of twenty-one, the medical evidence indicated that it was likely some sort of heart issue that caused his death, but no precise determination could be made. The jury concluded his death was undetermined.

With eighteen-year-old Robyn, there was no question she died in her boarding home of alcohol poisoning. She did not consume the alcohol in the home; instead, on a cold January night, she had been drinking in a wooded area. She was returned to her home by staff at DFC who left her in the hall. Her boarding parent, who also worked for DFC, was at work and testified she checked on her at about 2:00 a.m. but took no steps to seek medical attention for her. It was the contention of the family that her death was best seen as homicide because had the people responsible for her care taken the necessary care with her, she might well not have died. The jury returned a verdict of accident.

The river deaths were, in some ways, the most difficult to determine. There is no question that the five young men all drowned, but how did they get in the water? All of the deaths occurred between late September and February, and all five were clothed when they were taken out of the water. There were no witnesses who could explain how they entered the water. In addition, evidence was received by way of an agreed statement of fact from a former student at DFC who said that on October 28, 2008, almost exactly one year after Reggie went missing and a year before Kyle, he was walking by the McIntrye River on the way back towards DFC when he was confronted by three men. The three men threw him in the water and tried to prevent him from getting out, but he managed to get to the other bank and escape.

There was not any direct evidence to suggest that any of the five was murdered, yet there was little evidence to suggest that the deaths were accidents. The pathologist called by the coroner suggested all the deaths should be seen as accidental but allowed that Jordan's death could be undetermined. In his final submissions, coroner's counsel suggested that Jordan and Kyle's deaths were best seen as undetermined. On behalf of the families, we contended that all of the river deaths were undetermined, as troubling as that finding might be. In this position, we were joined by Nishnawbe Aski Nation (NAN).

Troubling Conclusions

In the end, the jury found that the deaths of Jethro, Kyle, and Jordan, were of undetermined causes but that Curran and Reggie's deaths were accidents. The jury is not required to explain its verdict, indeed that isn't permitted, so why some deaths were undetermined and others accidental is unclear. It may have been that the evidence showed that the last sighting of both Curran and Reggie had them on the banks of a river whereas Jethro, Kyle, and Jordan were not last seen close to water.

The findings that at least three of the river deaths were by undetermined causes leads to some troubling conclusions. If the deaths were not accidents, they certainly didn't arise from natural causes either. Since suicide was ruled out in all deaths, that means that if they were not accidents, then 'someone or ones' were responsible for the deaths.

There were many other aspects of the inquest that revealed very troubling and systemic issues. The one that stands out most for me is the reality of pervasive racism – racism makes the 'undetermined causes' ruling of the deaths conceptually easier for me to understand. Almost all of the witnesses who testified about their experience attending high school at DFC spoke about the racism – racism that sometimes took the form of name-calling but often included food and drinks being thrown at them on the street. These incidents happened day and night. They happened not only over the sixteen-year period that the inquest looked at in detail, that is, from 2000 to 2016, but extended back to the 1980s and 1990s.

Students who came to the city from First Nations communities where this sort of racism was foreign had to live with the knowledge that these assaults could occur at any time. None of these students ever went to the police and most didn't even report it to school staff. It was – and is – the price First Nations students pay for high school education.

With the release of the final report of the Truth and Reconciliation Commission looking at the impact of residential schools in Canada, there has been a great deal of discussion regarding the need for reconciliation. Yes, there needs to be talk about reconciliation – and not merely talk but action. That is why the Commission issued Calls to Action as opposed to recommendations. The Commission's Calls to Action engages not only governments but many institutions, particularly educational institutions, to take steps to ensure that they tell a complete and accurate story of Indigenous people in Canada.

Reconciliation is important. I do worry, however, that the term reconciliation can mask the darker realities that are still present in Canada. Reconciliation suggests that the evils have been done and what is now required is to work to remove the residue and the stains of those evils. With respect to residential schools, this is undoubtedly needed. The schools have now all been closed but the residue of the schools is still with us and we need to recognize and address those impacts. Racism being experienced by Indigenous people in this country is not entirely a residue from the residential school experience but it comes from the same mindset that allowed the residential school system to be developed in the first place – a belief that Indigenous people are less important than other Canadians. It is this belief that has allowed governments to ignore treaties, to criminalize Indigenous cultural practices, to strip Indian status from First Nations women who married non-status Indian men, and to not treat the disappearance of Indigenous women and girls seriously, to name just a few examples. This racism is, sadly, still alive in Canada.

Of course, not everyone in Thunder Bay throws things at First Nations students just as not everyone in Canada holds racist attitudes toward Indigenous people. But enough people in that city hold these opinions and act on them so that throwing things at Indigenous kids has become a practice that has transferred across generations.

The only way these pernicious practices can be rooted out is for everyone to take a stand against such behaviour and attitudes. While there are limits to what the legal system can accomplish in this regard, there are no limits to what society as a whole can accomplish if it puts its mind to it. For me, the legacy of the inquest into the death of Reggie Bushie and the other six students will be found in the way that Canada moves away from the racism that marks its past and present toward a better and more inclusive future. It is possible, it is essential, and it cannot wait.

PART FOUR
Love and Despair

Associate Chief Justice Faith Finnestad *attended Osgoode Hall Law School and served her articles of clerkship in Toronto with Greenspan, Moldaver. She was called to the bar in 1983. Prior to her appointment she practised criminal defence work, first as a sole practitioner and later in partnership at Hicks, Finnestad. Justice Finnestad was appointed to the Ontario Court of Justice in 1995. She presided for sixteen years in the Toronto criminal courts in Metro North and Metro East, serving as Local Administrative Judge in the latter for two years. In 2011 she was appointed to the position of Regional Senior Judge for Toronto, and in 2013 to the position of Associate Chief Justice-Coordinator of Justices of the Peace.*

Justice Faith Finnestad

Love is Not Love

Let me not to the marriage of true minds
Admit impediments. Love is not love
Which alters when it alteration finds,
Or bends with the remover to remove.

—Sonnet 116, William Shakespeare

MOST OF THE TRIALS that catch the attention of the Canadian public are ones of high publicity and sensationalism, taking place before a superior court judge sitting with a jury. These have all the drama of twelve citizens publicly gaining an insight into the world of crime and police procedure, and sitting in judgment on a fellow human being. It is often a public introduction to tangled issues of money, sex and murder, usually introduced, and challenged, by skilled lawyers on both sides.

I am a judge of the Ontario Court of Justice. I don't preside over those types of trials.

That said, not one of those dramatic cases in this province goes before a jury without first passing through the courtrooms of the Ontario Court of Justice. Every criminal case in Ontario begins in this court. More than ninety-five per cent of cases remain here through to completion. The others pass through the hands of those same Ontario Court of Justice judges for preliminary hearings, to determine whether there is "some evidence upon which a reasonable jury, properly instructed, could convict." In those cases where the evidence called by the prosecution passes that test, the accused is committed for trial in the Superior Court of Justice. Those trials will often be held with a jury, and in the case of murder, virtually always with a jury.

The preliminary hearings are usually held subject to a ban on publication of the evidence called, in order to protect the integrity of any subsequent jury trial. Knowing this, the press seldom attend.

In the fall of 2003, I was a judge in my eighth year on the bench. I presided over the preliminary hearing of Dwayne Dilleon, charged with the second degree murder of Joseph Pyne and the attempted murder of Dawn Paquin-Connors. I made the customary order banning publication of the evidence taken. Because the matter never went to trial, the evidence was never heard other than in my courtroom, and some of the most horrifying and intriguing evidence I have ever heard never went beyond the handwritten notes in my benchbook.

Every judge is familiar with the special nature of domestic violence cases. The complexities of the relationships involved typically go far beyond the charges themselves, which often end in withdrawals, acquittals and peace bonds, regardless of their merits or the truth of the allegations. This results from witness no-shows or implausibly recanting witnesses from whom the Crown struggles, often unsuccessfully, to elicit evidence. Often the relationship between accused and victim/complainant is more important to them than the criminal process, and this becomes clear in the courtroom.

The case of twenty-one-year-old Dwayne Dilleon fits within the category of 'domestic violence', but also belongs in a category all its own. In the late summer of 2002, Dwayne moved into the Scarborough apartment of his new girlfriend, Dawn Paquin-Connors. Two weeks later her former partner, Joseph Pyne, moved back into the apartment with them for the weekend. His purpose: to have a visit with their children who were 'in care' and to show the Children's Aid Society that they could co-operate. By noon on Sunday, Joseph Pyne was dead, Dawn Paquin-Connors was nearly dead, and Dwayne Dilleon had an abdominal injury that left him effectively eviscerated. There was no one else in the apartment when police arrived.

As police pieced together the evidence at the hospital and in the apartment, they concluded that despite his own injuries, Dwayne Dilleon was the perpetrator. Dawn was the only surviving eyewitness. She was caught between the murdered father of her three children, and the man she loved, who was charged with killing him and attempting to murder her.

When Dwayne's preliminary hearing commenced before me in

November 2003, the Crown began their case with the astonishing statement that despite having a living eyewitness who was prepared to testify, their case would be based on circumstantial evidence. Unlike many cases involving allegations of domestic violence where the alleged victim does not respond to a subpoena, Dawn came to court. She did not refuse to testify, nor did the Crown have to seek permission to cross-examine her as a hostile witness. She would describe everything that happened, but indicate that the room was dark and she could not see who was committing the acts. She described events so horrifying and at such personal cost to her that it was almost unimaginable. As I watched her in the witness box, still with her visible scars, it was clear that her love for both men was a guiding factor in her actions that day and in her testimony in court.

The Crown called Dawn as one of their first witnesses, and relied on her evidence as to the acts themselves and the persons present in the room. The rest of the evidence called on the preliminary hearing was the Crown's effort to build the other evidence around her testimony so as to rule out anyone but Dwayne as the perpetrator. Each day was part of a mystery unfolding as footprint comparisons, blood spatter analysis, DNA evidence, an *ante mortem* statement from Joseph Pyne, and neighbours' testimony were added to put together the picture the Crown was seeking to paint.

Here is the story as told in my courtroom. I am grateful to the excellent prosecutors on this case, Scarborough Crown Attorney Andrew Pilla and Assistant Crown Attorney Jackie Garrity, who met with me this year to put our memories together, and to flesh out the notations I had made in my benchbook over thirteen years ago. They not only refreshed my memory, but provided some behind-the-scenes information of which I was not aware while hearing the case. I did not speak to defence counsel for reasons of solicitor-client privilege.

The Story

Late on the morning of September 15, 2002, Toronto Police Services responded to a 9-1-1 call coming from a Scarborough apartment complex. As officers approached the building, a barefoot woman staggered out of the front door, her clothing soaked in blood and a bone protruding from one arm. As she collapsed, Detective Constable (D.C.) Eckersall caught her in his arms. She spoke hysterically about others in the apartment who were injured. He leaned her against a railing and she collapsed again, so he lowered her to the ground. He and Police Constable (P.C.) Greto then moved into the lobby of the building, where they saw bloody bare footprints leading down the hall towards the lobby from apartment B6. The two officers observed more blood on the door and threshold of Apartment B6.

D.C. Eckersall and P.C. Greto moved to the door, gloves on and guns in hand, not knowing what to expect. They crouched together at the door and opened it a crack. With the curtains drawn, the room was unnaturally dark for midday. D.C. Eckersall pulled out his flashlight. Blood was everywhere. A television blaring in one corner of the room competed for their attention with the excited barking of a pit bull near the kitchen. Just inside the door at their feet lay a man with massive amounts of blood spreading from his body, emanating from what would later be learned to be fifteen stab wounds to his neck and back. Over the din in the apartment the officers called out from the doorway. A female voice could be heard responding – that of the 9-1-1 dispatcher, still on speakerphone.

The officers hesitated, their guns drawn, crouching at the doorway of this dark, bloody, chaotic and uncertain scene. At that point the Road Sergeant arrived behind them and, sensing their hesitation, ordered them to enter the room.

D.C. Eckersall, a paramedic before he was a policeman, stepped in to check the man at the door for vital signs; P.C. Greto hurried to the kitchen and flipped a table on its side to confine the pit bull. (The dog was ultimately lifted out the kitchen window to avoid contaminating the scene.) As Eckersall knelt to take the pulse of what he quickly learned was a lifeless body, he looked up to see more bloody footprints leading down the darkened hallway to a bedroom at the end of the corridor. Visible, lying just inside the doorway, was a pair of unmoving feet, clad in socks.

D.C. Eckersall made his way towards the bedroom with his gun still drawn, apprehensively checking closets and doorways as he proceeded along the dim hallway. In the bedroom, between a mattress on the floor and a closet door, lay a man, motionless on his back and with his abdomen covered in blood. With the door closed, the television blaring and the dog barking, Eckersall could not tell what potential danger might be in that closet. On high alert and still with his gun drawn, the officer knelt to check for a pulse. At that very moment the motionless and bloodied man's eyes flew open and he gave a gasp. Eckersall backed off, shocked, to allow access to the paramedics who had just entered the apartment. As he watched, paramedics lifted the man's shirt and undid his belt buckle to determine the source of the bleeding. The man's intestines, with the pressure thus released, were expelled forcefully from his abdomen. A few soft moans emanated from him. He was rushed to hospital along with the woman who had collapsed on the front porch.

The Players

The body that officers had found on the floor just inside the entrance of Apartment B6 was that of Joseph Pyne, a twenty-eight-year-old man with no criminal record. For the past three years, and until mid-August, he had lived in that apartment with his partner of eight years, Dawn Paquin-Connors. He moved back in for that mid-September weekend with one purpose: to persuade the Children's Aid Society that he and Dawn had a stable enough relationship to allow for the return of the three daughters they shared.

The badly injured woman collapsed on the front porch was thirty-year-old Dawn Paquin-Connors, who had broken up with Joseph a few months earlier, but allowed him to remain in the apartment until mid-August. Her new boyfriend, Dwayne Dilleon, moved into Apartment B6 shortly after Joseph moved out. The planned visit with the children, scheduled to impress the CAS, resulted in all three people sharing the same two-bedroom apartment for the weekend. Before the weekend ended, those visit plans would be cancelled due to the illness of one of the children.

After being taken by ambulance to the hospital, Dawn gave doctors a version of events that was inconsistent with her injuries. She said something about a stranger coming into the apartment and hurting them all. While still in hospital recovering from her injuries, she was charged with accessory after the fact to murder and attempting to obstruct justice, charges she dealt with before ever appearing in my courtroom.

The man in the back bedroom with the eviscerating abdominal injury was Dwayne Dilleon. He survived, as the knife that sliced his abdomen open had miraculously touched no organs. At the hospital, in response to questioning, he made no statement. The police would later allege that his injury was self-inflicted. They charged him with the murder of Joseph Pyne and the attempted murder of Dawn Paquin-Connors.

Dawn's Evidence at the Preliminary Inquiry

By the time Dawn came to court to testify, the prosecution had little idea of how her evidence would emerge. They knew from her multiple statements that Dawn would not inculpate Dwayne Dilleon, but they knew as well that she would put all three of the players in the apartment. The prosecution would rely on their other witnesses to show both motive and opportunity for Dwayne, and the absence of any other viable suspects.

Dawn began her evidence standing in the witness box. As time went on, a mere year from the sustaining of her horrific injuries, she sat down for the remainder of it. She set out for me the relationships among the three people in the apartment that weekend. Joseph Pyne was the father of three of her five children; two girls who were living with his parents, and one who was in foster care. She and Joseph had been together for eight years by the time their relationship ended at the beginning of July, 2002. He had moved out of Dawn's apartment in August. Shortly after Joseph's departure, Dawn began a relationship with Dwayne Dilleon. By September 15, 2002, Dwayne had been living with her for two weeks.

Dawn explained how the three came to be together on the weekend of September 15, when Joseph began moving some things back in to her apartment. In order to get their girls back they had to co-operate and co-exist. A visit with the children was planned for September 15th. Dawn pleaded with him not to come that weekend because the day for the visit kept being shifted. She suggested they just meet at one of their parents' homes, but Joseph wanted to show that they could "get along" that weekend. On the night of September 14, Joseph stayed in one room, and Dawn and Dwayne in another. On the morning of the 15th, Joseph told her he had just learned that one of the children was sick and the visit, being co-ordinated between grandparents, would have to be rescheduled. She called her own mother to confirm this. The justification for Joseph's presence in this uncomfortable triangle had just disappeared.

Dawn went into her bedroom to tell Dwayne about the cancelled visit. His predictable reaction was to ask what the point was, in that case, of Joseph being there all weekend. Dwayne asked when Joseph was leaving and Dawn said it would be that morning. When asked if Dwayne had raised his voice she replied, "No, he never yells at me."

At that point, one of Joseph's friends who went by the nickname of 'Ninja', came knocking on the kitchen window looking for him. Dawn referred Ninja to the back bedroom where Joseph had been staying. She testified that to that point she had had no disagreement with Joseph, nor had she raised her voice. Joseph then came out of his bedroom saying that he was going out to talk to Ninja. He was gone about fifteen to twenty minutes. During that time Dwayne asked again how long Joseph would be staying. Dawn replied that he would be leaving shortly after he came back inside. When Joseph came back in, however, he went back into his bedroom.

Dawn then made a phone call to her son who was staying with her parents. At this point, her evidence became confusing and frightening, probably a reflection of her own feelings at the time. The Crown asked her few questions, letting her tell the story as she relived it. Dawn recalled ending the phone call by hanging up as she exclaimed to her son "oh my god something's happening!" Unfortunately, from my perspective, in the evidence that followed she did not describe clearly what that "something" was. The Crown, for tactical reasons, did not probe her often vague and evasive descriptions of the ensuing events.

Dawn said that she heard Joseph behind her, "going on" and she turned around and saw that he was being hit by "an arm." She instinctively ran around the couch to get between the two people, as Joseph was turning and trying to cover himself. Dawn told me that, "He's not much of a fighter so he goes into a defensive mode." As she came between them she realized she herself was catching the blows directed at Joseph, absorbing multiple punches to her head. Dawn moved further backwards, trying to protect Joseph, who was behind her. Ultimately, Joseph was pushed into a chair with Dawn bent protectively over him. She then saw "the person" pull a knife. Screaming, "No please don't!" Dawn put up an arm in an unsuccessful bid to block the blows. She closed her eyes, only aware that she was screaming, as she blocked repeated blows from the knife. Mercifully, she lost all feeling, and after being thrown aside, she also lost consciousness. When she regained her senses, Dawn was pulled up, punched, and stabbed to the side of her body. Thrown violently into a chair, she struck the wall and blacked out again. She heard and saw nothing for some time after that.

Dawn described her final return to awareness in that dark and bloodied room. Initially, she heard nothing and had no sense of time. She described her gradual assessment of her own injuries. Experiencing extreme pain to her arm, she examined it and saw a vicious cut, gaping and bleeding. Blood poured from her right hand. Police would notice the broken bone protruding from her arm when she came outside to meet them. Numerous stitches would be required to close wounds to her left bicep and upper forearm. Dawn's arm bone, shattered by blows from the knife, would require a plate and screws to hold it together. She would have over forty staples to her arm on top of a layer of inner stitches. When Dawn stood up inside Apartment 6B and began to move, she used her right arm to hold her left arm up. Both hands were cut open and bleeding and she could not use them. It was determined at the hospital that the knife had penetrated completely through the palm of one hand, and had caused extensive nerve and tendon damage to both hands.

The first thing Dawn saw as she rose to her feet was Joseph lying on his back. She called and got no response. Frightened and in pain, Dawn next called out for Dwayne. She heard a moaning from the back room, and followed the sound. She had difficulty moving, as her legs kept giving out, and she slid against the walls in her own blood. Eventually reaching the back bedroom, Dawn saw Dwayne, lying on the floor clutching his stomach, his torso bathed in blood. Dawn told

Dwayne she was dizzy, and begged him to help her back to the living room to call 9-1-1. He reached out a hand, and she touched it before he fell back. Dawn was standing just inside the bedroom door when she herself fell.

Rising again to her feet, Dawn managed to get to the hallway closet. She grabbed a towel in an effort to staunch the blood pouring from her arms and hands. She then described making her way back to the living room. I couldn't help visualizing and in some way reliving her experience, as she sat there recounting it so graphically and yet in so matter-of-fact a manner.

In the living room, there was now much more blood than there had been before. Blood was everywhere she walked or stood, and her own clothing was soaked with it.

Unable to use her hands, and with enormous difficulty, Dawn managed to dial 9-1-1. She told the operator that three people were badly injured, and that she believed one was, in fact, dead. She was put on hold. Bleeding badly and dizzy, she waited. She became aware of her other injuries. In addition to the injuries to her arms and hands, she had stab wounds from waist to head, behind her ear, at the nape of her neck, on her shoulder, to her bicep, upper forearm and back. Having pleaded with 9-1-1 and put on hold, Dawn decided that she had to get out of the apartment and find police. Dizzy and near fainting, she fell a couple times, and sat for a time in a chair to get her second wind. Once at the door leading out of the apartment, she struggled with both virtually useless hands to manipulate the door open. Dawn could not remember opening any locks, only grabbing the chain lock to keep from falling. When she finally got the door open a crack, she jammed her bare foot in, and used that to push the door open.

At this dramatic moment in Dawn's evidence there was a break for the lunch recess. When court resumed, Dawn advised me that when she was being attacked and leaning in over Joseph in the chair, she heard a door open. In my view this was a little late for the arrival of a mysterious stranger, and I did not give this addition much credence. Throughout her recitation of the attack there had been no mention of Dwayne, despite her earlier evidence of his being in the apartment that morning, and her having made no mention of his ever having left.

I was convinced by this time that Dawn was determined not to inculpate Dwayne in her version of the violent events in Apartment 6B.

Asked by the prosecutor in conclusion to describe the person who struck both her and Joseph, Dawn said it was a black person wearing something dark. She could not determine the gender. She added that she was shorter than both this dark assailant and Joseph, coming about up to their chest height. Dawn professed herself unable to say who had stabbed her and Joseph that morning; she hadn't had her glasses on, and could hardly see without them. She heard nothing beyond the door opening and a scream. Not surprisingly, there was no cross-examination of this witness by the defence.

Remarkably, Dawn's evidence did not identify who had stabbed her and Joseph. However, other than a last minute mention of an opening door, with nothing further, the Crown was content that her evidence had disclosed the exclusive presence of the three of them in the apartment that morning.

The prosecution proceeded to call other evidence, in an attempt to establish a case sufficient to meet the test to send Dwayne to a jury trial. Subsequent witnesses would be called to give evidence of a tension among the trio, and of a desire on the part of Dwayne to be rid of Joseph. The forensic evidence would seek to establish that no one else entered or left the apartment that morning.

The Other Evidence

The Crown called a neighbour who testified to seeing Dawn and Joseph and a second man outside that morning. She said that Dawn was loud and angry and could be heard telling Joseph to leave. She saw the second man only from the back, and he said nothing.

The Crown then called 'Ninja', a friend of Joseph's, who testified to knocking on the kitchen window around 10:30 that morning to ask Dawn if he could speak to Joseph. Ninja had heard Dawn yelling, and when she answered his knock, her face was red and she appeared to have been crying. He could hear a voice yelling in the background, expressing anger at Joseph's being there and wanting him to leave. When Ninja asked for Joseph, Dawn told him to go knock on the back bedroom window. While there knocking, Ninja could still hear

Dawn and a voice that sounded like Dwayne, in Jamaican Patois saying words to the effect of "You are taking me for an idiot. These things can't go on." He sounded angry and frustrated and said further things like "What is he doing here? He's not supposed to be here." Ninja testified that he spoke Patois himself and he understood the statements. When Joseph came to the window, Ninja invited him to come outside and talk, and the two met on the porch for about half an hour.

The Crown brought an application for admission of the statements made by Joseph to Ninja as they spoke outside. Ordinarily, the reporting by one person of the statement of another is hearsay, and not admissible for the truth of that statement. After hearing submissions, I ruled their conversation admissible. Ninja described that conversation as follows: Joseph came out of the apartment "in a downer mood" and said he couldn't deal with it anymore. Everyone was down on him. The visitation had been cancelled but Dawn had said to hang around and try to reschedule. He reported that Dwayne was inside making a stink about the possibility of Joseph staying longer. Ninja testified that he told Joseph he shouldn't be there anyway. Joseph protested that he had to stay because of the kids; he didn't understand "why he's getting bitched at." Ninja told him it was his own fault and that he shouldn't be there. He wanted to get Joseph out of that situation, and told him to go grab his stuff and leave. When Joseph agreed, Ninja asked if he should follow him in to avoid any arguments. Joseph declined, saying that he didn't want anyone to think Ninja was coming in to fight. Joseph said all of this in a soft voice, and went back into the apartment.

Dawn's son, Paul Connors, was at his grandparents when Dawn called him that morning. Paul heard male voices arguing in the background, and recognized Joseph's voice. He asked his mother who else was in the apartment and she told him. However his repetition of Dawn's response was hearsay, and since it was not put to Dawn during her evidence for her to either acknowledge or deny, I could not consider that statement for its truth. Near the end of the call, Dawn sounded worried and said "something bad's happening and I've got to let you go." He heard Joseph yell "What the fuck" before his mother hung up.

The evidence of the neighbour, of Paul Connors and of Ninja

contradicted Dawn's evidence that there was neither arguing nor raised voices that morning over Joseph's presence. Ninja's recounting of his conversation with Joseph showed the rising tensions in the apartment, as well as Dwayne's angry resistance to Joseph's continued presence. The boy Paul's evidence disclosed arguing in the apartment just before "something bad happened."

Police evidence described the scene, and the significance of some of the things they observed.

Despite the incredibly bloody scene in the apartment, and which was particularly notable close to the door, the only footprints seen leaving the apartment were the bloody, bare footprints of Dawn, heading to the front porch of the building. Right by the body of Joseph and around the chair where Dawn said the attack occurred, were what appeared to be boot prints, with a distinctive zigzag tread. In the apartment itself, bloody footwear prints with a distinctive zigzag tread led only one way – from the living room to the bedroom where Dwayne was found. Close to his body was a pair of boots with a distinctive zigzag tread. The Crown sought to qualify a 'footwear impressions expert' who had done a significant amount of work eliminating the footwear impressions of the fourteen firefighters, paramedics and police officers who had passed through the apartment, and who presented charts with numerous acetate overlays to display his findings. I was satisfied that I could draw my own conclusion in those unique circumstances.

Dwayne was wearing only socks on his feet at the time police arrived. His blood was located nowhere in the apartment except in the immediate area of the bedroom where he was found – a few drops on his socks, some on the toe of the boot, and some on a knife sheath found under the mattress. There was none of his blood in the living room or the hallway.

Under a sleeping bag, on the mattress on the floor beside Dwayne, was a large knife. Subsequent analysis showed it to have the blood of both Dawn and Joseph on it, although not of Dwayne Dilleon himself. Similar analysis of blood found on rings taken from his fingers at the hospital determined that it came from the same two sources. In a thorough search that had police in the apartment for three days, a fanny-pack was located. It contained not only a resumé and cheque stubs in the name of Dwayne Dilleon, but a photo of him posing with a large and particularly nasty-looking hunting knife. That knife had the same blade, serrations, and chrome on the handle as the knife found under the sleeping bag. Under the mattress itself was the knife sheath, which had a small amount of Dwayne's blood on it.

While the mystery of the missing knife involved in the stabbing of Dwayne remained unsolved, I was satisfied that Dwayne's injuries were sustained after those of Joseph and Dawn, and that the person who inflicted all of those injuries had never left the apartment. I was satisfied that there was sufficient evidence that Dwayne was the one who caused the death of Joseph, and concluded that the attack on Dawn while she was shielding Joseph was some evidence of his intention to kill her. I concluded that I should commit him for trial in the Superior Court of Justice on both charges.

Despite the fact that the charge upon which Dwayne was arraigned was one of second degree murder, the Crown in their closing arguments sought committal on the higher charge of first degree murder. In support of this they relied first on what they submitted was evidence of planning and deliberation. The Crown relied secondly on section 231(5) of the *Criminal Code*, which provides that where death is caused by someone while committing, or attempting to commit, the offence of forcible confinement, that murder is one of first degree.

There was evidence that one of the phone lines in the apartment had been cut, although not when, nor by whom. Dwayne had a knife with him on that day. The prosecution argued that Dawn's bloody handprints on the lock above the apartment doorknob was some evidence suggesting that the door to the apartment had been locked at the time of the attack. The argument was that Dwayne planned the event; that he brought a knife, cut the phone line, and locked the door before commencing the attack. By locking the other two in the apartment, Dwayne had forcibly confined them.

I was not persuaded that the evidence supported an escalation of the charge. With respect to planning and deliberation, it wasn't known that the visit with the children would be cancelled until that morning. Tensions seemed to escalate after that. I thought it unlikely that one would plan out a bloodbath of this nature without an escape route; that a self-inflicted wound spoke to desperation and poor planning; that there was no evidence as to when the phone cord was cut; that it was speculation to assume it had been cut in advance, particularly when Dawn was using one of the phone lines when the attack commenced; that there was no evidence that the knife was obtained that day and not simply part of Dwayne's personal belongings; and lastly that Dawn explained the presence of her blood on the lock when she testified that she did not recall having to undo any locks, but only grabbing at the chain lock to catch herself as she was falling.

I committed Dwayne for trial on charges of second degree murder and attempted murder.

The Love Story

There are actually two love stories here, and both involve Dawn. The easiest to understand is the love she clearly still had for Joseph, the father of three of her children, and a peaceful and soft-spoken man. Even so, it is almost impossible to comprehend the magnitude of the determination and courage she demonstrated in literally standing in the way of death in an effort to protect him. She did not cease trying to shield Joseph until she lost consciousness.

This love, as magnanimous and courageous as it was, is only a small part of what makes the other love story so difficult to comprehend: Dawn's love for Dwayne.

Two aspects of Dawn's evidence had a profound effect on me at the time, and have endured over the years. One was her description of the incredible violence that was inflicted on her, and its long-term effects. The other was her response when asked about her relationship with Dwayne as he sat in the prisoner's box. In the witness stand, with visible scars and the still-limited use of her seriously damaged hands, she replied, "Dwayne and I are still together. I haven't broken up with him. By all accounts he's asked me to marry him and I agreed." More than thirteen years later I still cannot reconcile those. Dawn described, and continued to act with, a love that transcends anything that love could be expected to overlook. To my mind it transcended sanity itself.

That love was clear to me in Dawn's evidence. But it was in

subsequent discussions with the Scarborough Crown prosecutors, Andrew Pilla and Jackie Garrity that I learned of its enduring nature. Here is a part of the story that took place outside of my courtroom.

Dawn went straight to jail from the hospital in September 2002 with both arms in casts, and still recovering from multiple injuries. While most bail hearings are held in the Ontario Court of Justice before justices of the peace, the charge of accessory after the fact to murder is one of the few which the *Criminal Code* requires to be held in the Superior Court of Justice. Dawn was ordered released in November but not before both of her arms were re-broken while in custody. Her only comment on that in her evidence before me was that, "The jail was not set up to meet my needs." Dawn's bail conditions included one of non-association with Dwayne Dilleon.

Shortly after her release on bail, Dawn began visiting Dwayne at the Metro East Detention Centre in Scarborough, in violation of that release order. After eight or nine visits, this came to police attention and Dawn was re-arrested on charges of breach of bail. In Toronto, all bail hearings and in-custody appearances for women are held at the College Park courthouse downtown. For this reason, and due to an inexplicable lack of communication between the downtown and Scarborough Crowns' offices, Dawn's re-arrest on the alleged breaches did not come to the attention of the office responsible for prosecuting both her and Dwayne. Dawn ultimately entered a guilty plea, at that downtown courthouse, to charges of breaching her bail order. A sentence of 'time served' was imposed and Dawn was again released on her original bail order.

Eventually, the Crown Attorney in Scarborough learned of the charges. Dismayed at not having been afforded the opportunity to seek cancellation of her original bail on the basis of those breaches, and concerned about collusion between their accused and their only living eyewitness, the Scarborough Crowns decided to bring that application then, knowing the prospect of success might be reduced by the fact that she had already served her sentence and had been released. The application was strongly contested by Dawn's lawyer but was ultimately successful. Dawn was detained in custody again until shortly before Dwayne's preliminary hearing.

Dawn spent ten months in custody on her original charges, and a few weeks before Dwayne's preliminary hearing, entered a guilty plea to attempting to obstruct justice, again at the College Park courthouse, but this time with the involvement of the Scarborough Crown's office. She received another sentence of 'time served.' She thus appeared before me out of custody for Dwayne's preliminary hearing, and it was there that she told me that "by all accounts he's asked me to marry him and I agreed."

Mr. Pilla and Ms. Garrity also told me what happened after I had committed Dwayne for trial on both charges. Within a month or two, he appeared before Justice David Watt of the Superior Court of Justice and after a judicial pre-trial, entered a plea of guilty to the charge of the second degree murder of Joseph Pyne. He refused to plead guilty to the charge of attempted murder of Dawn Paquin-Connors and in light of the life sentence he received for murder, the Crown withdrew that charge.

Mr. Pilla advised me that eight years later, in 2011, he was contacted by CBC's *the fifth estate* and asked to comment on the Dilleon case. He declined to do so. He directed me to a program that had aired in that year, featuring Dawn Paquin-Connors among other women. I found and watched the February 18, 2011, Season 36, Episode 17 episode of *the fifth estate*. It was entitled "The Devil You Know; Hate the crime, love the con."

The program interviewed women in love with men serving penitentiary sentences. Some met their man while he was in custody, and some, like Dawn, had a relationship that began before the man was sentenced. All maintained their relationships despite time, distance, and the fact that their partner was behind bars.

The brief portion of the program featuring Dawn dealt with a bus service operated by the John Howard Society, which drove women from Toronto twice weekly to a number of penitentiaries in the Kingston area. For a thirty-dollar fare, the twelve-hour roundtrip gave these women the opportunity for a two-hour visit before starting the ride back home. Dawn was one of those passengers. She told the camera she had been visiting Dwayne for eight years. She described herself as having given up everything for him, "including her five children."

"He would never do anything to intentionally hurt me" Dawn said. She described his love letters, sent from the jail over the years and which she had saved in an album, as having kept her going. She noted, "no one has ever said things like that to me." She spoke eagerly and optimistically of his pending first parole eligibility date, in 2012, saying that all she wanted was to live with him in peace and quiet, and to be the family they were meant to be. She concluded, "Your heart wants what it wants, when you really love someone."

All of this came after a brutal attack on her, the murder of the father of three of her children, and eight years of love letters and two-hour visits with the man responsible for it all.

As of the date of this writing in 2017, Dwayne Dilleon has no known release date, and is currently in a Canadian penitentiary.

Love alters not with his brief hours and weeks,
But bears it out even to the edge of doom.
If this be error, and upon me prov'd,
I never writ, nor no man ever lov'd.

Brian Beresh QC, founding partner of Beresh Aloneissi O'Neill, Edmonton, has practiced criminal law for over forty years. He is a past president of the Criminal Trial Lawyers Association and an original director of the Canadian Council of Criminal Defence Lawyers. A former Bencher of the Law Society of Alberta, he has taught advanced criminal law and other courses at the University of Alberta Faculty of Law for twenty-nine years. He has designed a wrongful convictions course to be offered in 2017. Since 1993 he has been a lifetime member of the National Association of Criminal Defence Lawyers. In his spare time, he loves to play hockey, climb mountains, and cycle. He has been a major contributor to the arts and music scene in Edmonton. He has never forgotten his Hungarian and Saskatchewan roots.

Mr. Brian Beresh

A Penalty of Death for Dina Dranchuk

"...YOU SHALL BE HANGED BY THE NECK UNTIL YOU ARE DEAD; AND MAY GOD HAVE MERCY ON YOUR SOUL."

So went the condemnation of a thirty-four-year-old woman who heard the words but could not appreciate their significance because they were spoken in English. They followed a verdict by six white Anglo-Saxon men sitting in judgment of a Ukrainian housewife who had been convicted of using an axe to end her abusive relationship.

It was 1934 in Edmonton, Alberta and the verdict concluded a five-hour trial. Court records would reveal that her trial commenced thirty-six days after her husband died. Swift justice did not, in these circumstances, serve the accused well. The prosecution's case was completed in under three-and-a-half hours with the calling of thirteen witnesses in its own case and one rebuttal witness. The defence case was completed in nineteen minutes which included an opening address and the evidence of a defence medical expert.

Defence counsel addressed the jury in closing for five minutes. The prosecution exceeded that by only two minutes. The Judge's charge lasted thirty-four minutes and the jury deliberated for under forty-three minutes.

The accused's utterances at the time of the verdict included "If you are going to hang me, I wish you could take my children and take them to my husband's place."

Condemned to death, Dina Dranchuk, become known as 'convict

3656'. She was sentenced to be hanged at Fort Saskatchewan, Alberta on December 12, 1934. She was transported directly from her trial to the Fort Saskatchewan institution where she was placed in the 'death cell' to await execution. Subsequently, the date of the hanging was rescheduled for December 31, 1934. Media coverage in the local St. Paul, Alberta newspapers was extensive and detailed, both pre-trial and during the trial.

My Fascination Piqued

I became fascinated with the Dranchuk case in 1994 when my good friend, Rick Boychuk, former editor of *Canadian Geographic* magazine and now speech writer for the Bank of Canada, brought the case to my attention. From the material I received, I became more concerned with how women historically have been treated in the justice system. From my initial review of the case I felt that there may have been a miscarriage of justice.

My interest in the case was further piqued when I learned that Dina Dranchuk was the last woman in Alberta to be sentenced to death. To the date of her sentence, six women had been sentenced to death in the province. Of these women, only, Filumenia Costanzo Lassandero (also known as Florence Lassandro) convicted along with her husband's employer, Emilio Picariello, of killing a policeman had ever actually been put to death in Alberta. All other death sentences imposed upon females had been commuted.

What fascinated me about the Dranchuk case was that it had all the elements that I thought might raise a type or form of Battered Woman Syndrome defence, which was not formally recognized by the Supreme Court of Canada until the 1990s Lavallee decision. Despite that, I wondered why, in all the circumstances, the jury might not have returned a verdict of manslaughter.

The dispute in the Dranchuk case between her and her husband arose over his refusal to give her money to purchase medicine. It must be remembered that in 1934, Medicare, as we know it now, was not a part of the Canadian fabric. It was not until 1962 that Premier Tommy Douglas' efforts aided by Woodrow Lloyd, to ensure all citizens access to medical treatment (and some drugs) came into effect.

In addition, Mike and Dina Dranchuk had immigrated to Canada from Ukraine, then a part of the Soviet Union, in about 1930 and homesteaded north of St. Paul, Alberta. They brought with them very little other than the clothes on their backs. The onset of the severe drought in 1930 and the ensuing depression hindered their meager dirt farming endeavor. Even by standards of the day, they were very poor. It was in this difficult situation that Mrs. Dranchuk raised her two sons who were fourteen- and six-years-old at the time of their father's death.

Myrna Kostach in her acclaimed novel *All of Baba's Children* described the hardship and racism faced by Ukrainian settlers in the area where the Dranchuk's had settled in Alberta. She described the particular plight of Ukrainian women:

> They were female workers and as such experienced a status and condition peculiar to their sex. As pioneers, they did not have, under Canadian law, the right to shared ownership in the homestead they helped to clear and manage nor to the income they helped earn; for years they did not even have legal guardianship of their children....Women are little better than slaves who toil laboriously at the beck and call of their inconsiderate husbands. Wife beating is common place.

What further intrigued me about the case was Mrs. Dranchuk's mental state, both on the date of her husband's death and at the time of the trial and how that played out in relation to the live issues at her trial. I was also concerned by the extensive pre-trial publicity, and given that, whether any steps were taken at trial to protect the accused's fair trial rights.

It struck me that this detailed pre-trial publicity, less than a month before the trial, could have directly affected the jurors pre-conceived notions about how and why Mike Dranchuk met his death.

In 1994, when I first learned of the Dranchuk case, my research was restricted to in-depth newspaper articles surrounding the case. Since my initial exposure to the case, many questions about it had remained unanswered and I knew that someday I would be moved to do more in-depth research and write about it.

Women and Criminal Activity

Throughout my years of practice, I found myself intrigued with how our criminal justice system has responded to women accused of criminal activity. In this patriarchal criminal justice system, the system has generated rules and policies which, for the most part, have been male dominated. It is trite to observe that treating male and female offenders alike can lead to disparity and injustice.

My first real exposure to what I believe to be unequal treatment of women in the criminal justice system occurred in my first year of practice in 1976 in North Battleford, Saskatchewan, where I was employed in an office operated by Saskatchewan Legal Aid. On one of my first appearances in Provincial Court, Judge Joseph Policka, a war veteran who ran his court more like a court martial proceeding than a criminal court, had before him a young Indigenous woman who pleaded guilty to a single charge of mischief. Normally, this type of charge would result in a fine or a suspended sentence with probation.

During the sentencing process, it was revealed that at 3:00 a.m. on the date of the offence, the accused had gone one or two blocks from her home to pick up a pizza, leaving her children asleep at home. The children were not harmed or affected by her absence, of which they were unaware.

The judicial display during sentencing that I witnessed was disturbing. Rather than focus on the minor mischief offence, the Judge became fixated on the accused briefly leaving the children. He scorned her publicly and scolded her for what he thought was poor parenting. He pontificated on what it took to be a good parent and obviously wanted the crowded courtroom to know that he is a tough judge. He sentenced her to a fourteen-day jail term.

The event was shocking and I questioned my career choice. Ironically, he had been scolding her for leaving her children alone for a few minutes without any concern that his decision directly resulted in the children not having contact with their mother for the fourteen-days of imprisonment.

Later in my career, in my defence of Yvonne Johnson, an Indigenous Cree woman, I saw not only the harsh standard applied by a white jury to a non-white accused, but also the jury's reaction to the accused's conduct. She, along with her husband and friend, were charged in the death of a man that she truly believed to be a child molester. Ms. Johnson was fearful for her children and other children in the community.

She and two others participated in the beating death of the believed child molester. As portrayed explicitly by Rudy Wiebe in his well-researched novel with Ms. Johnson, *Stolen Life: The Journey of a Cree Woman,* the fact that Yvonne Johnson, as a child, had been molested and abused drew no sympathy from the jury. Although her husband was found guilty of second degree murder in a separate trial, a male-dominated non-indigenous jury of nine men convicted Yvonne of first degree murder and she was sentenced to life in prison without parole for twenty-five years. Her concerns about her fear of how children might be victimized by the deceased appeared to have been ignored.

I sincerely believe that race and my client's non-traditional female conduct played a role in her conviction.

I encountered the same prejudice in my defence of Lily Choy, an Asian woman who was charged in the death of a three-year-old boy, placed in her care by Alberta Child Services. Ms. Choy was a very aggressive and successful nurse/instructor. She raised two of her own children as a single mother. She was a workaholic. She spoke out for herself and did not suffer fools.

In cross-examination at her trial, Crown counsel baited her often and unfortunately she took the bait and argued extensively with him.

She was acquitted of murder but convicted of manslaughter. I felt that the verdict was not justified and hard to rationalize on the facts. I honestly feel that in part, the jury did not like her aggressive approach, and she didn't fit the stereotypic mold of what jurors expected of this woman who professed her love for children. That love was confirmed by her desire to raise two to three other children in addition to her own.

Childcare and discipline became important issues in the Choy case. The prosecution called an expert who was critical of Ms. Choy's approach and parenting skills. The jury appears to have rejected Ms. Choy's evidence and to this day I am troubled by whether or not it was because the white jurors were not going to be lectured about childcare by an aggressive Asian business woman.

The Lisa Neve case was probably the best example in my career of how our justice system stereotypes female behavior and has a hard time understanding their conduct. Ms. Neve was the youngest female, (age eighteen at the time of offence and twenty-one at time of sentencing) in Canada to be declared a dangerous offender. In addition, she received an indeterminate prison sentence for the crime of robbery. I was not Ms. Neve's trial counsel but did take her case on appeal to the Alberta Court of Appeal.

The trial judge, a senior and well respected civil litigator in practice, found several reasons to declare Ms. Neve a dangerous offender and one of the main ones was his reliance upon the opinions of a senior psychiatrist, Dr. Flor Henry.

Ms. Neve's anti-social activities played heavily into this doctor's unusual (and almost bizarre) diagnosis of her. One sensed that her conduct personally upset him. Without sufficient data about the conduct of women, he chose to apply male offender statistics to his analysis. In court he opined that Ms. Neve's characteristics were "a female equivalent to a male lust murderer." This graphic opinion found prominence with the media covering the trial. It appears that this evidence, by itself, may have engendered fear within the trial judge. It would be hard to conclude otherwise given his ultimate rejection of the option of imposing a determinate sentence.

Fortunately, the Alberta Court of Appeal, composed of three female judges, rejected the trial judge's decision, set aside the dangerous offender designation, and sentenced Ms. Neve to a term of three years. She was released from custody July 1, 1990. Since that date, she has not had any further encounters with the criminal justice system, has been involved in counseling many women to leave the sex trade, and has become a well-known public speaker.

The Historical Dina Dranchuk Case

My recent defence of an abused woman who shot her husband in the Village of Glendon, only twenty kilometers from where Mike Dranchuk died, brought my thoughts back to my unfinished research of the Dranchuk case, and the question of whether justice was done.

One of my major concerns was whether the jury properly appreciated Mrs. Dranchuk's state of mind at the time of her husband's death. After the death sentence was commuted, she was sent to Kingston Penitentiary in Ontario. Only about six-and-a-half months after her trial, Kingston Penitentiary Warden R.M. Allen, in his April 2, 1935 letter to the Clerk of the Alberta Supreme Court wrote:

> When the woman was received here she was insane and she has since been transferred to a mental hospital. On admittance, we were unable to draw intelligent replies to questions which she was asked and as a result, our records are incomplete.

The questions she could not answer included her age, where she was born, when she arrived in Canada, the nationality of her parents and whether her parents were still alive.

I was curious to know how her mental condition was advanced at the trial and why, if she was suffering from a mental disorder, had she not been found not guilty by reason of insanity, as Section 19 of the 1934 *Criminal Code* defined it at the time. Alternatively, I wondered how uncertainty about her mental state and her ability to form the specific intent of murder was not reflected in the jury's verdict – resulting in a possible decision of manslaughter.

The direct evidence in the case consisted of Mrs. Dranchuk's admission to neighbours that she struck her husband with an axe. Her first statement to Lena Bohaychuk, a neighbour, was "I struck him on the head and I don't know what happened." Ms. Bohaychuk then posed the question to her "Did you kill him?" to which Mrs. Dranchuk replied "I don't know, I don't remember."

A further question was posed by the neighbour, "Well where's your children" drew the response "I don't know, I don't remember." This exchange occurred only a few hours after the incident.

Cross-examination of this witness did not highlight or attempt an expansion of the discussion revolving around the failure to recall nor was her state of mind at the time of this exchange explored.

Mrs. Bohaychuk did confirm that Mrs. Dranchuk often complained about being sick (since 1932) and her husband's refusal to provide money to her for the purchase of medicine. Unfortunately, throughout the trial, little effort was expended in attempting to clarify whether the 'sickness' related to physical or mental difficulties or a combination of the two.

Dina Dranchuk's conversation with Lena was overhead by Lena's husband, William Dohanuk. His testimony confirmed the conversation. Cross-examination of him did not touch on Mrs. Dranchuk's failure to recall, or the reasons for the altercation with her husband.

The only other direct evidence linking Dina Dranchuk to her husband's death were two statements provided to RCMP Detective Joseph Pooke. He confirmed that when he met with the accused on August 20, 1934 at about 5:30 p.m., she claimed that she was "sick" but refused a doctor's assistance stating that "The doctor can't help me." Unfortunately, the police officer did not pursue any inquiry as to what she was referring to in reference to her being 'sick'.

In a forty-five minute interview, when Detective Pooke acted as the Ukrainian interpreter, he claimed that she stated that she had gone to bed after a quarrel with her husband about her request for twenty dollars to travel to Edmonton to seek medical attention. According to the officer her next response was "Then she said she didn't remember exactly what happened."

Curiously, the officer claimed that while he made his notes of this oral statement some three hours later, he also recalled that she had said that she "struck her husband several times and in her own words stated 'I am sorry for what I did, but it is too late now.'" I suggest it as curious as the officer initially claimed he made the notes immediately after the interview and then altered them to suggest that they were made some three hours later. In his first recall of the discussion, he did not mention any admission about striking her husband. In a written police statement taken from Mrs. Dranchuk later that evening, she never admitted striking her husband. In fact, her only reference to "it" was her statement "...and it went to my head when I did it." This utterance was immediately followed by Detective Pooke's question "When you did what?" Mrs. Dranchuk's response was, "What somebody told me in the car when I was coming here about my husband."

This unusual response should have been pursued and clarified by the officer. One is left to speculate whether he may have feared that pursuing that line of inquiry would be harmful to the prosecution's case. That may be the same conclusion one draws as to why he did not inquire of Mrs. Dranchuk as to her state of mind at the time of the incident.

Mrs. Dranchuk's statements were ruled admissible at trial (I doubt that they would pass muster even on the voluntariness issue now). What was significant in terms of Mrs. Dranchuk's potential defence was that in her written statement, she described the abusive relationship and her 'sickness' as follows:

> If I told him he didn't love me to tell me and I would go away from him. He would never let me lay in bed for one day and would force me to go to work. Once he says he is going to leave me and then he thinks it over and he doesn't leave but quarrels and tells me to go away because no one forces him to love me. But I couldn't go away because my chest, feet and hands are sore and my chest was swollen. My hands would go numb and my feet also. When my sickness hits my head it appears its burning and I can't see through my eyes. When my husband quarrels with me, it makes me worse and I lose my memory and throw out milk when I intend to throw out water.

The narrative portion of that statement concludes with her stating "If the doctor examined me he would find out that there are clots of blood over my chest and arms and it went to my head when I did it." The officer then posed four questions and received the following responses:

> Officer: What did you do it with?
>
> Mrs. Dranchuk: I don't remember what I did it with. I went out on the road allowance and laid there.
>
> Officer: Did you go to any friends?
>
> Mrs. Dranchuk: I don't remember. I only remember laying on the road allowance.
>
> Officer: Is that all you wish to say?
>
> Mrs. Dranchuk: I don't remember any more.

In his brief opening statement, defence counsel never clearly outlined the defence case nor the possible impact Mrs. Dranchuk's personal and mental condition might have had on her conduct and ability to form the *mens rea* for murder. The opening contains the curious remark "She was sick and felt that she required medical attention and for a long period of time was suffering physically and mentally. The doctor will explain her condition to you and this condition was aggravated by quarrels with her husband, her inability to obtain medical treatment gradually culminated in the unfortunate incident on the night of the twentieth of August." He suggested that the defence would endeavor to show that there were "mitigating circumstances connected with the killing", without explaining how those circumstances might affect the potential verdict.

A Nineteen-Minute Defence

Without attempting to impose a modern-day standard, I was at a loss as to how her defence could properly have been presented in nineteen minutes. A portion of that time also included a brief opening address followed by the evidence of Dr. Carlton Taylor, a doctor who 'specialized in mental diseases and disorders'. He had examined Dina only once, a day-and-a-half before he testified. Unfortunately he was not asked to opine on her police statements about "the sickness hitting her head" and the absence of memory around the time of the event. Unfortunately and surprisingly, Dr. Taylor's evidence, as adduced, was very general and he was not asked by defence counsel as to his opinion of her mental state on the date of the death. When pressed by the prosecution and trial judge, his opinion supporting any finding of insanity weakened.

Dr. Charles Baragar testified in rebuttal as a doctor with experience in "examining mental cases". He saw Mrs. Dranchuk on three occasions. On the first, he could not communicate with her due to the absence of an interpreter. On the third occasion, she remained in a fetal position on the cell floor and refused to engage him. On the second occasion, through an interpreter, she could not remember the same information Kingston Warden Allen had been attempting to obtain. Without any objections from the defence, the witness opined that her forgetfulness was feigned. Despite the absence of relevant information, the witness claimed he found no evidence of insanity at the time of the crime. Unfortunately, the witness was not confronted with Mrs. Dranchuk's statements to her neighbors or the police.

At the end of the day, I am left troubled with how the evidence of her mental state was advanced.

Another issue that concerned me was whether Mrs. Dranchuk's fair trial rights were protected given the pre-trial publicity of a horrific event in a small community.

In 1934, the Dranchuk farm was approximately twenty kilometers from the Village of St. Paul. St. Paul and surrounding communities were served by two newspapers, both of which appeared to cover pre-trial and trial proceedings. These included the *St. Paul Journal* and the *St. Paul Canadien.*

Within days of Mike Dranchuk's death, the *St. Paul Canadien* headline read: "Flat Lake Farmer Victim in Axe Murder". The headline confirmed that its editor had concluded that the event was a murder. The article that followed quoted a Dranchuk neighbour, Fred Berezowski, as stating that Mrs. Dranchuk had told him after the death, "...I got mad and hit him on the head with an axe and ran here." No restraint in providing graphic details which could have affected her fair trial rights was shown by the editors.

Nine days after the death, the *Canadien,* in its leading front page story, chronicled the evidence heard by the Coroner's jury held before Magistrate J.W. Beaudry, on August 24, 1934 in St. Paul. It included a partial confession by Mrs. Dranchuk, her post-offence conduct of flight and her apparent confessions to neighbours. It cited her testimony before the Coroner's jury as often being "I don't remember." Finally, it quoted the Coroner's jury's findings as follows "From the evidence submitted we, the jury, find that Mike Dranchuk met his death from loss of blood caused by a wound on the right side of the head inflicted by some sharp weapon or instrument in the hands of his wife, Dina Dranchuk, between 11:00 p.m. on August 19th and 4:00 a.m. August 20th in his farm home situated on NW 3, 59-8-W4 near Flat Lake".

That front page news appeared only twenty-six days before the start of Mrs. Dranchuk's criminal trial. A Preliminary Inquiry was held in

St. Paul on August 31, 1934 before the same Magistrate Beaudry. At that time, the *Criminal Code* did not provide the media ban of publicity protection now afforded by Section 539. There is reference to the Preliminary Inquiry in some of the newspaper reports, although it is difficult to conclude how extensive that publicity may have been.

Dina Dranchuk's trial commenced on September 24, 1934 at 11:15 a.m. Jurors Biggs, Fletcher, Swanson, Olson, Jones, and Scott were sworn to hear the case before Mr. Justice Albert Freeman Ewing who had been a Superior Court Judge for only three years.

A review of the trial transcript reflects no concern being raised with whether any of the jurors might have prior knowledge of the case and/or formed opinions in relation to Dina Dranchuk's guilt. Despite that, and with knowledge that the case would only take two days, Justice Ewing sequestered the jury during breaks and after the first day of trial. In announcing that decision, Justice Ewing told the jurors "In the meantime, you will not permit anyone outside yourselves to speak to you and you will not speak to anyone else outside yourselves concerning this case." Section 945 of the 1934 *Criminal Code* provided that sequestration of the jury was mandatory where the death penalty might result.

Despite the distance between Edmonton and St. Paul, I am still very concerned that the graphic description of the death and evidence linking Mrs. Dranchuk would likely have been known by the jurors and yet no steps were taken at trial to address that issue.

At the end of this journey researching this case, I am left with a real sense of unease as to whether or not justice was done. I am troubled with how rushed the process was from date of the death to conclusion of the trial where the potential consequences were so grave. Had Dr. Taylor had more time to spend with Mrs. Dranchuk it may be that his evidence supporting insanity would have been much more clear and firm.

One is left with the conclusion that this was another appalling chapter in Canadian criminal justice where the accused's gender did not aid, but rather hindered the quest for justice. Unfortunately, I found little evidence of love in my research of this case, but substantial evidence of despair for both Dina and the criminal justice system.

PART FIVE

Questionable Experts

***Alan D. Gold** is certified by the Law Society of Upper Canada as a Specialist in Criminal Litigation and was the first Chairman of the Criminal Litigation Specialty Committee. In 1993 he was inducted into the American College of Trial Lawyers and received the G. Arthur Martin Award for Contribution to Criminal Justice in November, 1997. He is a past President of the Criminal Lawyers' Association of Ontario and was a Bencher of the Law Society of Upper Canada, elected from May 2003, three terms. He is now an emeritus bencher. His current practice is restricted to criminal trial and appellate work and he has appeared as counsel before all levels of courts in Ontario, as well as in seven of the other provinces.*

Mr. Alan D. Gold

The Murder of a Criminal Lawyer

FRED AND LYNN GILBANK were found murdered in their home in Ancaster, Ontario, a small town near Hamilton, on November 16, 1998. Lynn Gilbank – dead from three gunshot blasts. Fred Gilbank – face down on the second-floor landing with two shots to the back.

Fred Gilbank was employed by IBM. Lynn Gilbank was a very well-liked and popular criminal lawyer. They had two adult children, Mark and Kristen. A theory of a contract killing originated with the police and the local rumour mill: Lynn Gilbank was viewed as the primary target, Fred Gilbank just an innocent bystander. Unsurprisingly, the murder especially shocked the criminal bar, born of a concern that her profession was somehow related to her killing.

According to media reports, the murders of Fred and Lynn Gilbank triggered the most expensive and exhaustive homicide investigation in Hamilton history. After more than six years and multi-millions of dollars spent on the investigation, in early 2005, police charged two well-known criminals with the murders.

My future client Andre Gravelle was charged with two counts of first degree murder in the – at that point in time – six-year-old homicides. Andre Gravelle was well-known to the Hamilton, Ontario police department. Gravelle acknowledged, in a newspaper interview, that he had a long history of criminal convictions for drugs and smuggling drugs. In fact, his entire family was known to the police, and not in a good way.

Charged along with Andre Gravelle was a co-accused Ion Criotoru, whose gang nickname was Johnny K-9. He was an ex-wrestler and the police described him as the "Gravelle family's 'muscle.'" He has his own page in *Wikipedia.*

For the police investigation that preceded the charges, standard investigative tactics were used such as interviewing family members, friends, co-workers, and clients of the victims. Surveillance video and wiretaps were integral parts of the case. The investigation involved thousands of hours of wiretaps, producing tens of thousands of transcriptions of those intercepted communications. But that mass of evidence produced little, if anything, that supported the accusation of guilt against Andre Gravelle or his co-accused Johnny K-9.

Police also relied on less common tactics. The police resorted to a series of ploys, hoping to prompt useful evidentiary responses or cooperation. Hamilton had allegedly long had its share of organized crime families. Detectives travelled to the Kingston Penitentiary to talk to one alleged 'mob boss' about the killings and, when he refused to see them, they left a note saying one of the Gravelles had 'fingered' the mob boss for the killings. That stunt earned the Hamilton Police Department a pair of multimillion-dollar lawsuits – which they settled, paying out undisclosed amounts.

The Crown and police tried to obtain a Production Order to force a reporter to turn over notes of an interview with Paul Gravelle, Andre's brother, who was living in Mexico 'on vacation' since April 2005. The reporter had spoken to Paul Gravelle on a number of occasions in which Gravelle denied any involvement in the murders, but in one interview Gravelle indicated that he knew who had committed the murders. The Ontario Superior Court rejected this attempt: *R. v. Dunphy* [2006] O.J. No. 850 (S.C.O.).

A Press Conference and Offer of Immunity

Shortly after the sixth anniversary of the killings and before the charges, the police took the unprecedented step of holding a press conference and offering immunity to anyone involved in the crime – even the actual shooter – if they would testify against those who had planned the killings. No one came forward.

First arrested was Johnny K-9 and two months later the police arrested Andre Gravelle. Neither of the accused was alleged to have committed the actual murder. In fact, the police acknowledged they did not know who pulled the trigger. Their theory was that Andre Gravelle put out a contract on Lynn Gilbank and Johnny K-9 was involved in arranging it. Both accused vehemently protested their innocence.

Amazingly, in 2006, barely a year after police arrested them, the Attorney General for Ontario instructed the prosecuting Crown Attorney to withdraw the charges because there was no reasonable prospect of conviction. This turnaround was achieved by the unusual utilization of a bail application as the opportunity to discover and debunk the Crown's evidence.

Andre Gravelle was in a position to offer a reasonable bail for release pending trial. 'Bail pending trial' is available even in first degree murder cases. In practice, the determining factor generally reduces to one issue: how strong is the Crown's case? If Andre Gravelle was to obtain bail pending trial on these charges, it would only be by demolishing the Crown's case against him.

The Crown provided quite-fulsome disclosure as quickly as it was available and the application for bail pending trial was scheduled in the W in Hamilton for four days, commencing on May 24, 2005. It was eventually completed on August 11, 2005, after eight weeks of evidence, motions, and submissions. The defence used the bail hearing to dissect the Crown's evidence and expose its flimsiness. After "one of the longest and most bitterly fought bail hearings on record" (according to the media), the defendants were in fact granted bail by Mr. Justice D.J. Gordon on August 19, 2005: *R. v. Croitoru & Gravelle* [2005] O.J. No. 6404.

After the successful bail hearing, the case proceeded in the usual way and the preliminary hearing was set to begin on a Monday, June 12, 2006 and was expected to last several weeks. As the dates scheduled for the preliminary hearing approached, the prosecutors were determined to proceed. Andre Gravelle raised the idea of writing a lengthy letter to the Attorney General of Ontario setting out the issues disclosed by the bail hearing and the prosecution case and submitting that there was 'no reasonable prospect of conviction'. This is a test an Ontario prosecutor must constantly apply to an ongoing case to assess its continued vitality. The prosecutors on the case certainly felt the prospect remained.

Applying defence counsel's usual approach of 'it can't hurt', the letter was drafted and sent off, albeit with a feeling there was no reasonable prospect of a favourable reply, given the high-profile nature of the case and the accused.

Certain moments in a defence practice are forever memorable. At home the Sunday night before, I was set to drive to Hamilton to start the preliminary hearing. My staff was at the office preparing materials and one of them called me, quite excited. A fax had just been received, stating simply that the Attorney General of Ontario was instructing the prosecutors the next morning to withdraw the charges on the basis there was no reasonable prospect of conviction.

The lengthy bail hearing had not only successfully obtained bail; it had also obtained an objective, favourable review of the case. I also learned it never hurts to send a reasonable letter to the Attorney General.

The Evidence

The Crown's evidence, as brought out at the bail application, was an eclectic collection of evidentiary bric-à-brac.

The time of death was put at approximately 5:00 a.m. on November 16, 1998. About four weeks earlier, a jogger saw a suspicious-looking person in dark clothing and a balaclava looking in a residence window at about 5:00 a.m. He initially said it was at a different residence but after the murders, when he reported the sighting to the police, he thought it was at the Gilbank residence.

At approximately 5:00 a.m. on the November 16th date, a next-door neighbour was awakened by a banging noise. He got up to check and saw an older car in the Gilbank driveway. He did not see the individual, but saw an older model car leave.

Police investigation revealed no sign of forced entry to the residence and nothing appeared to be disturbed. It appears the sole purpose of entry was to kill the residents. It could not be said whether the killer had a key, or the front door was unlocked or some other form of entry was used.

Gloves were found at the scene; one in the front foyer, the other outside and adjacent to the driveway. DNA was found in the gloves, but was of no assistance in identifying the wearer. There was no shotgun residue found on the gloves.

The five shotgun shells at the scene provided no further information, nor was there any other useful forensic evidence.

Much time at the bail hearing was taken up with both accused's lengthy criminal histories. That the accused had been less-than-model citizens was clearly established, but any connection to the Gilbank killings was not. Some of the alleged history was highly questionable. A senior police officer testified about alleged informant information that seven years earlier, Andre Gravelle had supposedly issued a contract on his life and John Croitoru had accepted the contract. The Justice at the bail hearing concluded: "Despite Inspector [W.] … taking a serious view of the incident at the time, this evidence, in my view, is neither credible nor trustworthy as it was presented." This officer, interestingly, was subsequently found to be corrupt and convicted of criminal offences.

There was some suggestion that Lynn Gilbank had specific negative attitudes towards the Gravelles, but police questioning of her friends, other lawyers, and even judges completely failed to corroborate any such sentiment. In cross-examination at the bail hearing, the lead investigator went so far as to explain this lack of evidence by claiming that all these other persons interviewed, including some of the leading members of the Hamilton bar, were simply afraid to be truthful. I doubt the Justice hearing the bail application credited this idea.

One area of evidence, however, took the case into one-of-a-kind territory.

Forensic lip reading

Because of their criminal activities, it happened that Gravelle and Croitoru were under police video surveillance in connection with suspected drug activities and were captured speaking together about 2:30 p.m. the afternoon of November 16th, before the killings were discovered. There was video only, no audio, so the police in 2001 came to resort to a self-proclaimed forensic lip reader from England named Jessica Rees. In fact, she was the only forensic lip-reader in the world. She provided several reports claiming that she could lip-read the two accused having conversations that could be taken to reference the Gilbank killings. This would obviously be highly incriminating if true, because this was taking place before the killings were discovered and made public knowledge.

Detectives travelled to England, observed Ms. Rees testifying, and received a copy of an English Court of Criminal Appeal decision which lauded Ms. Rees's forensic lip-reading abilities: *R. v. Luttrell*, [2004] EWCA Crim 1344 (28 May 2004).

In preparation for the bail hearing, we needed to carefully investigate the crucial Ms. Rees to see if any inroads on this formidable *Luttrell* decision could be made. It happened ("chance favours the prepared mind") that a British barrister friend of mine, Edward Henry, had just finished a jury trial where Ms. Rees had testified as a forensic lip-reader for the Crown pursuant to the *R. v. Luttrell* decision. But my friend had done his homework regarding Ms. Rees and ultimately was able to supply the British Crown prosecutor with some interesting information, which information, in turn, I received with considerable delight.

When on June 22nd, 2005, the lead investigator in our case testified at the bail hearing, he confirmed in cross-examination that Ms. Rees had discussed the Luttrell case with them and that she also supplied other materials confirming her status as a forensic lip-reader. The investigator also confirmed the police had had no further communications from Ms. Rees of any significance nor any indicating any issues with her status as a witness.

Our cross-examination of the lead investigator, Steve Hrab, continued:

> Q. Do you remember [Ms. Rees] ever mentioning a case, October 26, 2004. R.v. Daniel Becon, Joshua McEvilley, Paul Collins, Rolly Monie, Spencer Tapper and Virginia Kayongo at Snaresbrook Crown Court, London East 11? Any of that information ring a bell?
>
> A. No.

Q. Did Ms. Rees ever tell you that as a result of her testimony in court, she was interviewed by the London Police under caution for fraud and perjury? Did she ever mention that to you?

A. No.

Q. Did she ever mention a case, and you hold the transcript in your hand, where as a result of her evidence about her qualifications the Crown prosecutor stood up and withdrew the case from the jury and told the judge he would not rely on her evidence, and that the Court of Appeal in the Luttrell case had been deceived by her. Did she ever mention any of that?

A. No.

Q. Okay. And you saw on page three of the day after that Ms. Rees was excused we see Mr. Wild, the Crown prosecutor advising the court:

> "Your Honour, may I say that the prosecution have decided to invite the jury to disregard Miss Reece's (sic) evidence when considering their verdicts in this case. Would you allow me, please, quite shortly, to explain why that decision has been made."
>
> Judge O'Mahony: Of course.
>
> Mr. Wild: ... It is difficult to know what the Court of Appeal would have said had they been informed that Miss Rees does not have a degree from Oxford University. All one can say, perhaps, is that it is something which may have made a difference to their attitude to her competence as a witness. It may, for instance, have caused them to say that she should not be used again until she has been re-tested. It may have caused the Court of Appeal to have more fundamental misgivings about her, I don't know. It is impossible to say, but probably it would have made a difference of some kind.
>
> What it comes to is this, Your Honour. The prosecution in this case, on these facts, have decided that the only safe course is to withdraw her evidence from the jury."

Were you aware of any of that, sir, before I put these matters to you in the witness box?

A. No.

Q. Had Ms. Rees ever told you anything like this?

A. No.

Q. Had Ms. Rees ever told you that there was an issue regarding her lying, sorry, regarding her evidence under oath regarding her academic qualifications?

A. Not that I'm aware of.

Q. Had she ever told you she had been investigated by the police about her testimony?

A. Not that I'm aware of, no.

Q. Had she ever told you that the prosecution in Crown Court had withdrawn her testimony because of the concerns expressed?

A. No.

Q. Would you agree with me, sir, that is, those are all things you would have liked to have known?

A. Sure.

Q. Would you agree with me, sir, that in light of this information, which I'm sure you will investigate, right?

A. Yes.

Q. You may never use Ms. Rees as an expert witness, isn't that possible, sir?

A. It's possible.

Q. And just to avoid misunderstandings for the future, I just want you to note on page six, Mr. Henry, one of the defence counsel just makes the comment:

> "Your Honour, may I, before Mr. Porter [the British prosecutor] addresses you, because this is a matter – I won't compliment my learned friend because that would be patronizing, but this is a matter of some importance not simply to this case, but to others. May I simply add this. As Your Honour knows, I had to, because it was of some length, abbreviate my

> cross-examination because of the hour last night, but the failure to disclose goes beyond that which has been averted to by my learned friend."
>
> Did you note that, Officer, and I'm sure you will fully explore what that is all about, won't you?
>
> A. Yes.
>
> Q. And we can take it Ms. Rees will be fully investigated before there is any thought of putting her in a witness box in front of a Canadian court, I take it?
>
> A. Yes.

As reported with singular understatement in the decision granting bail,

> "As a result of evidence arising from cross-examination of Sergeant Hrab and subsequent confirmation, Crown counsel indicated she was not relying on the lip reading reports on this bail hearing."

The world had lost its only *forensic* lip-reader!

Aftermath

Ion Croitoru returned to jail for conspiracy to commit murder arising from activities with a Vancouver criminal gang.

Andre Gravelle, unsurprisingly, went on, at age fifty-one, to be found guilty of trafficking marijuana, while being acquitted of four other charges for conspiring to traffic drugs and obstructing justice. Again, the media described him as "the kingpin of one of Hamilton's most notorious crime families."

Also, unsurprisingly, Andre Gravelle launched a wrongful prosecution lawsuit against Hamilton police and the prosecution services. Gravelle's malicious prosecution suit claims "negligent investigation, abuse of power, misfeasance in public office, conspiracy to injure, and intentional infliction of harm by unlawful means." The claim asks for $25 million, as well as $10 million from Rees for "fraudulent representation, negligent misrepresentation and negligence."

Hamilton Police had to pay Andre Gravelle $10,000 in court costs after they failed in a bid to change the venue of his lawsuit from Toronto to Hamilton: *Gravelle v. Hamilton (City) Police Services Board* [2015] O.J. No. 510 (O.S.C.).

Andre Gravelle also sued the Gilbank siblings for libel after CTV's *W5* program aired a 2007 segment about the killings. They appeared on the program and their comments were the basis for the libel lawsuit. That lawsuit was also against the producers, participants, and the network responsible for the program. They also tried unsuccessfully to move the trial to Hamilton from Toronto: *Gravelle v. CTV Television Inc.*, [2012] O.J. No. 1459 (S.C.J.) reversing [2011] O.J. No. 537.

Somewhat surprisingly, the lead investigator in the case was subsequently referenced in media reports as saying, along with some family members, that "they believe the Gilbank murder probe was thwarted by police corruption."

On February 22, 2017, *The National Post* reported on the death of Johnny K-9 at a half-way house in Toronto where he was finishing up his latest sentence. The headline read, "Natural causes succeed where mob hit men and gangsters failed – Johnny K-9 is dead."

The Gilbank murders tragically remain unsolved.

A Final Thought

It was August 11, 2005 that the Crown, in its closing submissions, advised the Court that it would not rely on the Rees lip reading reports. Our successful end to the case was still a year in the future. Obviously, the risk that Ms. Rees and her alleged expertise might somehow resurrect existed, if only in theory.

Perhaps it would have been wise to create some insurance against such an eventuality. For example, perhaps a firm of private investigators could have been hired to create a scenario of a couple having an illicit affair. A video could be created of the couple surreptitiously meeting and conversing on a park bench or other public location just as if the couple were being secretly videotaped by a private investigator performing actual surveillance for a real client.

But simultaneously with the videotaping, the 'couple' would be actually 'miked' and their conversation secretly recorded so an accurate record of what in fact was said would exist.

Perhaps then a law firm in another country could be used to retain Ms. Rees to have her lip-read the video ostensibly as part of a divorce action. Information would be provided to suggest the expected contents of the conversation to see how suggestible Ms. Rees is regarding her lip-reading. Her report of what she has the couple saying could then be compared with the actual conversation recorded to assess whether Ms. Rees' lip-reading is credible and accurate or not.

Imagine if when done and received her reports were seen to significantly differ from what was actually said in a manner obviously influenced by what the tainting information led her to expect to hear. Would that not have been a good idea?

James Lockyer *is a partner in the Toronto office of Lockyer Campbell Posner and founding director of the Association in Defence of the Wrongly Convicted. He has been involved in many cases in addition to Steven Truscott including Guy Paul Morin, David Milgaard, William Mullins-Johnson, Tammy Marquardt, Leighton Hay, and Maria Shepherd. He has received six honorary doctorates from the Law Society of Upper Canada and five Canadian Universities. In 2001, he received the G. Arthur Martin Criminal Justice Medal from the Criminal Lawyers' Association. In 2005, he received the John Howard Society's Award for Distinguished Humanitarian Service. In 2012, he received the Award for Justice (Advocates Society).*

Mr. James Lockyer

The Wrongful Conviction of Steven Truscott

As I drove to Guelph on a sunny Friday evening in August 1997 to meet Steven Truscott, I thought about how to approach him. I had read enough about the case to be able to talk about it with him but before agreeing to take it on, I wanted to know that he was innocent of Lynne Harper's murder. In 1959, when fourteen years old, he had been convicted of capital murder and sentenced to death – in those days a child tried in adult court for capital murder was subject to the death penalty – but the outrage that I felt over this could not blind me to the possibility of his guilt of the crime. I was only going to take on his case if I believed in his innocence.

I knocked on the door of Mr. Truscott's small home in Guelph where he had been living under the pseudonym Steven Bowers since his release on parole in 1969. Only a few people knew that he was Steven Truscott, including his parole officer and a few other selected people. Mr. Truscott and his wife, Marlene, answered the door. After introductions were made, I asked Mr. Truscott to come for a walk. We went down his street to where a stream ran and walked together along its banks.

Twelve-year-old Lynne Harper's body was found on Thursday, June 11, 1959, two days after she disappeared. It was concealed in a copse of trees and bushes known as Lawson's Bush on Bob Lawson's farm. She was lying on her back, naked from the waist down, and had been strangled by her own blouse that was knotted around her neck. She had been killed by a sexual predator.

A sexual attack often leaves traces of the perpetrator at the scene in the form of semen and other bodily substances. Vaginal swabs were taken from Lynne at the autopsy in 1959. If the swabs still existed, there was a strong likelihood that examination of them for DNA could identify the perpetrator. The forensic science of DNA did not exist in 1959; it was not until the late 1980s that the science was developed, but there was every reason to expect that a sample, although seized thirty-eight years earlier, would still yield the killer's DNA profile.

As it happened, I thought it unlikely that the vaginal swabs had been preserved in the intervening thirty-eight years. After all, the authorities in 1959 were not to know that twenty-five or thirty years later, a new science would enable actual identification of a person from a bodily sample left at a crime scene. But I decided not to tell Mr. Truscott this. Instead, I said to him:

> I expect all the exhibits seized in 1959, including swabs from Lynne's body, will have been preserved. I can find them and have them examined for DNA. They will probably give results. You have been on parole since your release in 1970, you have been living under an assumed name and almost no one knows who you are. Your case is part of Canada's history and so it will remain unless you decide otherwise. Because I will only pursue your case if you allow me to go public. Are you sure you don't want to let sleeping dogs lie?

What I was really saying to Mr. Truscott was – "If you killed Lynne, tell me to leave because you don't want headlines in a few months which say 'Science Proves Truscott's Guilt.'"

Mr. Truscott, now a forty-six-year old man, cut a dignified figure. In his demeanour, he presented as quiet, thoughtful, and gentle. He was greying and balding slightly. After a few minutes of silence, he stopped, turned and said, "Please do everything you can to find that evidence as quickly as you can."

It was two years before I got the final word at a meeting at the Centre of Forensic Sciences in Toronto. It was attended by the Chief Coroner, the Chief Pathologist for Ontario, two OPP officers recently assigned to the case, and several other government scientists and officials. We were told that all relevant exhibits had been destroyed in 1968, after the Supreme Court of Canada at a second hearing of Mr. Truscott's case had, once again, dismissed his appeal. A document was produced that recorded their being destroyed by the OPP by fire. So there was no easy solution to the case. Instead, it was going to be a hard slog but the hunt for DNA had served one purpose; Mr. Truscott's reaction on that first day I met him convinced me that he had not murdered Lynne all those years ago.

Lynne's Murder

Twelve-year-old Lynne Harper lived with her parents on the Royal Canadian Air Force Base in the small town of Clinton, near Goderich, Ontario, as did fourteen-year-old Steven Truscott. Both went to the same local school.

In the evening of Tuesday, June 9, 1959, Lynne ate dinner at her parents' home, finishing at 5:45 p.m. She then left home because she wanted to go see some horses in a field adjacent to Highway 8, more than a mile along the County Road and north of the Base. On her way, between 7:00 and 7:30 p.m., she encountered Steven who was on his bike. Lynne asked for a ride and Steven let her sit on his crossbar while he cycled north on the County Road. A number of local residents, adults and children who knew Steven and Lynne, saw them as they left the Base. Lynne was never seen alive again.

By 7:50 p.m., Steven cycled back to the Base. He was seen there by numerous people. To all outward appearances, he was acting normally. He exchanged bikes with his brother, Ken, and cycled home on Ken's (cheaper) bike to babysit his younger siblings. He arrived home at 8:30 p.m. and stayed there until the next morning.

Shortly before midnight, Lynne's parents, concerned that she had not returned home, notified the police. Over the next two days, a massive search for Lynne was conducted. On Thursday afternoon, a search party found her body in Lawson's Bush, 300 feet along a tractor trail off the County Road, the road along which she had travelled on Steven's crossbar two days earlier.

Lynne's Stomach Contents at Autopsy

What time Lynne was killed became a vital element of the case. Was she killed while she was known to have been with Steven? Or was she abducted by an unknown perpetrator at the highway and later taken to Lawson's Bush and strangled there, presumably after dark when no one was around?

An autopsy was conducted that evening by Dr. John Penistan. Its results were deadly for Steven. Dr. Penistan concluded that the condition of Lynne's stomach contents at her autopsy meant that she must have died within two hours of her last meal; in other words, she was killed on or before 7:45 p.m. on Tuesday. If that were so, Steven had to have been her killer. As the prosecutor, Glen Hays, so graphically put it in his closing address to the jury:

> What person or persons had the opportunity to kill her from 7:00 p.m. to 7:45 p.m.? I suggest that a review of the facts narrows those facts like a vice on Steven Truscott and no one else.

At 2:00 a.m., on Saturday, June 13, 1959, Steven was charged with Lynne's murder despite protesting his innocence during eight hours of police questioning. He told them that he took Lynne on his crossbar as far as the highway where he dropped her off, a ride that would have taken him about seven minutes. The tractor trail leading into Lawson's Bush was about halfway to the highway.

Tried in adult court, on September 30, 1959 Steven was convicted of capital murder by an all-male jury (women were ineligible to be jurors back then). The presiding judge, Ronald Ferguson, forthwith sentenced Steven to be hanged. On January 21, 1960, by Order in Council, after being held in the death cell in the Goderich County Jail for almost four months, Steven's death sentence was commuted to life imprisonment.

Dr. Penistan's "Agonizing Reappraisal"

From the day of his arrest, Steven's case was the subject of national and international interest. The sentence of death on a fourteen-year-old was enough in itself to attract such interest and criticism, and added to that was the nature of the crime. In early 1966, Isabel LeBourdais wrote a book, *The Trial of Steven Truscott*. It was revolutionary because it broke all traditions of that era by asserting that Steven was innocent.

National interest was renewed in the case by the book. Mr. Ferguson, Steven's trial judge, asked the then-Justice Minister, Pierre Trudeau, to prosecute Ms. LeBourdais for the crime of libel and slander for suggesting in her book that Steven was innocent. The judge's request was denied. Instead, the Government responded by directing the Supreme Court of Canada to conduct an unprecedented second review of the case. In October 1966, the Court heard from a number of renowned pathologists from Canada, England, and the United States who gave contradictory evidence as to whether Dr. Penistan's two-hour window for Lynne's death after she ate her last meal was scientifically correct. Dr. Penistan was not called on to testify again; the prosecution chose to rely on his trial evidence. The Court was unimpressed by the new evidence and, in May, 1967, with one judge dissenting, dismissed Steven's appeal for a second time.

In May 1999, the Archives of Ontario agreed to search for any files they had on the case. Due to its historical significance, it turned out they had six boxes of materials. In July, I sat down in a small room, H6 pencil in hand (all pens and other writing implements are seized at the entrance to the Archives) and with the boxes in front of me, began reviewing their contents. Soon I found out why the prosecutor had not re-called Dr. Penistan in the Supreme Court of Canada. There, in the boxes, was a new report dated May 19, 1966, from him. He had been commissioned by the prosecution to prepare this further report in anticipation of the second Supreme Court of Canada hearing. In the report, Dr. Penistan wrote:

> All autopsy findings are compatible with death within 2 hours of Lynne's last meal. They are not incompatible with death at a later time (up to 12 hours or even longer).

The reader should not be deceived by the double negative "not incompatible." What Dr. Penistan was really saying was that the autopsy findings were compatible with her death having occurred as long as twelve hours (or more) after her last meal.

In a covering letter to Inspector Harold Graham, the lead OPP investigator into Lynne's murder, Dr. Penistan wrote:

> In the review I have tried to clarify the facts as set out in the postmortem report on Lynne Harper and the transcripts and to restate the conclusions drawn from them and expressed in some places. I do not believe I have changed any of my essential conclusions as a result of my review (one is tempted to refer to it as an "agonizing reappraisal" in the current jargon: the adjective is probably better justified here than in most cases) but I must depend on someone else to assess whether there has been any significant change in the expression of these views. Your detailed knowledge of the transcript will enable you to do this better than most.

Dr. Penistan certainly had changed his "essential conclusions." Seven years after the trial, he was now saying that the state of Lynne's stomach contents when she died did not prove that she died before 7:45 p.m. He had completely resiled from his trial testimony. Her stomach contents were not a vice on Steven at all.

As I read Penistan's report and letter, I let out a shout, only to be immediately ticked off by a staff member at the Archives where there is a monasterial demand for silence at all times. It was a 'eureka' moment. The prosecution and police had withheld from Steven's counsel that Dr. Penistan had recanted his trial testimony. The Supreme Court of Canada was never told that. This kind of suppression of exculpatory evidence is not an uncommon feature of wrongful convictions – the prosecutors and the investigators are convinced of the defendant's guilt and so conceal 'inconvenient' evidence. The British have a phrase for it, arising out of a series of notorious wrongful convictions in that country. They call it "noble cause corruption."

Karen Daum's Statement

Dr. Penistan's "agonizing reappraisal" was sufficient in itself to cause the Court of Appeal to quash Mr. Truscott's conviction when they reheard his appeal in 2007, but there was much more in the Archives. There was also the statement of a young girl, Karen Daum, which had never seen the light of day. Why her statement was so important requires some background information.

The prosecution alleged that Steven took Lynne a short distance along the County Road from the Base and then turned down the tractor trail leading to Lawson's Bush where he killed her and left her body.

Steven told the police, and has always maintained, that he took Lynne down the County Road, past the tractor trail leading to Lawson's Bush, across the Bayfield River bridge where there is a swimming hole at which adults and children regularly congregated, and to the highway beyond the bridge. He dropped her at the highway because she wanted to see the horses. If Steven cycled past the tractor trail and took Lynne across the bridge to the highway, he was telling the truth and did not kill her; someone else must have abducted her and taken her to Lawson's Bush. If Steven only took her as far as the tractor trail, he was not telling the truth and was Lynne's killer.

Steven also told the police that on his return to the bridge, he looked back at the intersection where he had dropped Lynne and saw her get into a car that had pulled up beside her. He described it as a Chevrolet, likely a Bel Air, with lots of chrome and a yellow licence plate. Photographs introduced at the trial, which purported to reconstruct Steven's view from the bridge to the highway intersection, suggested Steven's story was implausible. As the trial judge said when the photos were introduced: "I can't even see the car in the picture."

In fact, the photos presented at trial were extremely deceptive. They made everything look much further away than it really was. 'Life-size' photos of Steven's view from the bridge, which were taken by professional photographers in 2005, showed that he could have easily seen a car at the corner of the highway from the bridge, and the colour of its licence plate. As the Court of Appeal said in 2007, the new photographs "show in stark terms just how unfair and misleading the photographs introduced at Steven Truscott's trial truly were."

Two of Steven's friends supported Steven's claim at trial. Twelve-year-old Gordon Logan was swimming in the river that evening, a short distance from the bridge. He described seeing Steven and Lynne go across the bridge on Steven's green racing bike and Steven returning across the bridge five minutes later alone on his bike. The prosecutor urged the jury to conclude that Logan was "simply not telling the truth." Doug Oates, also twelve years old, testified that he was fishing from the bridge with Karen Daum and looking for turtles to catch. He saw Steven, with Lynne on his crossbar, cycle by him across the bridge and carry on in the direction of the highway and he waved to them. Lynne smiled at him as they passed. The prosecutor was especially dismissive of Oates's testimony. He said to the jury:

> And then we come to Douglas Oates, and he is put forward by the defence as a witness to be considered seriously. He is twelve years old, and he is the young man who allegedly saw Steven and Lynne at the bridge between 7:00 and 7:30 p.m. You may have noticed Doug Oates in the witness box. It is hard, I suppose, for you to remember them all, but this one you may remember. I suggest to you, Gentlemen, he was too bright. Too bright, in that he is not to be believed. I suggest that he was prepared for a role and told where to hold the line, and that in doing so he made himself out to be a little liar.

Neither the prosecution nor the defence called Karen Daum as a witness. A statement that she gave the police on June 14, 1959, three days after the finding of Lynne's body, was in the Archives. She was nine years old at the time and was interviewed in the presence of her father, a member of the armed forces. She told the police that she went to the river that evening to fish and swim. She met Doug Oates there:

> Doug and I were staying there awhile and then Doug I think got down to catch one more turtle and couldn't and said "let's go home." I knew Lynne Harper and Steve Truscott. Me and Doug were coming up from the river and going to go home and I saw Lynne riding on the bar of the Truscott boy's bike.

> We were going home and they were coming towards the river. Lynne and Steve looked happy. Lynne was wearing a white blouse and blue shorts I think. We didn't speak to them or anything. Doug and I left the bridge together. He was riding first and I was behind him on my bike, but he got his pant leg caught and had to stop so I caught up to him and got ahead.

Karen also took the police to the exact location where she and Oates were when Steven and Lynne cycled past them. Karen Daum was, then, a third witness who saw Steven and Lynne go by. As the court of Appeal was to say in 2007:

> It seems unlikely that Oates, Logan, and Daum, who differed from one another in age, gender and school grade, could have conspired or colluded to provide false or unreliable versions of what happened that night.

Size Matters: How Maggots Helped Prove Steven's Innocence

By the time of Mr. Truscott's last appeal in 2006-2007, the time of Lynne's death had acquired a wholly new significance through evidence of insect activity on her body when it was found in Lawson's Bush.

Lynne's body was well-photographed (in black and white) where it was found in the bush, and later on the autopsy table. Her face was covered in maggots and eggs. In addition, there was a smaller collection of larger maggots in her vaginal area. Samples of the maggots were taken from both locations. Remarkably, Mr. Elgin Brown, who worked in the Attorney General's Laboratory in Toronto, bred the maggots and eggs from both areas separately and so determined the actual species of the maggots after they metamorphosed into flies in his laboratory. The eggs and maggots on her face bred into blue and green bottle blow flies. The maggots in her vaginal area bred into black flesh flies.

By now my law partner, Phil Campbell, was working with me on the case. In early 2006, we received a new and unexpected report from the prosecution. They had asked two forensic entomologists to look at the photographs and Mr. Brown's report to determine the "post-mortem interval." An entomologist will examine evidence of insect activity at a crime scene, take into account the environmental conditions from the time of the 'event' (in this case the homicide) until the collection of the insects (insects and maggots grow faster in warmer conditions, slower in cold conditions) and estimate back to when the body was first colonized by flies and other insects. When the insect colonization began can then be used to establish the time of death. The experts' conclusions in Lynne's case also had to take into account that flies are diurnal, not nocturnal. In other words, flies only come to a body and lay their young on it in daylight hours.

The two entomologists retained by the prosecution placed the time of Lynne's death as Tuesday evening. In their opinion, the larger maggots collected from her vaginal area must have been laid there on Tuesday before darkness fell to have reached the size they were when she was found two days later, the smaller ones in her facial area having more likely been laid the following morning or thereafter. Their conclusions were based on an assumption that the maggots were all of the blow fly family (blue and green bottles). If their opinions were correct, this was new forensic evidence as significant as Dr. Penistan's stomach contents claim and was a twenty-first-century vice on Steven Truscott. If Lynne was murdered before darkness fell on Tuesday evening, Steven was almost certainly her killer. It was inconceivable that an unknown killer abducted her at the highway and killed her in Lawson's Bush before dark because of the presence of adults and children who would have been travelling home along the County Road to the Base as they returned from their evening enjoyment of the river.

However, it turned out there was a significant flaw in the prosecution's experts' conclusions. They had relied on a poorly photocopied version of Mr. Brown's report on his rearing of the maggots in the laboratory and assumed that all the maggots on her body had been laid by blow flies. We went to the Archives and obtained a clean copy of his report.

The prosecution's version of Mr. Brown's report did not contain his finding that the maggots in her vaginal area had grown into flies of the black flesh fly family. This was key. Blow flies lay eggs that hatch into maggots after a day or so in the open. Flesh flies hatch their eggs inside their bodies and then lay actual maggots. This means that maggots deposited by flesh flies will always be a day or so larger than maggots that have grown from eggs deposited by blow flies. Mr. Brown's findings explained the greater length of the maggots in Lynne's lower extremities; these maggots had been deposited by flesh flies. Their length, like the smaller maggots that had hatched from the eggs deposited by blow flies on her face, was consistent with their having been laid on Wednesday morning, not Tuesday evening. By wrongly assuming that the larger maggots had hatched from eggs left by blow flies, the prosecution experts had miscalculated the time that they were laid.

Mr. Campbell and I also found out that Mr. Brown, now in his 90s, was still alive. In 2006, we visited him at his home and he subsequently testified for Mr. Truscott in the Court of Appeal.

Mr. Brown's report turned the entomological findings from being proof of Steven's guilt, which was the claim of the prosecution's experts, towards being proof of his innocence. There remained one issue that could undermine this. Flies only lay their young in daylight. If Steven had murdered Lynne in Lawson's Bush at, say, 7:50 p.m. on Tuesday, June 9, would flies have laid eggs (or maggots) on her body in the time left until darkness, which was around 9:45 that night? If this was insufficient time for the flies to be attracted to her body, then she could have been murdered by Steven before 8:00 p.m., or by an unknown killer who abducted her after Steven dropped her at the highway. Either way, the flies would not have colonized her body until the next morning and entomology would not advance the case for Steven or the prosecution.

Pigs are known to best replicate the human body when it comes to insect colonization. Farmer Bob Lawson was still very much alive, still had the farm and strongly believed in Steven's innocence. He readily gave us permission to use his farm for an experiment. One evening in June, 2006, a week before the Court of Appeal hearing was to begin, Dr. Sherah VanLaerhoven, a forensic entomologist at the University of Windsor, arranged for three pigs to be freshly slaughtered and placed within thirty minutes of their doom in Lawson's Bush at a 'non-contaminatory' distance from each other. The weather conditions were forecast as similar to those forty-seven years earlier on June 9, 1959. Darkness was at the same time, and the pigs were placed in the Bush at 8:00 p.m. Would flies begin to lay their eggs/larvae on the pigs before dark?

Dr. VanLaerhoven had a video camera recording activity for each pig. By dark, all three had eggs around their snouts and lower extremities. So if Steven had killed Lynne during their cycle ride, the maggots from the blow flies and flesh flies would have colonized her body before dark and so would have been bigger than the ones found on her face and lower extremities. In short, the entomology evidence suggested that Lynne must have been killed in Lawson's Bush after darkness fell on Tuesday. Indeed, it was Dr. VanLaerhoven's opinion that the comparatively small size of the blow fly and flesh fly maggots established that she was likely murdered as late as sometime around midday on Wednesday, June 10.

The Acquittal

Steven Truscott served more than ten years of his life sentence until his release in 1970. He remained on parole for the next thirty-seven years. In 2006 and 2007, the Ontario Court of Appeal heard his case once again.

On August 28, 2007, the Court unanimously quashed Mr. Truscott's 1959 capital murder conviction and acquitted him in a 303-page judgment. They found that if he were to be tried with the benefit of the new evidence, an acquittal was the likely result. He had waited all these years for his exoneration and it was a testament to his strength of character that he had never given up. His two regrets? First, that Lynne's killer has never been found. Second, that he did not have the chance to return to that courtroom in Goderich where he had been sentenced to hang so long ago and be exonerated there. But apart from not having that satisfaction, he could now be Steven Truscott with no pseudonym and hold his head high for the rest of his life.

PART SIX

Self Defence

Honorable Jim Ogle *is the Assistant Chief Judge of the Calgary Criminal and Regional Division of the Provincial Court of Alberta. He is a graduate of the University of Alberta Law School and before his appointment to the bench, he was a criminal lawyer for over thirty years. He was appointed Queen's Counsel in 1992. He is a long-time instructor in the University of Calgary and Legal Education Society of Alberta 'Intensive Trial Advocacy Course', a nationally recognized advocacy training program for law students and lawyers from across Canada. While still a lawyer, Judge Ogle was appointed to the board of Directors of 'HomeFront', a co-coordinated community response to domestic violence in Calgary. Once appointed to the Bench, he opened the Calgary Drug Treatment Court in 2007 and has been the presiding and mentoring judge in Calgary's Drug Treatment Court since its inception.*

Judge James Ogle

A Line in the Sand

Arms and a Man

SATURDAY, NOVEMBER 8, 1986 was an unseasonably cold day in Calgary. A light skiff of snow was already on the ground, signalling an early start to winter. It was also windy, and the wind was causing a problem at the IDA drugstore located on 33 Avenue in what is now called the 'Marda Loop' area of southwest Calgary. When customers opened the north-facing door to the store, the frigid wind would catch the door, banging it loudly as it tried to close. And so the drugstore owner, Steven Kesler, who was busy with customers at the checkout counter at the front of the store, had instructed his ten-year-old daughter Patricia to stay by the door and catch it when customers entered so it wouldn't bang.

Patricia's twelve-year-old sister Marlene was also in the store that day, stocking shelves in one of the store's three aisles. Steven's wife, Mary Kesler, was working in the pharmacy section located at the back of the store, accessible by proceeding directly down the westernmost aisle leading directly from the front-store entrance.

Such was the usual Saturday routine for the Kesler family. Steven and Mary, immigrants from their native Yugoslavia since 1977, had purchased the drugstore in early 1984. Mary was a licenced pharmacist and ran the small pharmacy at the back of the store while Steven tended the counter at the front.

The drugstore was meticulously maintained. The Keslers had put their life and savings in to the store, and were proud of their accomplishment. This was a true family-owned and family-run business, open six days a week. Steven and Mary worked in the store every day, and their two daughters Patricia and Marlene helped out whenever they were not in school. On Sundays, the entire family would deliver store flyers to the neighbouring community, in hopes of increasing business.

Saturday was usually a busy but uneventful day at the Kesler drugstore, but all of that was about to change in an instant. Just around 3:00 p.m., as Steven Kesler was serving a customer at the pharmacy's lone front checkout, he heard a commotion at the front-door entrance. He looked up to see two men, with toques pulled full-down over their faces, aggressively enter the store. The smaller of the two, who would be later identified as Stephen Fleming, had a gun clearly visible in his hand as he immediately rushed down the first aisle toward the pharmacy area where Steven's wife Mary was working. The larger man, who would be later identified as Tim Smith, came directly up to the front counter and yelled at Stephen "Give me your money or you're dead." Smith kept one hand in his pocket and was jamming at the keys to the cash register with his other. Steven handed him the money in the till, which turned out to be $115. At the same time, he was able to press a secret 'panic button' installed under the checkout counter. This sent an alarm directly to the police alerting them that the store was being robbed.

The panic button was not the only thing Steven Kesler kept under his drugstore counter to deal with would-be robbers. As Tim Smith moved back toward the store exit with the stolen money clutched in his hand, Kesler pulled out a 12-gauge shotgun. He pointed it at Smith and in his thick accent said "Now you listen me!"

Smith didn't listen. Instead he bolted out the door, took a hard left and ran south down the sidewalk along the west side of the pharmacy building. Kesler rushed out the door after him. As Smith continued to flee down the sidewalk, Steven Kesler lifted the shotgun to his shoulder and fired. Of the two-hundred-eight pellets normally contained in the No. 5 shotgun cartridge that Kesler had earlier loaded into the shotgun, approximately one hundred struck Tim Smith in the back. Several of those entered his heart. He immediately fell to the sidewalk, mortally wounded and still clutching the $115 he had taken from Kesler's pharmacy moments earlier.

Kesler then turned and re-entered the store. He headed down the first aisle toward the pharmacy area where Fleming was in the process of robbing Mary Kesler at gunpoint, yelling at her to put all her narcotics in the bag he was holding. When Fleming saw Steven Kesler coming down the aisle, he pointed his gun at him and opened fire. Steven Kesler responded by discharging the two remaining cartridges in his 3-shot shotgun. Fleming discharged five of the six bullets in his revolver. During this shoot-out, Mary Kesler managed to sneak out of the pharmacy area, run up the aisle adjacent to the one her husband was in and escape the store. In her panic she forgot that her two daughters were cowering in the third aisle of the store.

Miraculously, neither Kesler nor Fleming was struck in this hail of gunfire. In fact, in later testimony at his trial, Kesler stated he thought that Fleming must have been firing blanks, or using a replica handgun, as he had not been hit. But the bullets were real.

When Kesler heard Fleming's gun finally click several times with no apparent discharge, he charged at him and a desperate struggle ensued. Fleming managed to escape up the aisle and out the door, with Kesler in hot pursuit. Fleming ran south in the same direction Tim Smith had gone and as he crossed the roadway he yelled at Smith "Get up, let's go." Not surprisingly, Smith did not move. He was either near death or already dead.

Kesler continued to pursue Fleming, striking him with the butt of the shotgun whenever he could. Fleming jumped into the driver's seat of his intended getaway vehicle, parked across the street from the pharmacy. Kesler jumped in after him, continuing to strike him with the shotgun and then choking him. The struggle continued until Kesler was literally pried off Fleming by Detective Paul Manuel, who was one of the first Calgary police officers to arrive at the scene in response to the panic alarm. Throughout this time, Fleming continued to cling desperately to the bag of narcotics he had just stolen from Mary Kesler.

Steven Kesler was placed in a police car at the scene, and although he had not been formally arrested, Detective Manuel instructed the attending officer in the police car to take careful notes of anything Kesler said.

What Steven Kesler was alleged to have said in the police car and elsewhere at the scene would bear heavily on subsequent events.

Kesler was eventually transported from the scene of the shooting to police headquarters, though he was still not under arrest. While seated in an interview room, Steven called his family real estate lawyer Bryan Hagel. While waiting for Mr. Hagel to arrive, and despite his protests, Steven was searched. Found among his possessions were three .22 calibre bullets, two shotgun shells, and a potentially damning further item – a small, ballpoint pen-like item that Kesler advised the officer to be careful with. The 'item' can be best described as a 'pen gun' and it was loaded with a single .22 calibre bullet. Immediately after this discovery, Steven Kesler was informed that he was under arrest and was being charged with the second degree murder of Timothy Smith.

Tiger by the Tail

I became involved with the case later that night when Bryan Hagel contacted me. I had known Bryan as a fellow lawyer and friend for several years, and he had recommended my services to Mr. Kesler. And so began a journey for me that was the most memorable and emotional case of my thirty-plus-year career as a criminal lawyer.

I was successful in setting up an immediate bail hearing for Mr. Kesler on the Monday following the shooting, thanks to the co-operation of then Crown prosecutor Peter Martin (now Justice Martin of the Alberta Court of Appeal). Peter did not oppose release, and Steven Kesler was back working in his drugstore before the day was out.

I was frankly concerned when I learned Peter Martin was handling the bail hearing, as I assumed that as a result he would probably be doing the trial. Peter, a good friend of mine then and to this day, was a formidable opponent in the courtroom, always a very well prepared and persuasive advocate in the trials we had done together to that point. But after the bail hearing, he told me he would not be doing the trial. Perhaps it was his heavy workload at that time, or perhaps it was at least partly due to what I sensed was a sympathy for the plight of Steven Kesler and his family. Though he did not take the case beyond the bail hearing, I distinctly remember a conversation with Peter in the courthouse hallway a day or two after the bail hearing. He said, "Jim, you've got a tiger by the tail on this one." How right he was.

Initial news coverage was extensive on the Sunday and Monday following the shooting, and over the following days it became a national story. The press, at first, focused on the disturbing detail that the robber Smith had been unarmed and was shot in the back while running away from the store and, presumably, no longer a threat. In the following days, further details emerged. It was reported that although Smith was not armed, the other robber in the store, Stephen Fleming *was* armed, with a loaded handgun that he had fired off in the store.

There was another incredible development. We learned that on the day of the robbery, Smith's partner Fleming was out on bail awaiting trial on a charge of armed robbery of this very same Kesler drugstore, seven months earlier in April 1986! The fact is, I first learned this information through a newspaper report. These were pre-*R. v. Stinchcombe* days where full and early Crown disclosure was not legally required, and, as such, was sporadic and, at times, even 'whimsical'.

Public sympathy for Steve Kesler grew steadily in the following weeks. It was fuelled by the fact that shortly after the Kesler shooting, a similar incident occurred in Montreal. There, a shopkeeper, Guy Gilbeault, allegedly shot and killed a would-be robber who had confronted him with what turned out to be an unloaded pellet pistol. Gilbeault was reported as saying he got the courage to do what he did from reading about Steven Kesler.

Following a review of the case, Quebec authorities decided not to lay any charges at all against Gilbeault. Only two weeks before the Gilbeault case, a storekeeper had been shot dead by a robber in Montreal; a fact that may have influenced this decision by Quebec authorities. Whatever the reason, the press and numerous other supporters of Kesler publicly wondered if all citizens of Canada were subject to equal application of the law. How could Kesler be charged with murder and Gilbeault walk free?

A local Calgary songwriter composed a song titled 'The Ballad of Steven Kesler' and it played extensively on local stations. Near Christmas, a local newspaper ran an unofficial public opinion poll which suggested overwhelming public support for Kesler. Indeed, Kesler was even nominated by one local newspaper as Calgarian of the Year.

A Citizens' Defence Fund for Kesler

A group of shopkeepers in the Marda area where the Kesler store was located organized a defence fund, and within a very few weeks it raised almost $40,000, a significant amount in those days. Donations came from across the country. Most were accompanied by expressions of support for Steven.

The enormous and generally positive press coverage and expressions of public support were encouraging to the Keslers. In the eyes of an uninformed public unfamiliar with all the evidence, this seemed to be an easy case to win, a virtual 'slam-dunk'. However, as I prepared for trial I knew that the case was not nearly so certain, and that Steven Kesler faced some significant hurdles. Among them were:

a) Kesler had shot an unarmed robber in the back, as he was running away, arguably no longer a threat. The Crown would argue that this was excessive and entirely unnecessary, and that Kesler's actions had nothing to do with protecting himself or his family, but were instead for the sole purpose of recovering the $115 Smith had taken.

b) Besides the loaded shotgun, Kesler was also armed with the prohibited and loaded pen gun in his shirt pocket on the day of the robbery, with extra shells for both in his pocket.

c) In June of 1986 the Kesler drugstore was the target of a robbery, two months after the April robbery when Stephen Flemng was one of the culprits. Two robbers entered Kesler's drugstore wearing motorcycle helmets and sunglasses, again in search of narcotics and getting away with the drugs. Both Steven and Mary Kesler were in the store at the time. As soon as the robbers left, Steven retrieved a rifle he kept in the basement of the pharmacy and ran out on to the street with it, though by this time the robbers had escaped on a motorcycle.

d) Detective Paul Manuel, the initial police detective on the scene on November 8, 1986, had prior dealings with Kesler during the robbery investigation at the Kesler store in June 1986 and at a break-in at the store in the summer of 1986. Manuel claimed that during those investigations Kesler told him that he had bought a shotgun after the June robbery of his drugstore, that he kept it loaded under the counter and that he would "shoot and kill" the next guy who tried to rob him.

e) Manuel also claimed that Kesler told him that since the break-in at the pharmacy in the summer of 1986, he stayed in the store at night with the loaded shotgun across his lap, "ready to shoot anyone who broke in." If believed, this was damning evidence of a pre-formed intention by Kesler to kill any would-be thief or robber, regardless of the circumstances.

f) Finally, and most damaging, Detective Manuel also claimed that as he was examining the mortally wounded Smith on the sidewalk, Kesler approached and yelled "He's got my money, I want my money, don't do anything for him, give me my money."

Other Challenges

Several lawyers offered, both publicly and privately, to take Keslers case – for free if necessary – and at least one lawyer approached Kesler through an intermediary suggesting a change of counsel to him, a particularly galling and, in my view, a simply unethical approach.

The Keslers themselves were, at times, challenging to deal with, although in their circumstances that could certainly be forgiven. They questioned why Steven had been charged at all, especially in view of the Montreal case. They were vulnerable to the suggestions of others that they should be getting different counsel who would somehow convince the Crown to withdraw the charge, a task I knew from my discussions with the Crown already, was doomed to certain failure. In hindsight, I realize the Keslers were easy prey for the bald assurances of some lawyers who 'guaranteed' a successful outcome. I knew this was a big case and that the eyes of the country would be on me. I had successfully defended numerous serious cases to that point in my career and felt well-able to defend Kesler. I just needed to reassure Steven and Mary Kesler of that.

A fellow criminal lawyer and close friend of mine, Noel O'Brien QC, with whom I had co-counselled on several cases to that time, said to me one day, "Jimmy, the biggest risk for you turning over this case to another lawyer making bald promises will be between now and the preliminary inquiry. Once they see you perform there, and see how well prepared I know you will be, you'll be fine." His words were encouraging, and proved prophetic. I was well prepared for the preliminary inquiry, and although I had warned Steven that he would almost certainly be committed to stand trial, there was no more talk from the Keslers about retaining other counsel once the preliminary was done.

For both the preliminary inquiry and trial, the Crown was represented by Bob Davie, at that time the Director of Criminal Justice for Alberta. I had known Bob for most of my career as a lawyer, and always respected him as a fair and competent prosecutor. For my part I was ably assisted by my associate Larry Hursh. Larry did much of the initial interviewing of potential witnesses and helped keep the Keslers informed of our ongoing trial preparation.

As we approached the trial commencement date, prosecutor Bob Davie contacted me to advise that the Crown would consider taking a plea to manslaughter, leaving the issue of sentence wide open. Subsequent discussions confirmed that on a plea to manslaughter, the Crown would seek a prison term in the range of two years.

As I was ethically bound to do, I advised Steven Kesler of these discussions, and outlined the pros and cons of the Crown's proposal. I tried to be as informative, but as and neutral as possible in this critical discussion, careful not to pressure Steven one way or the other. I felt we had a reasonable chance of an outright acquittal at trial, but also was keenly aware and pointed out that if convicted of second degree murder, the sentence would be life imprisonment with no parole for at least ten years. Ultimately I advised Crown prosecutor Davie that the matter would proceed to trial and there would be no plea to manslaughter. My instructions were clear.

I acutely felt the pressure of those discussions. What if I was wrong about our chances? What if I made a mistake at trial that impacted the result? What if the jury accepted the evidence of Detective Manuel and found Steven to be an uncaring and tight fisted man with a pre-conceived plan to shoot and kill anyone who tried to take his money or possessions?

The Case Goes to Trial

The trial of Steven Kesler commenced in early June 1987 before the Honorable Justice Arthur Lutz and a jury of ten men and two women.

To me, the decision to have a jury trial on this case was easy, even though the Crown at that time in Alberta routinely consented to trial by judge alone on murder cases if the defence requested it. I firmly believed that Steven's best chance was with a jury of his peers rather than a single judge more attuned to the complex legalese of the law of self defence in the *Criminal Code*.

At the time of Steven Kesler's trial (the law has since changed), section 34(1) of the *Criminal Code* (the self defence provision) stated that "Everyone who is unlawfully assaulted ...is justified in repelling force by force if the force he uses is not intended to cause death or grievous bodily harm and is no more than is necessary to enable him to defend himself." Section 34(2) extended this defence, stating that if the person assaulted did cause death or grievous bodily harm in repelling the assault, he was justified if "he caused it under reasonable apprehension of death or grievous bodily harm from the violence with which the assault was originally made...and he [reasonably] believes ... that he cannot otherwise preserve himself from death or grievous bodily harm."

It was the defence position that the robbery by Smith and Fleming was an ongoing – and potentially deadly – assault on not only Steven Kesler but also his wife and children.

The Evidence and Testimony

The Kesler case was front page news throughout Canada as the trial proceeded. Media from across the country filled the courtroom daily. A sketch artist sat in the front row of the courtroom and much of her work accompanied the extensive newspaper and television coverage of the trial. Daily live media scrums on the courthouse steps reported on developments in the case.

The trial took almost three weeks to complete. In its early days, things looked grim for Steven Kesler. The Crown opened with several witnesses who were on the busy street at the time of the shooting. They described Kesler as calm and deliberate as he raised the shotgun, hesitated briefly, then fired.

The Crown called Detective Manuel. He testified to his version of conversations with Kesler in the weeks prior to the shooting, that

Kesler had told him that he waited in the store at night with a loaded shotgun, prepared to shoot anyone who broke in, and that he would "shoot and kill the next man who robbed him." He described an angry Kesler hovering over Smith's body on the street, and the cold-blooded statements allegedly made by him of "He has my money! Don't do anything for him."

As I rose to cross-examine Detective Manuel I knew that his testimony was extremely damning evidence if believed by the jury. His evidence had to be aggressively challenged and thoroughly discredited if Steven was to have a chance at acquittal.

Initially I stressed the fact that although he had kept careful notes of his dealings with Kesler prior to the day of the shooting, Manuel had made no notes whatever of these earlier statements of lethal intention he was now attributing to Kesler.

Moreover, Manuel's partner had a far less clear and less damaging recollection of these earlier conversations with Kesler.

I pointed out that while Manuel had made detailed notes at the scene of the shooting on November 8, his notes did not include any of the damning statements he was now attributing to Kesler at the scene. Further, Manuel was forced to acknowledge that numerous other people were in the immediate vicinity at the time he claimed Kesler yelled out the heartless comments at Smith's body, yet not one other witness confirmed what Manuel claimed. Finally, in a moment of unexpected candidness during cross-examination, Manuel acknowledged he was biased "to a degree" against Kesler.

By the end of Detective Manuel's testimony, we believed that his credibility had been significantly challenged. Nevertheless, it would take further defence evidence to totally diminish its impact.

The Tide Shifts

Thankfully, for Steven Kesler, that further evidence came in the form of mundane but crucial records from an in-store security system at the Kesler drugstore. The Keslers had installed a security system after one of their earlier break-ins. Among other features, the system was motion-activated and was remotely monitored and managed by the private security company that installed it. The system automatically forwarded records to the security company's off-site location of all times it was activated. The system also monitored any in-store movement while activated which in turn tripped a silent alarm at the security company headquarters. The company records showed that at the end of each working day, the system was activated by the Keslers as they closed up for the night. A review of the records established that in the months leading up to the shooting, that is, the very time period Manuel testified Kesler said he was staying in the store at night with a loaded shotgun, there was not a single occasion where there was an unexplained entry to or movement in the store at night. This was convincing proof that Kesler had not actually stayed in the store at night at all, let alone with a loaded shotgun.

We also had to deal with the disturbing evidence of the police finding the loaded pen gun on Kesler's person when he was questioned at the police station after the shooting. Undoubtedly the Crown would argue that this was further evidence of a pre-determined and firm plan by Kesler to shoot anyone who tried to steal from him. In a *voir dire* to determine the admissibility of this evidence, I relied on the then-recently proclaimed *Canadian Charter of Rights* to argue that the search and seizure of this pen gun was illegal and the pen gun should be excluded. I further argued that in any event, this was highly prejudicial evidence with little probative value. Fortunately for Mr. Kesler, Justice Lutz acceded to the argument and the evidence of finding this loaded pen gun in Steven Kesler's shirt pocket was never placed before the jury.

I also knew it would be important to address the civilian witness's evidence of Kesler's apparent calmness and "deliberateness" when he raised the shotgun and shot Smith.

Steven Kesler took the stand himself and testified that he fired quickly, and in a panic. He said he intended to hit Smith in the legs, but in his haste and inexperience with a shotgun, fired high. He testified that he did not mean to kill Smith, but rather to eliminate him as a threat so that Kesler could then return to the drugstore to confront the other robber inside, who was armed with a weapon.

In support of Kesler's testimony I called a firearms expert, Mr. David Tomlinson, who was then president of the Canadian National

Firearms Association. Tomlinson testified that persons inexperienced with the use of shotguns usually shoot higher than intended, as shotguns, unlike rifles, do not have double sights along their barrels. The expert advised further that such inexperienced users tend to not fully level their eye to the barrel of the gun when firing, especially if in a hurry. This evidence was essentially unchallenged by the Crown.

Kesler had also testified that the 'hesitation' people observed before he shot, which observers took as an indication of calm deliberation, was in fact an attempt to fire quickly, then realizing the safety was on, quickly releasing it, and then quickly firing.

This expert evidence would be helpful in perhaps reducing a murder case to one of manslaughter, but it did not address the real thrust of our defence. The defence theory was that Kesler did not simply shoot a lone unarmed robber who was running away and therefore no longer a threat. Rather it was our position that on that day Steven Kesler and his family were under attack by not one, but two armed robbers – robbers who were desperate for drugs, and for that reason were dangerous, unpredictable, and thoroughly prepared to shoot and kill to achieve their purpose. Support for that theory came primarily from Steven Kesler himself and from his family members.

I called Steven's wife Mary to testify. She confirmed her husband's evidence that their store had been broken into twice before, and that they had been robbed at gunpoint on two prior occasions. Mary told the jury of the April 1986 robbery – the robbery that had occurred less than seven months before the November 8th shooting where, unknown to her at the time, Steven Fleming was one of the robbers.

In dramatic and graphic testimony, Mary Kesler described the fear and horror of these prior robberies and how Steven was deeply impacted by her fear at the time. As Mary Kesler testified about these prior robberies, it became increasingly clear that she too had been deeply traumatized by them.

Mary also described experiencing that same fear during the fateful November 8 robbery, when Fleming confronted her in the pharmacy with a gun that turned out to be loaded with six bullets. She described seeing her husband Steven return to the store, shotgun in hand, to confront Fleming. She described Steven as "my salvation" at that point. She then testified about the terrifying gun battle in the store between Steven and Fleming, where Fleming emptied his revolver in the direction of Steven, miraculously failing to hit him with any of the five bullets he discharged. She told of her escape from the small pharmacy area during this time, running frantically down the middle aisle and out of the store, completely forgetting in her panic that the two Kesler daughters were still inside.

I was frankly surprised, but more than a little pleased, when Crown Prosecutor Bob Davie called the two Kesler daughters, Marlene and Patricia, as Crown witnesses. I would unquestionably have called them myself if the Crown had not, but the fact they were Crown witnesses was supportive of their credibility. I believe their mere presence, let alone their testimony, significantly impacted the jury. Their evidence and childlike innocence put a very human face to the defence claim that Kesler was a loving father protecting his family from two very dangerous robbers. The girls described the aggression of the two robbers when they entered the store, and testified they saw Fleming pointing his gun at Mary Kesler in the pharmacy section as he demanded narcotics. Patricia, who was eleven years old at the time of the trial, testified that Smith said "Give me your money or you're dead" when he confronted her father at the front counter, and confirmed that Smith had one hand in his pocket at that time. This was critical confirmation of Kesler's testimony that he believed Smith was armed and dangerous.

By the end of the evidence presented, two very different versions of Steven Kesler had emerged. Was he a crazed shopkeeper angry about past thefts, with an advance plan to calmly shoot the next man who dared steal from him, as argued by the Crown? Or was he a loving family man, traumatized and fearful from past violent robberies by dangerous thieves desperate for drugs? Did he callously shoot an unarmed Smith in the back as he was running away, merely to recover his money? Or was he defending his wife and two young daughters from the double threat of two desperate and determined robbers he believed to be armed? It was this contrast that I spoke of in my jury address, suggesting the more reliable evidence pointed strongly to the latter view, "family man under siege."

In my jury address I deliberately refrained from discussing the possibility of a "compromise" manslaughter verdict. I did not want to leave any suggestion with the jury that this would be an acceptable result for the defence – we were seeking an outright acquittal. I also knew that in his jury charge, Justice Lutz would be duty bound to raise manslaughter as a possible verdict to the jury even though I had not raised it in my address. I left it alone.

Justice Lutz completed his jury charge through the afternoon. The jury then retired to commence deliberations at about 4 p.m. When they had not reached a verdict by 9 p.m., they were sequestered in a local hotel for the night. They continued their deliberations the next morning. The intense hours dragged on. Waiting for the return of a jury is an incredible, draining, even frightening experience, but at 2 p.m. the next day, we were advised the jury had reached a verdict. After everyone had re-assembled in the courtroom, the jury filed in and sat down. Then the foreman arose to announce their verdict. "Not guilty of murder, not guilty of manslaughter."

There was a noticeable cheer in the packed courtroom. Steven Kesler, in the prisoners box, raised his fist in a gesture of victory, then ran over and hugged me. I felt a tremendous release of tension that had been building for months. As I looked over at the jury, one member winked at me, a gesture I will never forget. Once things settled down, Justice Lutz said, "Mr. Kesler, you are free to leave."

Aftermath of the Case

In the aftermath of the Kesler verdict, there was undoubtedly concern that the not guilty verdict would encourage other shopkeepers to arm themselves and confront would-be robbers or thieves. I was asked by the large press scrum that formed on the courthouse steps after the verdict "Is this verdict a signal for shop owners to arm themselves?" I responded, "There is no signal except that this man, in these circumstances, was justified." I went on to say that a different jury on different facts may well come to a different conclusion.

There was another question directed at my client by the media present – one I had anticipated and had already warned Steven about.

When asked "Do you still have a gun in the drugstore?" Steven Kesler politely but firmly stated that he would not answer that question.

On the day after the verdict, the *Calgary Herald* newspaper published an editorial titled "Kesler No Hero." The editorial reflected the likely mixed feelings of Canadians on the verdict in view of the full evidence that had come out. Citing all that Kesler had gone through as a result of his decisions that fateful day, and noting that a young man had died over the sum of $115, it strongly discouraged others from taking any similar vigilante action.

Though I have defended numerous murder and other serious cases in my time as a criminal defence lawyer, the Kesler case stands out for me as perhaps the most challenging – perhaps satisfying – of my career. My own father had supported our family by owning and operating a corner grocery store, and I and my five brothers and sisters had all worked many hours there as we were growing up. I knew how important that store was to our family, and so could very much identify with Steven Kesler and his family business.

Steven Kesler and his wife and family had gone through an unbelievable series of break-ins and robberies; violent and unpredictable events that were destroying the Keslers' ability to safely make a living, leaving them in a state of justifiable fear. I often thought of how my own family would have been affected if we had gone through even part of what the Keslers had experienced before that fateful day in November of 1986. I always believed that the jury got it right in Steven Kesler's case, as juries usually do.

Clayton Rice, Q.C. *received his Bachelor of Laws degree from Dalhousie University and his Master of Laws degree from New York University. He was a professor of law at The University of Alberta, Faculty of Law, for ten years where he taught Criminal Law, Evidence and Constitutional Law. He practices wiretap law and drug law with Evans Fagan & Rice in Calgary, Alberta. Clayton is a member of the American Civil Liberties Union and continues to participate as a panelist in legal education programs. He posts regularly to his blog On The Wire at www.claytonrice.com and you may follow him on Twitter @WiretapLawyer.*

Mr. Clayton Rice

The Case of Kristen Budic

Too Crazy to Be Insane

THE THEME FROM *SHAFT* was playing on the radio. In Cambodia, the Khmer Rouge had attacked the airport in Phnom Penh. Clint Eastwood's film *Play Misty for Me* was running at the theatres, and *The Day Of The Jackal* by Frederick Forsyth was a bestseller. Three days after *Procol Harum Live with the Edmonton Symphony Orchestra* was recorded at the Northern Alberta Jubilee Auditorium, Kristan Budic walked into the historic Tegler Building in downtown Edmonton with a loaded handgun in a briefcase. It was November 22, 1971.

He had come to see Dr. Bozo Bulaijic. He was holding the gun when he walked in. The nurse's aide fled when Dr. Bulaijic came out of his office. She heard the shots from the hall. She then pushed the door open. Budic was sitting in the waiting room. The gun was on the floor by his feet. "Don't touch it," he said. "The police will need it for evidence."

Detective Zane Kotyk arrived at the scene. He was all ears and Budic was ready to tell him everything that happened. "Get police doctor to check my blood full of poison," Budic said. He continued:

> I can't live. My hand is frozen. I haven't got medical. I buy gun in Toronto. I went down there to see doctor and guy stop me on street to sell watch and then I buy gun for $70.50. I came back to Edmonton and he take my life so I take his life. Why he never gave poor guy to live. I always work. I spent six thousand dollars running away from him. I went to kill him because he try to make me die like dog on street.

Delusion Triggered

On December 30, 1971, by order of the Lieutenant Governor, Kristan Budic was remanded to the Alberta Hospital which is an Edmonton facility that provides mental health services for adults. The medical and psychiatric conclusions were that he suffered from a physical atrophy of the brain and this disease triggered a delusion that he had been poisoned. The delusion had become more intricate over time as he travelled across Canada and Europe in search of treatment.

At the core of the delusion was Budic's belief that he had signed an insurance policy on a previous visit to Dr. Bozo Bulaijic and that Dr. Bulaijic was preventing him from getting treatment. According to Budic's thinking, Dr. Bulaijic carried out the worldwide conspiracy against him by telex machine. Dr. Geoffrey Hopkinson, a psychiatrist at the Alberta Hospital, would testify years later: "I suspect that [Budic] took the law into his own hands to perhaps save his own life." The psychiatric diagnosis was the easy part. Getting Budic to trial was something else.

Four years after the shooting, Budic was indicted on a charge of non-capital murder. The trial before Justice J.C. Cavanagh in the former Alberta Supreme Court, Trial Division, began with a preliminary hearing on whether Budic was fit to stand trial. Dr. Hopkinson testified that Budic was fit. He understood the charge and the nature of legal proceedings. He was capable of instructing his lawyer. On the trial itself, Budic testified about the poison and that Dr. Bulaijic was conspiring to kill him. Dr. Hopkinson took the stand again and said this about the insanity defence:

> He knew it was wrong, he knew it was not a legal act, but he felt that he had no other recourse. He felt that he was ridding himself of someone who was trying to kill him. He told me that he expected no leniency from the law. On one occasion, he said that he would prefer a life sentence which he felt he could survive if he was rid of what he considered to be persecutions.

Well, Justice Cavanagh was having none of that. He interjected and aborted the trial:

> This man is today suffering from delusions and these delusions are right at the very heart of the crime with which he is charged and I do not see how he can make a full answer in defence under the circumstances and I doubt if he is capable so I find him unfit to stand trial.

Budic appealed.

Budic had discharged a number of defence lawyers as he wove them into his delusional system. Although he was free from Dr. Bulaijic, the source of his torment, he was still hospitalized and he wasn't getting out. Renowned Edmonton counsel Robert H. Davidson, QC was Budic's lawyer on the appeal. Writing the unanimous opinion of the former Alberta Supreme Court, Appellate Division, Justice Carlton Clement said:

> The question under consideration is, at large, to be determined in the interests of fairness to the accused, and which ought to include the undesirability of having postponed indefinitely a verdict on the crime with which he is charged. The persistence of a delusion to the time of trial is not unusual. Its effect as a defence does not have a necessary relation to the fitness of the accused to stand his trial. Dr. Hopkinson clearly distinguished between the two issues. Counsel for the defence felt he was adequately instructed. Evidence given by Budic gave no suggestion that he was unfit to stand trial.

The case was sent back to Justice Cavanagh to proceed with the trial. But, then, everything careened off another guardrail.

Nullity and Correction

Budic's case was making its way through the courts during the moratorium on capital punishment. He was indicted for non-capital murder in 1975 and the trial began in 1976. Parliament amended the *Criminal Code* by the time the case was sent back to Justice Cavanagh repealing capital and non-capital murder and replacing them with a new legal regime – first and second degree murder. And, just to add to the pile, the Appellate Division ordered that the aborted trial be resumed, an order that was incorrect in law. Lawyers and judges have a word for this: it was a nullity, a nullity being a proceeding or an order of the court which has no legal force or effect. By the summer of 1977, Davidson was back before the same judges, with Budic in tow.

The nullity was corrected. The order for the resumption of the aborted trial was an oversight and the court simply ordered a new trial. That left three more things. Davidson motioned to amend the notice of appeal asking that the new trial be by judge and jury. The Crown sought directions about whether the new trial should be on the old Indictment for non-capital murder or whether the new law required a new Indictment for first degree murder. And to top it all off, that raised the question whether the new law was retroactive.

In 1977, the *Charter of Rights* was five years away, so the question of retroactivity was decided as one of statutory interpretation. The problem deeply concerned the court. One of the judges was Justice William G. Morrow. He had a national reputation as a former judge in the Northwest Territories and wrote about his experiences in *Northern Justice: The Memoirs of Mr. Justice William G. Morrow,* a book published by the Osgoode Society for Canadian Legal History. Although the court was unanimous in the result, Justice Morrow wrote separate reasons:

> Under the new section it is quite conceivable that the appellant could find himself subjected to a heavier sentence if he is convicted than would have been the case had his trial continued under the old section, hence the present concern. It is to be remembered that the general rule in interpretation is that the legislation leans against retrospective operation, particularly where the rights of parties in pending actions might be affected and where it is a criminal matter....The instructions as to preferring a new indictment and the procedure to be followed is made imperative throughout by the use of the word 'shall'. I am unable to reach any other conclusion than that the new legislation is intended to take immediate effect both retrospectively and prospectively, except where an original proceeding not resulting in a new trial may already be underway.

Because the corrected order of the court was for a new trial, and because the legislation required that there be a new Indictment, Budic would stand trial for first degree murder.

The trial took place before Chief Justice J.V.H. Milvain and a jury. Edward Molstad QC was Budic's new lawyer. Dr. Hopkinson testified again: "There is no definition of a delusion," he said.

> It is easier perhaps to describe just what a delusion is like, rather than to say what it is. It is a false belief that occurs to a person which is completely out of context with his cultural background, with his educational background, so it is a crazy belief. It carries with it a strange sense of complete conviction. It is a symptom of disease of the mind.

Here is another key passage from Dr. Hopkinson's testimony about the insanity defence:

> Q. Would he have been able to appreciate the nature and quality of the act that occurred on that date?
>
> A. Umm, perhaps – his perception of what was happening at that time was altered by his mental illness so that though he believed to some extent that he knew what was happening, this appreciation was appreciation of a diseased mind. He would appreciate what he was doing to the point that he knew he was killing someone; and indeed what the consequences might well be. At the same time his appreciation of the situation was of a man who was being poisoned perhaps by the person he killed. To some extent in this sense, in the sense of his appreciation of what was happening, it is not the appreciation you or I would have, but it was an appreciation.
>
> Q. But he knew it was wrong.
>
> A. Yes, he knew that it was an illegal act.
>
> Q. And he knew that he could be and probably would be punished for the act.
>
> A. Yes, he did.

Budic then testified. He explained how he had been poisoned from drinking wine at a friend's house. He talked about his struggle to understand what had happened to him and why. He talked about the many doctors he had consulted and trips to the former Yugoslavia and Soviet Union in search of treatment. He said exactly what he had told Det. Kotyk, his many lawyers, the psychiatrists, and Justice Cavanagh. This is what he said to the jury about the day he killed Dr. Bulaijic:

> Q. Did you know why Dr. Stevens did not do anything for you when you went back to see him the second time?
>
> A. He Dr. Bulaijic, he connect doctors. They never give me medical anymore. He stop me for medical. Every doctor gave me medical.
>
> Q. So was that Dr. Bozo Bulaijic?
>
> A. Yeah.
>
> Q. Was he connected with Dr. Stevens?
>
> A. Well he connect all doctors. I was going from doctor to doctor. I never got help anymore.
>
> Q. And on November 22nd, 1971, did you think you could get medical help?
>
> A. No, I never think I going to get medical help.
>
> Q. And why not?
>
> A. Because Dr. Bulaijic connect doctors and I no got medical anymore.
>
> Q. And what did you think was going to happen to you?
>
> A. Well I just die like dog in street and I cannot get medical.
>
> Q. So what did you do?
>
> A. So when I come back and went in his office, Dr. Bulaijic.
>
> Q. And did you talk to him?
>
> A. Yeah, I started talking to him. I said to him good morning, and I asked him what he did to me, he cannot talk. I shot him. But he cannot talk anymore.
>
> Q. What did you ask him?
>
> A. When he come in I say good morning; and he never answer me. I said, do you know what you did to me? And he never

say nothing.

Q. So what did you do?

A. Like I pull gun with my briefcase and I shot him.

Q. Why did you shoot the doctor?

A. Well why I should go die; I never did him nothing.

Q. What did you do after you shot the doctor?

A. I call nurse. I tell nurse to phone police.

Budic had complained to the police many times and had previously met Det. Kotyk. The detective was concerned and went to see Dr. Bulaijic. But Dr. Bulaijic was reluctant to have Budic committed to the hospital. Det. Kotyk testified that Budic was not rational when he arrived at the scene. "He kept insisting that his blood was poisoned and he was going to die," the detective said, "and he went over this many, many times." Det. Kotyk described the conspiracy:

Q. And did he tell you that he couldn't get medicine from all of these doctors because of the connections of this Dr. Bulaijic?

A. That's right. Dr. Bulaijic had connections with all the doctors in the world, and for that reason Mr. Budic couldn't get treatments from any doctor.

Q. Did he tell you how Dr. Bulaijic was connected with these doctors?

A. I recall something about a machine. I think he was talking about a telex or a similar type of machine, but he was talking about a machine.

Q. By this 'connected with other doctors through this machine', that meant that the doctors conferred with each other in a conspiracy and purposely would not treat Mr. Budic; is that what it came up to mean?

A. Yes, sir.

The jury convicted and Budic was sentenced to life imprisonment without parole eligibility for twenty-five years. Everyone in town was surprised by the verdict.

My First Murder Case

A couple of weeks later, I was standing outside the door to the maximum security building of the old Fort Saskatchewan gaol with Alexander D. Pringle QC. Held together by a lick and a promise, and known as 'the Fort', it functioned as a provincial gaol and a remand centre. Alex and I often bumped into each other visiting clients in those days and then we would head to the Library Pub in Edmonton to talk about how not to practice criminal law. I remember the clanking elevator up to D Block. And the smell.

And Budic shuffling in for our first meeting. He didn't look anything like I expected. I said to Alex later that evening, maybe Kris is just too crazy to be insane.

It was my first murder case. The trial transcript soon arrived and we settled into preparing the appeal brief. The arguments made were based on errors in the charge to the jury about the law of insanity under section 16 of the *Criminal Code*. The subsection dealing with delusions ricocheted the case off another guardrail. Here it is:

> A person who has specific delusions, but is in other respects sane, shall not be acquitted on the ground of insanity unless the delusions caused him to believe in the existence of a state of things that, if it existed, would have justified or excused his act or omission.

If that subsection applied, I thought, then Budic's case was not about insanity at all. The law commanded that a presumption be factored into the analysis – the presumption being that the worldwide conspiracy to prevent him from getting medical treatment was true. Dr. Hopkinson was right. This was a self-defence case.

The court that heard the appeal was comprised of Chief Justice William A. McGillivray, and Justices Arnold F. Moir and William R. Sinclair. The Crown attorney was Jack Watson QC, who is now a supernumerary justice of the Alberta Court of Appeal. He appeared on all the Budic appeals. By the time we finished a full-day harangue over whether Budic acted in self-defence, the court was in a state of apoplexy.

The unanimous opinion was released on September 28, 1978. The conviction was set aside and a verdict of "not guilty on account of insanity" was substituted. The court held that the self-defence argument could not succeed because "no sane person could plead self-defence because a doctor was preventing him from getting medication, unless there were some element of captivity involved." The appeal was allowed on the basis of errors in the instruction to the jury on whether Budic knew that shooting Dr. Bulaijic was legally wrong. The jury was not told that they had the right to reject the opinion of Dr. Hopkinson. Chief Justice McGillivray, writing for the court, put it this way: [1]

> Now, let us look at the facts. The appellant, in vain attempts to obtain medical treatment, had tried numerous doctors, clinics and hospitals in Canada, and, moreover, he had gone to Yugoslavia twice and to Russia once. He had complained to the City of Edmonton Police and to the RCMP on several occasions, to no avail. His view was that Dr. Bulajic was trying to make him die like a dog in the street. There was nothing secretive about the shooting; no attempt to escape detection. When the nurse's aide returned to the doctor's office after calling for help, the appellant was sitting in the waiting room with a gun beside him on the floor. The appellant said: "Don't touch it. The Police will need it for evidence."

Chief Justice McGillivray continued:

> In my view, the jury was entitled to have put to them by the trial judge this evidence in support of the defence's position that the appellant did not know that what he was doing was wrong. The trial judge, having commented on what, in his view, was the fair-minded professional way in which Dr. Hopkinson gave his evidence, said that the Doctor said: 'He could appreciate the act and know it was wrong and he could be punished for it. He says I expect that he took the law into

1 All references to the court judgments and trial transcripts may be found in the reported cases: *R. v. Budic* (1977), 35 CCC (2d) 272 (Alta CA); *R. v. Budic* (No. 2) (1977), 35 CCC (2d) 333 (Alta CA); and, *R. v. Budic* (No. 3) (1978), 43 CCC (2d) 419 (Alta CA)

> his own hands in order to save his own life, that is in his mind.' Having quoted this expression of opinion, the trial judge should have made it clear to the jury that they were not bound to accept this, but that they should, in weighing whether the appellant knew what he was doing was wrong or illegal, weigh the factors which I have outlined above.

Budic was transferred back to the Alberta Hospital. The last time I saw him was at a Board of Review hearing where we succeeded in getting more liberal hospital privileges. He then faded from the public spotlight until the news broke in the Edmonton media. He had quietly gone into a cubicle in a men's room and hung himself. I stopped Dr. John H. Brooks at the Law Courts one day as I always did when I saw him. John was a compassionate psychiatrist, a skilled witness and a good friend of the defence bar. He told me some details about Kris' suicide. I never asked John who found him.

Replacing the Insanity Verdict

The Tegler Building was soon gone too. Robert Tegler was an entrepreneur who arrived in Edmonton at the turn of the last century. The building was constructed at the corner of First Street and Elizabeth Street in 1912. It was the largest building in western Canada and later became a haunt for lawyers and other professionals. It was designated an historical resource but city council rescinded the designation and the building was razed on December 13, 1982. John Zazula reported on CBC News that "a gigantic cloud of dust rolled through the city's centre like a wave on the ocean." The Bank of Montreal now stands in its place at the corner of the renamed 101st Street and 102nd Avenue.

In 1992, Parliament amended section 16 of *The Criminal Code* repealing subsection (3) dealing with delusions and replacing the insanity verdict with the modern test of 'Not Criminally Responsible' because of 'mental disorder' (NCR). In 1956 the McRuer Report had condemned the provision based on the weight of medical opinion that it described a person who could not exist, that is, no one who has specific delusions could be in other respects sane. Professor Don Stuart of Queen's University, in his *Canadian Criminal Law: A Treatise*, had therefore praised the opinion of the Budic court for ignoring "a fundamentally discredited section." And Chief Justice Antonio C. Lamer, writing for a 5-4 majority of the Supreme Court of Canada in 1990, had recognized the "difficult and perhaps impossible task of deciphering the plain meaning" of the provision or of "fathoming the intention of Parliament" in enacting it.[2] The Budic ruling, however, is still good law and is cited for the principle that a specific delusion does not preclude a defendant from suffering from a mental disorder that rendered him or her incapable of knowing that an act was wrong.

Although the case of Kristan Budic was my first murder case, it was not my first case involving serious mental disorder. When I was in law school at New York University I enrolled in a law and psychiatry clinical program at Bellevue Hospital. One of the patients was a young girl suspected of homicide who was found on the street in East Harlem. Maria C. was catatonic. Catatonia is a state of neurogenic motor immobility manifested by stupor. Stupor means unconsciousness or insensibility. Maria never moved during the many hours I spent with her. She would sit quietly, her eyes fixed. It was a humid day in September the last time I saw her. I remember the rumble of traffic on First Avenue as I picked up my notes and went to the door. "Good bye, Maria." I sometimes think about her and the solace of silence when I hear Kris again: "Why I should die like dog in street?"

The year after the last Budic appeal, Alex referred a client with an appeal from a drug conviction. It was my first wiretap case that would end in the Supreme Court of Canada and my practice slowly transitioned from crimes of violence to search and seizure law. The early years and Kristan Budic came with me when I moved to Calgary, although I continue to take cases in Edmonton where I enjoy the camaraderie of the bar in a city with a memory on every corner. I wrote Budic into a screenplay in 2003 called *Pirouette* that is set in New York. Meetings with my attorney to prepare the copyright application were good excuses to walk it around the old neighbourhood. I have no idea whether I will ever get it out of the Library of Congress. My brother Bill, a New England orthopedic surgeon, said: "That purge was probably better than an enema."

2 R. v. Chaulk, [1990] 3 SCR 1303, at para. 110.

PART EIGHT

A Tough, Fascinating Profession

Judge Raymond Wyant *was appointed a Judge of the Provincial Court of Manitoba in 1998 and appointed for a seven-year term as Chief Judge in 2002. During his term, he led a domestic violence project that won a Gold Award for Innovation from IPAC and a United Nations Award for Public Service. He is also a Deputy Judge of Yukon Territory and currently serves as a Senior Judge in Manitoba. Judge Wyant is past Chair of the Canadian Council of Chief Judges and currently Chairs the national Steering Committee on Justice Efficiencies and Chairs the National Symposium on Criminal Justice Reform. He teaches Ethics and Advocacy at the University of Manitoba Law School and presently does consulting, including having worked for the United Nations on judicial reform in Ethiopia.*

Judge Raymond Wyant

The Scars that Never Heal

OVER THE COURSE of the past forty years of my journey in the criminal justice system as a criminal defence lawyer, Crown prosecutor, and judge, I have, like most others in our profession, accumulated many memories. Some of those memories are good ones but so many more are not. The constant contact with the effects of crime takes a vicarious toll on all of us who work in the criminal justice system – we cannot help but be affected by what we encounter. I am amazed that I can still be amazed by the unspeakable things one human being can do to another.

Our profession is built on pain. There are, sadly, few happy results that occur with crime. For the most part, we deal with human sorrow and misery. Criminal acts almost always involve victims, some of whom are irreparably damaged by the acts inflicted upon them. People die, sometimes in heinous and ghastly ways, and many others are scarred physically and/or psychologically by the criminal acts inflicted on them or on their loved ones.

There are few moments of happiness or satisfaction, no matter what the outcome of a criminal case might be. There is no turning back the clock; no ability to put people back into the position they were in before a crime was committed. People talk about closure but I have come to realize that, in many instances, there is no closure with the end of a criminal case. Victims are still victims, and sending an accused to jail is never a happy occasion. We may find satisfaction in a job well done in litigating a case but that satisfaction is a personal one. From time to time, we may find happiness in seeing a person turn their life around and feeling, to some extent, that we helped them do so. But these moments of satisfaction are few and far between. There are far too few happy endings.

Police officers and first responders see the immediate and devastating effects of crime first hand and often right after an event has occurred. Viewing a grisly murder scene or a tragic and deadly traffic accident can have long-lasting effects on the psyche of even the strongest of personalities.

Lawyers and judges are not immune to the devastating effects of crime either. In fact, even though we often view events through the rear-view mirror of photographs or eye-witness descriptions, the constant exposure to scenes of violence or depravity can seep through our bodies in silent and discreet ways even though we haven't witnessed the actual events depicted first hand. Our contact with these events, though removed, is more sustained because it can often be a constant occurrence. Most of us can be affected in unseen and subtle ways that we may not fully understand or appreciate. But all of us are changed in some fashion, changed forever. Like doctors constantly exposed to disease and death, we may think we become immune but very few of us do. How many of us can say we haven't been, on occasion, moved to tears at the description of the effects of pain on people who appear in court? We may not even understand the life-altering effects that some of our work has on us. We may not even appreciate how we can be affected by memories that sometimes lie buried deep inside us.

As a result of my career, I carry painful memories of events that never leave me. Some of those memories have seared into me like a branding iron on cattle. The soul-altering images of children exploited in images of child pornography, for example, are so disturbing it almost defies description. Then there are the images of the poor and wretched, those vulnerable people who appear so constantly before us in court. And, of course, there are memories of specific cases and specific individuals; the effects of which can lead to life-long torment.

The Case of Michael Jewell

I am not sure of the exact date of the first time I met Michael Jewell but I will always remember the last meeting, but I am getting ahead of myself.

As a young criminal defence lawyer in Winnipeg, I had come to represent Michael on a number of relatively minor and petty charges in the late 1970s and the early 1980s. Michael was an auto mechanic by trade, sometimes employed and sometimes not. During the time I represented him, he was never charged with anything significantly serious but, for a while, he provided me with some regular work and the opportunity to hone my craft. During the course of defending Michael, I had come to know his wife, Michele. Michele Jewell was a lovely individual, a couple of years younger than Michael who worked as a nurse on the cardiac unit at Winnipeg's St. Boniface Hospital. She always came to court with Michael and always paid cash for his legal fees. I could never figure out what attracted her to him. He was a scofflaw of sorts with a criminal record, and she was a bright and vibrant young woman with a warm personality and a winning smile. I guess she was attracted to the 'bad boy' in Michael. At least, from my perspective, that was the only explanation I could figure out.

As a result of Michael's numerous court matters, I came to know Michele quite well and we were on friendly terms. We often chatted about things unrelated to court when she attended my office or came to court with Michael. I liked her. Michael, on the other hand, was just a good client.

Unbeknown to me though, there had been trouble in the marriage. They had separated a number of times but always got back together. For a couple of years prior to 1984, I lost of track of the two of them, as Michael didn't call me for assistance.

Then in February 1984, I received a call from Michael. He had been arrested in a small town outside of Winnipeg and detained on what I remember to be a charge of dangerous driving. He wanted me to appear in court the next day to apply for his release on bail. I agreed. Given his background, I didn't see that there would be much difficulty in securing his release.

Later the same day I received a call from Michele. I will never forget that phone call. In retrospect, it seems like we talked for a long time; maybe an hour. But who knows how long it was in reality. Memory is a funny thing and the gist of that call has been replayed in my memory in slow-motion countless times over the years.

Michele told me she knew Michael was in custody and begged me not to get him out on bail. She filled me in on what had been happening in their marriage, that they had been separated since early January and that she had filed a petition for divorce on the grounds of mental and physical cruelty. She also informed me that the divorce hearing was to take place in a few days. She told me she was fearful and scared of him. She didn't want him out of custody because she feared for her safety. I recall listening to her detail her concerns and the background of their relationship and his violent temperament. It came as a surprise to me because Michael had not shown, in any obvious legal fashion that I knew of, any propensity for violence, but the fact she told me he had a significant drinking problem did not come as a surprise.

I told Michele that Michael would, in my opinion, get out on bail regardless of who was representing him. There just weren't sufficient grounds for keeping him in. I told her that I would represent Michael on his present charge but, under no circumstances, would I ever represent him on anything involving her. I went further though in what, retrospectively, was a well-intentioned but mistaken attempt to assist her. I said to her I was confident Michael would never do anything to harm or hurt her because he cared for her. I told her I was certain she was not in any danger from him. My intent was to reassure her and to put her mind at ease because it was clear to me she was quite concerned and frightened and I thought I was helping her. By the end of the call, I believe I had done exactly that. She was calmer and less anxious and thanked me for listening to her and for helping her, calming her down and being a friend. I wished her well. That was, regrettably, the last time we spoke.

Petition for Divorce and a Gruesome Death

Michele's petition for divorce was scheduled for the morning of Monday, February 27, 1984. In the very early morning hours of that

Monday, Michael went to Michele's apartment block in north Winnipeg. He proceeded to scale the outside balconies of the apartment block all the way to the twelfth-floor apartment where Michele lived.

Using a tool he brought with him, he broke into the apartment. During the course of their separation, Michele had changed the locks on a couple of occasions but nothing was going to prevent Michael from entering her place that morning. What happened inside over the next couple of hours was horrific, violent and gruesome.

Michael attacked Michele and badly beat her with a blunt force object. He vaginally and anally raped her. Eventually, he slit her throat. The pathologist later testified that she probably took a long time to die; perhaps up to two hours. He could not say whether she was conscious when her throat was slashed and legs amputated. We can only hope she was not. Only Michael knows what he did to her during that horrible time frame in the apartment, but we can all surmise that Michele died a slow and painful death, likely in her bathtub.

Neighbours later testified they heard strange noises coming from the suite and a woman's voice saying "get away from me, get away from me." Around 5:00 a.m., they were awoken by about ten intermittent thumping noises and something or someone being dragged. They then heard the shower go on and off a couple of times.

After Michele was dead, Michael went to extensive efforts to clean up the crime scene. It is likely Michael drained much of the blood out of Michele's body, in the same fashion hunters would, in order to make her body lighter to carry. He used a knife and hacksaw he had brought with him and amputated her legs which allowed him to place her body parts in plastic garbage bags. The pathologist later testified there was little blood left in her 115-pound body upon his examination. Michael carried the bags down the twelve flights of stairs to his vehicle. He then drove to his brother's residence in Emo in northwestern Ontario, a few hours from Winnipeg, the place he had been living since his last separation from Michele.

Once in Emo, he took further steps to dismember the body. Using a chainsaw, he cut the body up into five parts. He wanted to bury the body but it was winter and the ground was frozen so he figured he would wait until the spring and, in the meantime, would store the frozen body parts in bags until he could find a time to bury her. Before his crime was discovered, his intention was to further dismember her body.

Michael might have gotten away with the murder if it hadn't been for his brother discovering one of the bags on his property the day after the murder. Opening up the bag, his brother Wayne screamed as he saw a woman's hand and the upper torso of Michele's body. He called the Ontario Provincial Police who searched the rural property further and found two other bags, one containing two thighs and the other two legs severed below the knee. Michael was arrested. Initially he denied knowledge but later gave a detailed confession.

Ironically, while driving on the highway on his way to Winnipeg to commit the murder, Michael had been stopped by an Ontario Provincial Police officer for not wearing his seatbelt. The vehicle he was operating was not his, and Michael told the officer he had lost his driver's licence and had verbally given the name of the registered owner of the truck he was operating, producing the vehicle's registration papers. The officer believed Michael's story and the false identity given to him and let him proceed. One can only wonder how things might have gone differently if he had not been allowed to go on his way. After the murder, Michael was also stopped on his way back to Emo by another officer, for the same reason of not wearing a seatbelt and, again, provided a false identity. That officer later testified that he noticed a green garbage bag in the back of the pick-up truck but had no reason to search the vehicle. How close Michael came to being discovered then.

The Arrest

What happened next is both clear and yet cloudy. When Michael was arrested, he was asked if he had a lawyer. He gave my name. I recall receiving a telephone call from the police informing me that they had Michael in custody and informing me of the outline of the charge. I recall they told me that they were transporting Michael to Winnipeg and that he wanted to meet me there. They then told me what time he would likely be arriving. I was numb upon hearing the news. It was as if I was dreaming and I can't recall if the reality of what I heard from the police really sank in at that point.

After Michael arrived in Winnipeg, he was taken to the Public Safety Building in downtown Winnipeg, a building that, at that time, served as the main police station and also housed the remand facilities for Winnipeg. I remember Michael coming into one of the small interview rooms in the remand facility. In my memory, that meeting seemed to last forever but, in reality, it probably only lasted a few minutes. I just looked at him. He said nothing. I only said that I wouldn't represent him and would get another lawyer in my firm to do so. That was the last time I saw him. I went home and got drunk and I tried to wash the blood off my hands.

The Outcome of the Crime

Michael, at age twenty-seven, was convicted of first degree murder and sentenced to life with no parole for twenty-five years, the mandatory sentence. At his trial, it was revealed that Michael had written a letter to Michele eleven days before the murder claiming he had changed and professing his love for her and his hope they would reconcile. Others would testify at his trial that he was hopelessly in love with her and despondent at their separation.

But it was also revealed that Michael told the investigating officers he was thinking of writing a book titled, "How to end a love addiction…with a chain saw." He also said he cut up Michele's body and took it to Emo so he would never be far away from her because he still loved her. That isn't love. His fixation and possessiveness clearly knew no bounds. If he couldn't have her, he made sure no one else could. That is why she lived in fear and dread.

Michael appealed his conviction to the Manitoba Court of Appeal. The Appeal Court found that the trial judge had made an error in his charge to the jury. Rather than ordering a new trial though, the Appeal Court reduced his conviction to one of second degree but then sentenced him to the same sentence, life with no parole for twenty-five years because of the premeditated nature of the murder and its brutality. At that time, this was the longest sentence ever given for second degree murder in Manitoba's history.

I don't know what happened to Michael after his sentencing although his twenty-five years came up a number of years ago. I also don't know what happened to members of Michele's family although I recall reading a Letter to the Editor to the *Winnipeg Free Press* about eight years ago from Michele's brother which talked about her death. I do know that she was deeply loved by her parents and siblings and her tragic and senseless death and the subsequent trial inflicted an immense toll on all of them.

Michele was only twenty-five years of age at the time of her death, a death that profoundly affected me and changed me forever. It was the beginning of the end of my career as a defence counsel. My days were numbered. By 1985 I had joined the Crown's office.

I have never forgotten Michele and that fateful call a few days before she was killed nor have I forgotten that last meeting with Michael in the jail. I have replayed those events over and over again throughout the intervening years. Sometimes the thoughts come in the middle of the night. What could I or should I have done differently? I know that nothing I did contributed to her death; Michael did what he set out to do. At least I know that intellectually. But emotionally, the scars and the guilt will always be there.

Back in 1984, the justice system treated most cases of domestic violence quite differently than today. Subsequent Inquiries into the tragedies changed all of that. By the 1990s police and prosecution procedures and charging practices changed and it became required that all of us who work in the justice system be trained to know and understand the dynamics of domestic violence and how to recognize it and respond to it in order to protect victims and prevent tragedies.

I got into criminal defence work because I wanted to help people and I believed in the presumption of innocence and the right to a fair trial for everyone. I still believe in those ideals but the case of Michael Jewell tested my beliefs. This case was gruesome but I didn't leave defence work because of that – many cases are awful and gruesome. I left because of the personal nature of this case and my involvement in it and the personal effect the tragic death of a person I knew had on me. Unfortunately, a dozen or so years later, tragedy struck again when I lost a good friend of mine to yet another senseless murder. It seems you can never escape.

We are all products of our experiences; they shape us as human beings. This case was no different. It has contributed to my vicarious trauma but also, in some fashion I believe it has made me more sensitive, more human, more compassionate, empathetic, and sympathetic. It has contributed to my knowledge of human behaviour, and the human condition, and the effect of crime on victims and maybe, just maybe, it has made me a bit better at what I do. If there is anything positive I can take from all of this, I do hope it lies there.

I don't get nightmares anymore dreaming of how Michele died, but while it is said time heals all wounds, I disagree. They may be less visible but some scars never heal; and the blood, though faded, will never disappear from my hands.

Rest in Peace Michele.

Justice Joseph Di Luca *Joe received his LL.B. from the University of Toronto in 1996 and his LL.M. from Osgoode Hall Law School in 2003. He was called to the bar in 1998 and became a Certified Specialist in Criminal Law in 2008. He practiced criminal law for over eighteen years prior to his appointment to Ontario Superior Court of Justice in 2016. He also appeared before The Walkerton Inquiry, The Goudge Inquiry, and Standing Committees of the Senate and House of Commons. Joe had the privilege of regularly appearing before the Court of Appeal for Ontario as duty counsel for indigent inmates and as* amicus curiae *on mental health related appeals. In 2010, he was a co-recipient of the Osgoode Hall Law School Teaching Award given in recognition of teaching excellence.*

Justice Joseph Di Luca

The Inmate Appeal Duty Counsel Program

SOME OF THE BEST MOMENTS of my career as a lawyer were spent appearing as duty counsel on inmate appeals before the Court of Appeal for Ontario. Part tragedy and part comedy, the inmate appeals never failed to highlight the significant challenges faced by the indigent in the system while also providing some insight, at times lighthearted, into the human condition.

Over the years, my colleagues and I assisted countless inmates with their appeals. I also had the privilege of serving on the board of the Inmate Appeal Duty Counsel Program. As it turns out, my final appearance as counsel before the Court of Appeal was, fittingly, on an inmate appeal. The fellow was appealing his sentence. He had been caught up in a prescription drug trafficking ring and had received a significant penitentiary sentence. As is often the case, he could not afford counsel. I reviewed his file and prepared arguments in support of his appeal. I then met him on the morning of his appeal and we chatted for maybe five minutes in the cells in the basement of the courthouse. I told him I would make submissions on his behalf and that he was free to add in anything he thought might help his cause.

After I made my pitch about the errors made by the sentencing judge, the Appellant addressed the court directly. He spoke eloquently, expressed sincere remorse over the offences and talked about his plans for the future. He thanked the Court for listening and sat down. The Court retired to deliberate and upon returning, reduced the sentence by one year, citing an error in principle by the sentencing judge. The

Appellant was taken away and I turned to the next case. A week or two later, I received an email from the fellow's sister. The email conveyed a touching and heartfelt expression of gratitude and thanks from the Appellant and his family for having given the time to help him with his case. His sister indicated that without duty counsel he would have had no one on his side. The email also conveyed the fellow's promise to use this opportunity to turn his life around.

Emails like this from an Appellant's family are the 'payment in kind' for any lawyer doing pro bono work. They make the effort worthwhile and meaningful. They give credence to our belief that the system can and does work. They serve as an inspiration to continue to serve the public. Thankfully, emails like this one are not an entirely rare occurrence amongst the lawyers who give their time to the duty counsel program.

The Duty Counsel Program

Before I relate some other stories, I want to share some of the history of the duty counsel program. In the days before the program, inmates who wished to appeal their conviction and/or sentence but who did not have counsel would appear before the Court on appointed days and 'make their pitch'. They would stand up in court and explain as best as they could why they should get an acquittal, a new trial, or a sentence reduction. These submissions were often, in essence, a plea for mercy.

The Crown, in the finest traditions of the bar, would do its best to bring to the Court's attention any legal issue that might deserve a second look and that might have escaped the inmate's grasp or notice. While the process worked in a rough and tumble sort of way, many were concerned that the confines of the adversarial process made it difficult for the Court to fairly assess the merits of the appeals. Along came the late great Justice Marc Rosenberg, who with co-architects Marie Henein, who needs no introduction, and Alison Wheeler, then a defence counsel, now one of the best appellate Crowns around, decided that a better system was needed.

In 1998, this legal triumvirate met over a drink or two (I presume) and using a cocktail napkin (again, I presume) sketched out the basic structure of the duty counsel program. In short order, a small roster of experienced appellate counsel was assembled and asked to offer volunteer services as duty counsel on a few occasions a year. Practices and protocols were put in place with the Crown office to ensure that the required appeal materials would be assembled and provided to duty counsel in advance of the scheduled dates. Self-represented inmates now had access to a free appeal lawyer who would review their case and advance any argument that could be gleaned from the limited inmate appeal record. At times, the duty counsel would help the inmate obtain Legal Aid or a court-ordered appointment of counsel. At other times, duty counsel's role was simply to stand beside the inmate 'for support'. The program was an immediate success. The roster of counsel grew as more appellate counsel learned of the program and signed up. The number of cases dealt with through the program also grew.

The program is now staffed by one full time paralegal/manager/hair stylist extraordinaire (I kid you not), Paul Jones, and approximately thirty duty counsel, ranging from approximately seven- to thirty-plus-years of experience. The program provides duty counsel services on thirty-four hearing days per year (twenty-two days in Toronto and twelve days in Kingston). In 2014 alone, duty counsel argued approximately eighty appeals. Even more importantly, duty counsel have managed to win many cases, several of which resulted in reported decisions that have contributed to our jurisprudence. This latter fact is remarkable given that the cases that end up on the inmate list are often screened in advance for lack of merit by Legal Aid Ontario (those deemed to have merit get funding for counsel).

Over the eighteen years of its existence, the program has received some well-deserved recognition. A number of years ago, Chief Justice Roy McMurtry nominated the entire program for the Sidney B. Linden Award given out by Legal Aid Ontario. The Court has also hosted a number of receptions to reflect its gratitude for the assistance provided by duty counsel. The program has received supporting grants from the Law Foundation and Legal Aid Ontario. The program retains a remarkable roster of duty counsel that reflects the 'who's who' of the criminal appellate bar.

The program has been an unparalleled success. While Justice Rosenberg is sadly no longer with us, one aspect of his wonderful legacy of humanity and pursuit of justice lives on with the program. Indigent inmates, with no lawyer and often no hope, have been provided with meaningful access to counsel. The Crown has been relieved of the obligation to straddle adversarial roles. The Court has enjoyed the benefit of having defence counsel review, vet, and present appeals. The justice system has been well served.

But there's more. Perhaps the most amazing aspect of the duty counsel program is that it infuses the rigid appellate process with a healthy dose of humanity, warts and all. The appellants are present in the courtroom and get to watch and participate in the unfolding of their appeals. The intellectual exercise of discerning legal errors gets tempered and at times hampered by the human condition. Some days, the depth of human tragedy and suffering that is revealed is staggering. Other days, the proceedings take on a decidedly light-hearted feel.

The stories that can be told would fill a book. For present purposes, I only need to fill a chapter so I will share only a select few that capture the wonderfully real and at times surreal human element of inmate appeals.

We often encountered inmates who spent a fair bit of time observing the court process and who managed to pick up some bits and pieces of legal knowledge along the way. But, as the saying goes, a little knowledge is sometimes dangerous. I recall reading one notice of appeal, handwritten in pencil, which listed as the only ground of appeal, "The Trial Judge lacked causable reason." Apparently, the Appellant took a shot at legalese and cobbled together some words he collected during various court appearances. Ironically, in the circumstances of his case, he wasn't too far off!

Another fellow filed a notice of appeal simply listing "The Trial Judge" as his only ground of appeal. Again, he also wasn't entirely far off!

On a mental health related appeal, an appellant handed up a number of pages which had a long list of typed numbers like "1154:53, 1167:67, 1983:21" and so on. The list of numbers went on for pages and was occasionally annotated with the odd word or phrase. The president of the panel looked at the pages intently, then turned to the appellant and asked, "Are these transcript references?" To which the Appellant replied, "No, it's my factum." Without missing a beat, the president of the panel said "Yes, of course." He 'read' the factum for a few minutes and then thanked the Appellant for his helpful submission. The appeal went on to be addressed on the basis of other errors identified in the record, with the Appellant satisfied that his 'factum' had been duly considered.

On another occasion, I watched an Appellant, a self-appointed minister of a church based on the sacred use of marijuana, remove his shirt in court and wrap it around his head. When asked whether the impromptu head-dress was for religious purposes, he replied "No, but you guys are all dressed up so I want to be as well." The Court let him continue with his submissions and head-dress. He did not get his marijuana back.

In yet another case, a fellow started reading from his notes, which were densely handwritten from corner to corner and edge to edge on multiple pages. When the president of the panel asked a question, the fellow answered and then started his 'speech' from the beginning. This happened a couple of times, until one judge asked him why he kept starting from the beginning each time he was interrupted. He explained that he didn't appreciate being interrupted and he warned that in order to keep the flow of his presentation, he would start from scratch each and every time he was interrupted! His appeal did not go so well.

The legal creativity of some of the appellants was at times astounding. A number of years ago, I was assigned a case where an appellant had been convicted of a number of offences, including a theft of certain photographs depicting his former partner's surgically enhanced breasts. Part of his argument before the Court was that he had paid for the surgery and therefore had a 'colour of right' argument for possessing the purportedly stolen photos. Needless to say, I advanced a mildly different argument that was met, unsurprisingly, with resistance from the Court. I was going to lose, but that was okay as I had managed to say something for the fellow and that was pretty good in the circumstances. As I sat down, Chief Justice Roy McMurtry asked the appellant if he had anything more to add, at which point the Appellant raised an entirely new ground of appeal: the incompetence of duty counsel, i.e. me. I quickly came to accept that this wasn't one of the times I would be receiving a nice thank-you note from the Appellant and I sat back and listened as he explained how I had just "screwed up" his case. Once the submissions were done, the panel retired to consider the case. Upon returning, Chief Justice McMurtry read out an endorsement dismissing the appeal. In addressing the incompetence of duty counsel argument, Chief Justice McMurtry noted "In our view, Mr. Di Luca did a very adequate job representing the Appellant." What? "Very adequate"?!! What even is "very adequate"? Is it akin to an "excellent C+" on a paper or placing seventh in a race? Or is it worse than that? Is it so adequate as to verge on inadequacy?

Leaving the courthouse that day, I had no option but to stop at the local watering hole for a very adequate pint and plate of wings, if only to quell the gales of laughter and teasing coming from my duty counsel colleague who was in court with me for the festivities. As for the Appellant, I understand that he went on to seek leave to appeal to the Supreme Court of Canada, which thankfully was denied.

Some of the appellants were passive participants in the appeal process. Many times, they were simply content to let duty counsel "give it a shot" while they sat and watched. On the rare occasion, we encountered an Appellant who had lost interest in his appeal.

One such occasion of an inmate losing interest took place in Kingston, Ontario, where the inmate sittings are often held due to proximity to the penitentiaries in the area. Kingston is a special place. Beautiful and historic. The Courthouse is a fantastic old building on the edge of the Queen's University campus. On days when the inmate appeal hearings are in Kingston, the Court travels by train with an entourage of clerks and students. The Crowns and defence counsel also travel to Kingston, often sharing a dinner or two together. The collegiality and camaraderie is wonderful. Indeed, the Kingston sittings are viewed as a bit of working holiday for all involved.

In any event, on this one day, we gathered in the courtroom and began arguments on a serious appeal involving a conviction for bank robbery. During the course of arguments, we could see the Appellant glancing over at the law students seated near the judges. As arguments went on, it became clear that the Appellant was not at all concerned with his appeal. He wasn't even paying attention. Instead, he was more interested in making eye contact with one particular student, who, as it turns out, was a Fox Scholar from England. At the conclusion of the case, he summoned duty counsel over to speak with him and handed over a note which he asked that we pass on to the law student. Curiosity got the best of us and we looked at the note. In it, the Appellant very politely noted that he thought the student was quite attractive and he indicated that he wanted to take her on a date "once he got out." He also provided his Fingerprint Service Number, "just in case" she wanted to look him up before his parole date. While perhaps this wasn't a match made in heaven, we had to admire the chutzpah of the appellant who was so clearly aiming high in the circumstances.

Another instance of a disinterested appellant happened a few years back when I encountered an elderly gentleman who had been given a life sentence for a bank robbery. It was maybe his tenth or eleventh robbery. He had lost hope, and on the morning of the appeal indicated that he had decided to abandon his appeal and simply serve his life sentence. I met with him for a while and eventually convinced him to let me argue for a sentence reduction, assuring him, "it can't get any worse than a life sentence!" Well, I was wrong. While I won the appeal and the sentence was reduced from life to fourteen years, the Court imposed a parole ineligibility order of eight years. Of course, the *Criminal Code* only imposes a parole ineligibility period of seven years on a life sentence for non-murder related offences. So, for all my efforts, the Appellant was rewarded with an extra year of parole ineligibility, despite a reduced sentence! I thereafter changed my advice to include "it can *always* get worse" as a standard precaution in every case.

At times during the inmate sittings, the humour wasn't provided by the Appellant or by me but, instead, by the other lawyers and judges. On one particular occasion, I was joined on the train to Kingston by Lou Strezos, a talented, generous, and gregarious defence counsel. In keeping with the strict traditions of the program, we likely consumed one or two drinks before, during and immediately after the train ride. As we pulled into the train station, we noted a black limousine parked on the apron of the track. We joked that it must be there for the judges, though we noted that the judges had missed our train and were on the train behind us, some forty-five minutes back. As we exited the train, I saw Lou run ahead and speak to the limo driver. As I approached, I heard him say words to the effect, "But we are counsel for the Court of Appeal judges..." At this point, I decided that it would be safest to head to the taxi stand, alone. Sometime later, Lou joined me at the taxi stand and expressed deep regret that he had not been able to convince the limo driver to take us to the hotel rather than wait for the next train and the judges.

The following day, we argued a number of appeals and at the end of the day, just as everyone was getting ready to pack up, the president of the panel, Moldaver J.A. (as he then was), stopped the proceedings and said, "Mr. Strezos, do you have a *Criminal Code* handy?"

"Yes, Justice Moldaver, I do." replied Lou.

"Good, can you look up Theft of a Judicial Limousine and tell me what the maximum sentence is?"

"Attempt theft, Justice Moldaver, it was only an attempt," begged Lou.

"Di Luca, what do you say?" asked Justice Moldaver.

"I'll help him plead guilty to take auto without consent, but I wasn't involved..."

"Of course not…Mr. Di Luca…of course not…." declared Justice Moldaver with a smile.

And for a brief but fleeting moment I carried the heavy baggage of wrongful conviction through guilt by association.

On a more serious note, in a perfect world, there would be no need for the inmate appeal duty counsel program. All indigent inmates pursuing conviction and/or sentence appeals would have access to state-funded counsel. The success of the program is in large measure built on the countless hours of unpaid time dedicated by the lawyers involved as duty counsel. This fact must be recognized. However, it must never be taken for granted.

William Trudell *attended the University of Windsor's Faculty of Law, first graduating class. He is the Chair of the Canadian Council of Criminal Defence Lawyers, a Fellow of the American College of Trial Lawyers and practices law in Toronto at Simcoe Chambers. He is a member of the National Steering Committee on Justice Efficiencies and Access to Justice and a member of the Steering Committee for the Annual Re-Inventing Criminal Justice Symposium. He was the Law Society of Upper Canada's representative on the Judicial Appointments Advisory Committee and in 2014 was the recipient of the Law Society Medal. He is frequently invited to appear before the House of Commons Standing Committee on Justice and Human Rights and the Standing Senate Committee on Legal and Constitutional Affairs in relation to proposed legislation in criminal justice matters. He authors a quarterly column, Sidebars, in Canadian Lawyer Magazine.*

Mr. William Trudell

A Nice Job

DEFENCE COUNSEL will tell you that the job we do, the vocation we have chosen although 'tough' is fascinating, perhaps even life changing sometimes. The people we meet, the clients we represent, the stories we hear, and the institution where it all plays out results in often-frustrating but otherwise enriched professional lives. You might say it's a nice job, indeed sometimes we appreciate a 'nice job' salutation at the end.

I remember a client years ago who was charged with importing eleven pounds of hashish secreted in his suitcase as he landed from India at Toronto Pearson Airport. He denied knowledge and after a fascinating investigation and trial, he was acquitted by a jury. He had been in jail for well over a year awaiting trial. A year to the day after his acquittal I received a postcard I will never forget:

> Dear Mr Trudell...sitting in a Paris café on a beautiful night ...can't help but remember a year ago...one day onions, next day honey...Thanks"

And there it is, the life of defence counsel, onions and honey. Realistically, we don't get to savour the honey that often; onions keep appearing with the resultant tears as our defence is peeled away. Nevertheless, the journey and the memories are unique and some cases are just so fascinating that you never forget them.

Let me share one of those with you.

On October 10th, 1986 a jury in Toronto found Gary Foshay guilty of second degree murder in the slaying of Hanna Buxbaum. He was soon thereafter sentenced to life imprisonment with parole eligibility set at fifteen years. It was a journey like no other.

Two years earlier, on July 5, 1984 Helmuth Buxbaum's car pulled over to the side of a major highway outside sleepy London, Ontario. Suddenly his wife Hanna was dragged from her passenger seat and murdered by a masked gunman.

The quiet, conservative middle class city of London and all of southwestern Ontario erupted in headlines at the senseless and unheard-of slaying of the wife of the prominent and successful owner of retirement care residences. It was not long however before the grieving husband was arrested and charged with first degree murder. It was shockingly revealed that he had contracted local inhabitants of a seedier, aimless, drug plagued lifestyle, foreign to the many fine citizens of London, the 'Forest City'. Buxbaum apparently preferred a life of drugs, sex, and association with these people. Hanna Buxbaum, his devoted wife, stood in his way.

The Journey

Foshay and Buxbaum were tried separately. Buxbaum first and ultimately Foshay's trial was relocated to Toronto because of the sensational publicity that accompanied the Buxbaum trial. Although he was defended with great skill by the late iconic Eddie Greenspan, Helmuth Buxbaum's fall from grace and prominence was stark and final. He was convicted of first degree murder and sentenced to life imprisonment with no parole eligibility for twenty-five years.

The Crown then turned their sights on Gary Foshay, the alleged shooter. I remember the phone call from the courthouse during Buxbaum's trial from someone I asked to discreetly monitor it. "Does your client have steel blue eyes? Because that description was just proclaimed from the witness box." Oh well, it was never going to be easy.

I knew that every possible protection the law provided Mr. Foshay, he would need.

The journey started with the change of venue application to move the trial from London, where it was obvious that finding an impartial jury would likely be impossible. That application was not contested by Crown counsel, Al MacDonald and Brendan Evans. We turned our attention to another forum. A series of books were about to fly off the presses detailing the sensational and seedy story that unfolded in Buxbaum's case. A decision was made to try to block their publication by applying to the Court for an injunction. The irrefutable Dean of libel, slander and all such related litigation is and was the remarkable Julian Porter QC. He represented one of the publishers and was theatrically aghast that we would seek such a stifling remedy violating the freedom of the press. Watching my dear friend in action despite his argument against us was a young lawyer's dream.

We lost, of course, but there was never really a hope. I was laying the groundwork for something else…an expanded 'challenge for cause' in the jury selection at Foshay's trial.

Jurors can be questioned about their impartiality, certainly not to the extreme as in the United States, but with the Court's permission in Canada we can explore a bit. Laying the groundwork to highlight the intense public attention and potential bias was a seed planted in the unsuccessful injunction application. I, later at trial, secured a broader latitude for questioning prospective jurors by the brilliant and masterful trial judge, Patrick Galligan.

The Remarkable Jury – The People's Court

The criminal trial remains a mystery for the majority of society. Their exposure to it is more predictably on television, in the movies or on their laptops. It is that other world of judges and lawyers, police and guilty people in that big building, to avoid, in the centre of town. The secret is that it is a magical place where something called '*justice*' unfolds; it becomes more magical when it is a jury trial.

Twelve members of the community are chosen to sit in judgment of an accused whose future in many ways, is in their hands. Without hesitation, I believe that a jury trial is the greatest and most humbling experience a defence lawyer can have.

Jurors, randomly selected, enter into our courthouses with skepticism, perhaps like protesting kids on the first day of school, similarly figuring out how to get out of this. I suspect, however, after they have been chosen and have sat in judgment of a fellow human being, they never forget and likely cherish the experience. Ordinary people from every walk of life become judges in a vital theatre of democracy. Our job as defence counsel is to help demystify the process, take them through the story and guide them to the ending we hope for. The process is astoundingly human. The experience is remarkable and, as in Mr. Foshay's case, the memories of interaction with the Jury can last a lifetime.

Murder trials are jury trials in the high courts of this country, presided over by a federally appointed judge who may be seen as a sort of responsible and engaged referee, deciding rules, what the jury can hear, and the law that is applied. Some see the judge as the most powerful player in this scenario, but it is the jury, the people, who ultimately decide and are as powerful, if not more so.

They bring the outside into that big building in the centre of town and remind us all that it really is the people's court, where common sense and everyday life experience strips away the mystery.

The jury in Gary Foshay's trial epitomized this in every way.

A Large Panel Becomes Small

A large panel had been summoned by the Court as it was assumed that it might take some time to choose twelve people to sit on this major case which had gained so much attention and was likely to require a two-month commitment.

Defence counsel and Crown counsel have a list of prospective jurors and as their names are randomly selected, we would consult the list and put a face to the name, occupation and address.

There is a limited number of what are called 'preemptory challenges' where the prospective juror is excused so that counsel can simply indicate and challenge. There is a complementary process called 'challenge for cause' where counsel can question a prospective juror to insure their impartiality and suitability. This may be especially important in a high profile case, and what I had in mind in our unsuccessful injunction application.

My practice has always been to try to study the prospective juror for any reaction when their name is called. You find out pretty quickly in a challenge for cause procedure how humbling and remarkable the system can be.

One gentleman seemed to wince when his name was called. He reluctantly moved from the safety of the assembled panel to the unpredictable front of the courtroom. I rose to question him and asked, "Sir", I said, "I apologize if I am mistaken, but I noticed that when your name was called after the judge told you about the nature and expected length of this trial...you seemed uncomfortable ...am I right, is there a problem?"

"Yes actually", he replied, "I am not sure I can put up with you people for that long." I chose him. You don't get more honest than that.

When I asked another potential juror if he had followed the Buxbaum case in the media he replied, "Was it on the Sports pages?" We chose him. He burst the bubble we lived in, that surely everyone knew about our big case.

They were an amazing group, selected from the sixty-eight who were rejected. They were interested, hard-working, human, and dedicated to their roles. They eventually deliberated for four days before arriving at their verdict, which was, in its own way, a brilliantly creative compromise.

They apparently accepted neither the Crown's theory that Foshay was the gunman and it was planned and deliberate, nor ours that they had the wrong man. The second degree murder decision was a compromise by an amazing group of strangers who likely looked at the deals made with others who were involved, and decided to level the playing field, as it were.

Indeed, when they came back to Court during their deliberations, to ask a particular question for guidance from the judge, he offered, "It is hard to imagine a clearer case of first degree murder, than a contract killing."

Justice Patrick Galligan, later in sentencing Mr. Foshay, suggested that this jury, after deliberating for over four days, had applied a real sense of practical justice. A review of the evidence illustrates exactly that.

The Witnesses

Originally Helmuth Buxbaum and six Londoners were charged with first degree murder and conspiracy. The Crown made plea arrangements with all of them except Buxbaum and Foshay.

Robert Barrett, nicknamed 'Squirrel', the man who arranged the contract killing with Mr. Buxbaum, was called first by the Crown. He had decided to blow the whistle on his co-accused after discovering Christianity in prison. Just weeks after the murder he pleaded guilty to Conspiracy to Murder and was serving a ten-year sentence. He was likely the first to 'make a deal' as they say, with the Crown.

He, of course, found Jesus after taking a correspondence course in Bible study.

Barrett's evidence was that although he had set up the murder with Mr. Buxbaum, he'd really had nothing to do with carrying it out. There had been a dry run on the given day, but it had collapsed when a police officer happened to drive by. Barrett then suggested he'd had nothing to do with the actual killing later the same day, as Mr. Buxbaum was returning to London after picking up his nephew in Toronto.

He laid the responsibility on Gary Foshay.

Barrett's evidence was unreliable, his life plagued with drugs. He simply was the money man, others were responsible, he protested.

It was not difficult to suggest that his claim to finding religion in the Middlesex Detention Centre was not the motivation for his evidence. Rather, the charge and lenient sentence the mastermind had secured in return for his testimony was the irresistible carrot.

Patrick Allen was the next star witness called by Crown counsel, another recipient of a suspiciously light sentence, clearly in return for his testimony. In targeting Gary Foshay as the killer, he became the target of our defence. He too lived a drug-infested existence. He testified that he was actually on the side of the road in the morning, about to carry out the plan to kill Hanna Buxbaum, but a gift of chance changed his involvement when a police officer drove by and the plan was dropped. He then suggested that Gary Foshay, previously not involved, took over and carried out the murder later that day.

Allen didn't find religion like Barrett who hired him, but interestingly the two of them were put together in the same area of the detention centre. Let us just say that of course they did not plan and deliberate their evidence.

Patrick Allen testified that he heard later that Hanna Buxbaum pleaded for her life before Foshay killed her. He wasn't there, but heard it from others, he protested. Mr. Allen's story was simply unbelievable. I suggested that not only was he present in the afternoon, but his role never changed, he was the killer.

The only clear message from the witness box when Mr. Allen left it was that he was a very lucky man and a stranger to the truth. He had been evasive and often resorted to the lair of the liar, "I don't remember."

I suspect the jury would not need divine intervention to question the reliability of most of the witnesses in this case, and that would have been especially true in assessing Terry Armes, a key player and vital witness for the Crown. Sadly, Mr. Armes was a man whose life had been thrown away into a bottle, supplemented by drugs. His testimony was as self-serving as Squirrel's and Allen's, but was fog-filled by twelve to thirty-six beers a day.

Indeed, he admitted that many of the events were in a fog for him, but he said he was there and his evidence was essential for the Crown. He was there for the dry run in the morning, a misnomer if ever there was one, and crucially, he was there for the killing. He testified that although he was drunk all day, he jumped into the car and held Mr. Buxbaum's fourteen-year-old nephew down while Gary Foshay, wearing a baseball cap and a nylon mask covering all but his steel-blue eyes, dragged Hanna Buxbaum out, pleading for her life.

Originally charged with first degree, Armes pleaded guilty to second degree murder and was sentenced to life imprisonment with parole eligibility set at ten years. This was a remarkably lenient sentence given his role, alcoholic fog or not. I suspect that the jury's 'practical justice' decision was influenced in large measure by the resolution of Armes involvement.

The Last Witness

Crown counsel stood and announced their last witness would be Tracey La Roque.

The courtroom door opened and in she came. Seventeen at the time of the events, not unlike her name, she was memorable. Quite beautiful, the former dancer made her way in a hushed courtroom to the witness box. She told the court that sometime within hours of the death, first in the middle of the afternoon, then in the evening, she and Gary Foshay were drinking at a local establishment in London. She described how at one point, the gun stuck in his pants, they started dancing. He told her that he killed a woman. This evidence was devastating. She was nervous, even weepy on the stand and all you could hear was the sound of the media's pens recording the next day's headlines.

It seemed to be over, and yet we still had some questions. I noted that she had been in a bar and asked if she had been drinking. "Yes," she asserted. I inquired as to what she had consumed. The answer was almost brazen, yet clearly astounding, " I had six B-52s."

She responded by easily describing the three liqueurs involved and I asked her if she thought it might have affected her memory. "No," she replied matter of factly, "not at all." I sat down.

Days later in my jury address, I reminded them of Ms. LaRoque's evidence that the six B-52s had no affect on her memory. I rhetorically asked, "Ladies and gentlemen, I invite you to have six B-52s and see if it affects your memory."

After the verdict had been rendered, all counsel met with Justice Galligan in his chambers to discuss the case and wish each other well after a difficult but quite civil trial. As I was about to leave, Justice Galligan's clerk told me that there were several jurors who wished to speak to me. I froze and felt more than a shiver of apprehension. "I can't talk to jurors," I protested. "Well," he said, "they are blocking the courtroom door."

As I left the chambers to gather my belongings, there indeed stood a number of jurors at the courtroom door, in effect blocking the entrance. I remain, years later, overwhelmed by what came next… "Mr. Trudell, we are here for our six B-52s."

That experience was just one of the unusual experiences that kept unfolding in defending Mr. Foshay. London was my hometown and the discovery of the seedy underbelly that permeated many of the witnesses' lives was a shock to my sheltered environment. London, the home of head offices at the time like Labatts, General Motors, 3M, London Life and the respected University of Western Ontario was seemingly safe and conservative.

I discovered a much different side of my hometown and practicing in Toronto, I think I felt somewhat sheepish having to expose it. Nevertheless, the memories around this trial are amazing.

Cars Sometimes Break Down

On one occasion, as I drove home to London for a visit, the trial scheduled to proceed in the coming months, my car started to helplessly sputter and then ironically, simply stopped on the side of the highway. As an experienced lawyer, I immediately exited, opened the hood and stared at a world I had absolutely no clue about. I likely pretended to the occupants that I could fix whatever the hell it was, and after touching some hoses and clamps I tried to start it up to no avail. It happens I thought, cars sometimes break down.

Stranded, unbelievably, an Ontario Provincial Police cruiser pulled up and a very helpful officer offered to assist and drove us to London, leaving the car to be towed. As I sat beside him, un-arrested in a police car, we chatted about our lives. I was so eager to foolishly brag about the big case I was working on. I think I mentioned it, but my better angel told me to shut up.

Months later in the trial, the Crown called the OPP driver who discovered a gun in the Thomas River near London. The witness was none other than my Good Samaritan. I began my cross-examination before the jury, tongue firmly in cheek, noting that cars often break down, and we had already met on such an occasion. That moment was surreal and just another fascinating twist in an amazing journey.

London Life has for years promoted 'Freedom 55', a retirement plan built around life insurance. It usually never applies to defence lawyers, but I learned what it was because of this trial. Midway through a cross-examination of a witness, Crown counsel stood and politely, but firmly, complained that I was going too far and taking too long and should know better.

Justice Galligan looked down at me and said, "Well Mr. Trudell…?". I apologized to the court, the Crown, the witnesses and the jury, but told Justice Galligan that it was my birthday, I had turned forty. He wished me Happy Birthday and said he would let me go a little further that day. Weeks later, Mr. Foshay was convicted of second degree murder, parole eligibility set at fifteen years...when I would be turning fifty-five.

Still Trying to Get It Right

As I finished my jury address, I had a feeling of relief and some accomplishment. We felt that Mr. Foshay had a chance, given the unreliable cast of characters called by the Crown. Moreover, Mr. Foshay wanted to testify and he did, denying his involvement. It was in the jury's hands.

I took off my glasses and walked to the back of the courtroom and approached my wonderful parents who had travelled from London to hear my address to the jury. A sense of pride and perhaps a need for parental approval accompanied my ego as I strode in my robes to the pew where my parents sat. I think I asked how I had done.

My incredibly beautiful mother looked at me and said, "that was very interesting but Billy, could you not get...a nice job?"

INDEX

Books in the 'True Cases' Series

Tough Crimes: True Cases by Top Canadian Criminal Lawyers

Book One in the True Cases Series
Eds: CD Evans and Lorene Shyba

Tough Crimes is a collection of thoughtful and insightful essays from some of Canada's most prominent criminal lawyers. Stories include wrongful convictions, reasonable doubt, homicides, and community.

Price: $29.95 *Trade Paperback*
ISBN: 978-0-9689754-6-6 (2014)

Shrunk: Crime and Disorders of the Mind

Book Two in the True Cases Series
Eds: Drs. Lorene Shyba and J. Thomas Dalby
Foreword: Dr. Lisa Ramshaw

Shrunk is a collection of chapters by eminent Canadian and international forensic psychologists and psychiatrists who write about mental health issues they face and what they are doing about it.

Price: $29.95 *Trade Paperback*
ISBN: 978-0-9947352-0-1 (2016)

More Tough Crimes: True Cases by Canadian Judges and Criminal Lawyers

Book Three in the True Cases Series
Eds: William Trudell and Lorene Shyba
Foreword: Hon. Patrick LeSage

More Tough Crimes provides a unique window into the world of criminal justice. Many cases are recent, but some from the past were so disturbing they resonate in the public consciousness.

Price: $29.95 *Trade Paperback*
ISBN: 978-09947352-5-6 (2017)

Upcoming!

Women in Silks: True Cases by Canadian Women in Criminal Justice

Book Four in the True Cases Series
ISBN: 978-0-9947352-4-9

Selections
Durvile and UpRoute Books

Milt Harradence: The Western Flair

Foreword by Hon. John C. Major, CC QC
Retired Justice, Supreme Court of Canada

"It should find a permanent home in every trial lawyer's library."
— Ron MacIsaac, Lawyers Weekly

In Milt Harradence: The Western Flair, C.D. Evans perpetuates the legend of his flamboyant, larger-than-life colleague with whom he shared thrills, spills, brilliant courtroom spars.

Price: $30.00 *Trade Paperback*
16 pages of colour photos.
ISBN: 978-0-9689754-0-4

A Painful Duty
40 Years at the Criminal Bar

A Memoir by CD Evans
Reflections Series, Book 1

"Very rarely have I read a memoir or autobiography whose author had as overwhelming concern for truth and fairness as Evans displays in this book."
— Alex Rettie, Alberta Views

Evans reveals insights into the practice and the characters of the Criminal Bar, with special tributes to no-nonsense judges.

Price: $42.50 *Trade Paperback*
16 pages of colour photos.
ISBN: 978-0-9689754-3-5

Less Painful Duties
Reflections on the Revolution in the Legal Profession
by CD Evans
Reflections Series, Book 2

In this sequel to his book *A Painful Duty: Forty Years at the Criminal Bar*, Evans reflects on revolutionary changes that have come about within the Canadian legal profession, in particular the Criminal Bar, over the past fifty years. Topics he covers include ascendancy of women in the profession, the *Canadian Charter of Rights*, and the impacts of cell phones.

Price: $29.95 *Trade Paperback*
ISBN: 978-0-9952322-1-1

5000 Dead Ducks
Lust and Revolution in the Oilsands

A Novel by C.D. Evans and L.M. Shyba

"5000 Dead Ducks may be a satire, a fever dream of sorts, but its message is clear: When it comes to the oilsands, the stakes are so high that anything is possible."
— Gillian Steward, Toronto Star

A comedy satire about an unscrupulous group of "Candidian" lawyers engineer a revolution to take over the "Alberia" oilsands.

Price: $16.95 *Trade Paperback*
ISBN: 978-0-9689754-4-2

Stop Making Art and Die
Survival Activities for Artists

By Rich Théroux

UpRoute Imprint

"Stop Making Art and Die asks big questions about creativity, fulfillment, and happiness."
— Eric Volmers, Calgary Herald

The first adult activity book that makes it impossible not to succeed and flourish as and artist by encouraging a deeper understand of art.

Price: $42.50 *Trade Paperback*
ISBN: 978-0-9689754-3-5

A Wake in the Undertow
Rumble House Poems

by Rich Theroux and Jess Szabo

UpRoute Imprint

Arms flung wide
Rib cages swung open
Hearts thunder
Wild vibrations
Where that river
meets the ocean.

Welcome home.

Price: $16.95 *Trade Paperback*
ISBN: 978-0-9689754-9-7